ULTIMATE
CV

ULTIMATE CV

CV

FOURTH EDITION

Over 100 winning CVs to help you
get the interview and the job

MARTIN JOHN YATE

KoganPage

LONDON PHILADELPHIA NEW DELHI

Publisher's note

Every possible effort has been made to ensure that the information contained in this book is accurate at the time of going to press, and the publishers and author cannot accept responsibility for any errors or omissions, however caused. No responsibility for loss or damage occasioned to any person acting, or refraining from action, as a result of the material in this publication can be accepted by the editor, the publisher or the author.

First published in the United States in 1993 as *Knock 'em Dead* by Adams Media Corporation
First published in Great Britain in 2003 as *The Ultimate CV Book* by Kogan Page Limited
Reprinted in 2003, 2004, 2005, 2007
Second edition published in 2008 as *Ultimate CV*
Third edition 2012
Fourth edition 2015

Published by arrangement with Adams Media Corporation, 57 Littlefield Street, Avon, MA 02322, USA

2nd Floor, 45 Gee Street
London EC1V 3RS
United Kingdom
www.koganpage.com

1518 Walnut Street, Suite 1100
Philadelphia PA 19102
USA

4737/23 Ansari Road
Daryaganj
New Delhi 110002
India

© Martin John Yate, 1993, 1995, 1998, 2001, 2003, 2008, 2012, 2015

The right of Martin John Yate to be identified as the author of this work has been asserted by him in accordance with the Copyright, Designs and Patents Act 1988.

ISBN   978 0 7494 7454 6

British Library Cataloguing-in-Publication Data

A CIP record for this book is available from the British Library.

Typeset by Graphicraft Limited, Hong Kong
Print production managed by Jellyfish
Printed and bound by CPI Group (UK) Ltd, Croydon, CR0 4YY

CONTENTS

INTRODUCTION

Most books on writing CVs haven't adjusted to accommodate today's changing work environment, or the way that companies now store, access, and review CVs. The goal of this book is to help you accelerate your job search with an understanding of the world in which your CV must compete, and the tactics that will enable it to compete most effectively.

No one wants to write a CV. On the list of things we 'want' to do, it comes just above hitting yourself on the head with a hammer; and in part that is because of the self-analysis involved. Although we know ourselves better than anyone else does, actually taking that knowledge and packaging it for public consumption is always an extremely difficult task.

In *Ultimate CV*, I explain the ins and outs of putting a CV together as painlessly as possible. I'll show you the best ways to look at your background and present it to the public in your CV. You'll understand why certain things should be in your CV and how they should look, and why other things should never appear. Today's world of work is complex, and your circumstances are unique, so there will be situations when what is right for one person's CV is wrong for another's. In these cases I'll always share with you what the experts think on the topic, and whenever industry experts disagree I'll give you both sides of the argument, along with my reasoned solution to the dispute. That way you can make a prudent decision based on the factors that affect your particular situation. In addition, you will see a wide variety of styles and approaches that can be used within these practical guidelines to help you create a truly individual CV.

You'll get to read real CVs from real people. Each of the CVs in this book is based on a 'genuine article' that opened the doors of opportunity for its writer. CVs are included for today's and tomorrow's in-demand jobs, confirmed by the professionals on the front lines: corporate recruiters and other employment industry professionals from across the country. You are quite likely to find a CV that reflects exactly the kind of job you are after; if not, you can still learn lots from the examples, and you can lift and adapt key phrases and use their layouts as templates for your work.

You will also find a number of CVs from people with special challenges. These reflect the pressures and needs of a modern, profession-oriented society struggling into the information age, such as the CV that got a minimum-wage factory worker a £40,000-a-year professional sales job, or the one that helped a recovering alcoholic and drug-abuser get back on his feet again. Included here are winning CVs of people who are recovering from serious emotional challenges, re-entering society after time in prison, starting over after a divorce, and sometimes changing careers into the bargain. What's more, these examples have proved themselves effective in every corner of the nation; their writers landed both interviews and jobs.

A powerful, on-target CV, properly distributed, is only one element in a successful job search; for this reason, *Ultimate CV* is part of an integrated series of books crafted to help you land jobs and prosper in them. This book will at times touch on subjects that are handled in greater depth elsewhere in the series. In these instances, I will refer you to the appropriate work. For example, the self-knowledge you develop in preparing your CV will also help you prepare for job interviews.

The wide range of CV examples here, and the nuts-and-bolts advice about CV production and distribution, will give you everything you need to create a distinctive, professional CV – and get it in front of the people who count! You will find something on every single page that you can put to work in your job search right now, today.

1
How to make your CV shine

Read this book with a highlighter –
it will save time as you refer back to important passages.

Your CV is the most financially important document you will ever own.

When it works, the doors of opportunity open for you. When it doesn't work, they won't. No one enjoys writing a CV, but it has such a major impact on the money you earn during your work life, and consequently on the quality of your whole life outside work, that you know this is something that needs to be done well.

You didn't come to this book for a good read. You came because you are facing serious challenges in your professional life. The way the professional world works has changed dramatically in the past few years, and nothing has changed as much as the way companies recruit. Because everything related to recruitment and selection has changed almost beyond recognition, everything to do with your job search needs to be re-evaluated from top to bottom.

In these pages you are going to learn how to build a CV that works. But you're going to learn something more. Since my approach to CVs is part of a larger strategy for achieving long-term career and personal success, everything I teach you about developing a knockout CV will apply to the broader challenges of the job search, being interviewed and career management.

When you are finished, you will walk away with a CV that will land you that new job, plus you will learn some key strategies and tactics for your job search, interviews, and even some amazing insights into winning raises and promotions.

Self-awareness: the key to professional survival and success

Understanding what employers need and how they express and prioritize those needs, will tell you what you have to do to get their attention and that job offer.

Your employer just wants to make money

Staff only get added to the payroll to enhance profitability. Think about this: if you owned a company, there just isn't any other reason you would add workers to your payroll. So it is implicit in the employment contract that your job contributes to profitability in some way.

Depending on your job you can help your employer by:

- making money for the company;
- saving money for the company;
- saving time/increasing productivity.

No matter what your job, no matter how impressive your title, at its core your job exists to help your employer increase and maintain profitability by:

- *identifying* problems within your area of responsibility;
- *preventing* problems within your area of responsibility;
- *solving* problems within your area of responsibility.

No CV gets read, no one gets interviewed, and no one gets hired unless someone somewhere is trying to solve a problem. That problem may be finding a quicker way to manufacture silicon chips, speed up accounts receivable, facilitate social networking for brand management, or any one of a million other profit challenges.

The only reason your job exists is because your employer needs someone who can identify, prevent and solve the problems that occur in a specific area of professional responsibility. It exists because not having someone like you is costing them money. Problem solving, the application of critical thinking within your area of expertise, is what you are paid to do. It is why every job opening exists, and why every job gets filled with the person who seems to have the firmest grip on how to identify, prevent and solve problems related to that job.

Why no one wants to read your CV

You may think that CV writing is a tough job, but what if you had to *read* them? Go to the CV samples section and try to read and understand six CVs in a row. Then you'll understand why no one wants to read your CV.

No one reads CVs unless they have to, so when your CV does get read, it means that a job exists – a job has been carefully defined and titled, a salary range has been authorized, the position has been budgeted and the funds have been released. *Whenever a recruiter searches a CV database or reads a CV, s/he is doing it with a specific job and the language and priorities of that job description in mind.*

Why they may never get the chance

The impact of technology on the workplace causes the nature of all jobs to change almost as rapidly as the pages on a calendar. CVs today rarely go straight to a manager's desk; they are more likely to go to a CV database.

This means that before anyone actually reads your CV, it must first have been chosen from that database by an employer with a specific job and the language and priorities of that job in mind. Keep in mind that some of those databases contain millions of CVs.

Can you see that if your CV is a mish-mash of everything you've ever done, *everything you happen to think is important*, without reference to what an employer actually wants, it is never going to work?

The CV that works

'The customer is always right', 'the customer comes first', and 'understand your customer' are phrases that underlie successful businesses. When you apply this thinking to a CV, you create a document tailored to your customers' needs. Your CV works when it matches your skills and experience to the responsibilities and requirements of a specific target job. This requires that your CV focuses on how employers – your customers – think about, prioritize and describe this job's requirements – what you are expected to deliver by way of results as you execute your assigned responsibilities. A CV focused on a specific target job and built from the ground up with the customer's needs in mind will perform better in the CV database searches and will be far more attractive to human eyes already glazed from the tedium of CV reading.

This is not your last job change

In a world without job security, when job and even career changes are happening ever more frequently, being able to write a productive CV is one of life's critical survival skills. This is probably not your first, and almost certainly won't be your last, job change. You are somewhere in the middle of a half-century work life, during which you are likely to have three or more distinct careers and statistically likely to change jobs about every four years. This is a world where economic recessions come around every 7 to 10 years and age discrimination is going to begin to kick in around the age of 50.

When I started to talk about these issues 25 years ago, I was asked how I could suggest that people be disloyal to their employers. History has shown it is the companies that break the employment contract, yet companies demand the unblinking loyalty and blind fidelity of their employees. I'm sorry, but if you accept this double standard your life and the lives of your loved ones will suffer. Wake up! Times have changed. You need a tougher, more pragmatic approach to your professional life. You still need to do your best for your employer and your team, but you also need to put yourself first, because you need to survive and hopefully prosper in life. To do this you need to find a more sophisticated approach to managing your professional life and guiding your destiny.

Start to think of yourself as a company, a financial entity that must always plan and act in the best interests of its economic survival. Like any company, you have products and services that are constantly under development. These are the ever-evolving skills that define the professional you. Again, just like any organization, these products and services are branded and sold to your targeted customer: employers who hire people like you.

The success of your company depends on how well you run it, and like every successful company you'll need research and development, strategic planning, marketing, public relations, and sales.

- **Research and development:** every company is continually involved in identification and development of products and services that will appeal to their customers. You must have the same ongoing initiatives. This translates into skill building in response to market trends, which you do by being connected to your profession and by monitoring the changing market demands for your job.

- **Strategic planning:** the development of career management strategies. You'll begin to think of your career over the long term, where you want to be and how you are going to get there – how you will stay on top of skill development, how you will develop and maintain a desirable professional identity.

- **Marketing and PR:** this requires establishing credibility for the services you deliver. You must position these services so that your professional credibility becomes visible within your company to encourage professional growth, and within your profession to encourage your employability elsewhere.

- **Sales:** you need a state-of-the-art sales programme to sell your products and services.

Your new CV is your primary sales tool. It is one of the most financially important documents you will ever possess, you can learn how to do it well, starting right now.

2
Get inside your customer's head

'The customer is always right' is probably the first business lesson you ever learned. When you accurately tailor your product to the customer's needs you experience more successful sales. This chapter is about how to customize your CV to your customer's needs.

Your CV is the primary marketing device for every job and career change throughout your life. It is your promotional tool. In short, it is absolutely vital in determining your professional success. Yet when it comes to creating a CV, no one ever seems to think about what the customer wants! Instead we try to get it done quickly, with as little thought and effort as possible.

Your current CV is probably a straightforward recitation of all you have done, but despite all your efforts this CV isn't working. That's because a simple recitation of all your accomplishments and activities results in a hodgepodge of what *you* think is important, *not what your customers believe is important*.

Have you seen a Swiss army knife? It's got knife blades, bottle openers, screwdrivers... it does practically everything. But companies aren't hiring human Swiss army knives. They are hiring human lasers, with exceptional skills focused in a specific area. *You need a CV that mirrors the priorities of your customers*, because they won't make the time to struggle through an unfocused CV to see if you might be what they want.

The most productive CVs start with a clear focus on the target job and its responsibilities from the point of view of the employer. The customer comes first, so let's get inside the customer's head.

Target job survey

There's a practical and easy way to get inside the employer's head. It's called a target job survey. It's a way to get a focus on what your customers are buying and what will sell before you even start writing your CV. Take half a day to do a survey and your investment will yield:

- a template for the story your CV *must* tell to be successful;

- an objective tool against which you can evaluate your CV's likely performance;

- a complete understanding of where the focus will be during interviews;

- a very good idea of the interview questions that will be heading your way and why;

- relevant examples with which to illustrate your answers;

- a behavioural profile for getting hired and for professional success throughout your career.

The survey

Step 1: collect advertisements

Collect 6 to 10 advertisements for your target job.

Not sure where to start? Try *these* job sites and look for jobs with your chosen keywords:

www.monster.co.uk

www.jobsearch.co.uk

www.jobrapido.co.uk

www.check4jobs.com

www.clickajob.co.uk

www.careerjet.co.uk

www.workhound.co.uk

Step 2: identify job titles

Look at the job titles that employers use when hiring people. From this you can come up with a suitable target job title for your CV; that will help your CV's database performance and also act as a headline, giving the reader an immediate focus.

Step 3: identify skills and responsibilities

You are looking for requirements common to all or most of your job postings. These are the key skills and responsibilities you need on *your* CV.

The greater the number of keywords in your CV that are directly relevant to your target job, the higher the ranking your CV will achieve in recruiters' database searches. The higher your ranking, the greater the likelihood that your CV will be rescued from the avalanche and passed along to human eyes for further screening.

Step 4: identify problems to solve

At their most basic level, all jobs are the same – they focus on problem identification, avoidance and solution in that particular area of expertise; this is what we all get paid for, no matter what we do for a living.

Go back to your survey and look at the skills and responsibilities. Think about the problems you typically need to identify, solve and/or prevent in the course of a normal workday. List specific examples, big and small, of your successful handling of the problems. Quantify your results when possible.

Some examples may appear in your CV as significant professional achievements. Others will provide you with the ammunition to answer those interview questions that begin, 'Tell me about a time when...' – because interviewers are concerned with your practical problem identification and solution abilities.

Step 5: identify a behavioural profile for success

Think of the *best* person you have ever seen doing this job and what made them stand out. Describe their performance, professional behaviour, interaction with others, and appearance: 'That would be Carole Jenkins, superior communication skills, a fine analytical mind, great professional appearance, and a nice person to work with.' You are describing the person all employers want to hire.

Now your CV can focus on what the customers want to hear

Once you complete your survey, you will have a clear idea of the way that employers think about, prioritize and express their needs when they hire someone for the job you want.

Now you know the story your CV needs to tell to be productive in the CV databases, which means it will get retrieved for human review. You now have the proper focus for a killer CV.

Overleaf is a simple 'before and after' example that will illustrate how powerful this process can be. The CV is for a young graduate with a computer science degree, looking for her first position in the professional world. When we first spoke, she had been out of university for nearly three months and had only had a couple of telephone interviews and one face-to-face interview. The first CV shown overleaf is the one she was using; the second she created after completing a survey.

> As a rule of thumb, you need about 70 per cent of a job's requirements to pursue that job with reasonable hope of success, especially in a slack economy when competition is more fierce. If you complete the survey and realize you don't make the grade, you have probably saved yourself a good deal of frustration pursuing a job you had no real chance of landing.

I have taken professionals from entry level up to boardroom executives through this process. They all say a couple of things: it was a pain but it was worth it, and they almost all got job offers surprisingly quickly.

Before

JYATITI MOKUBE
1 Any Street
Anytown AT1 0AA
00000 000000
jyatiti@anyaddress.co.uk

Education

- Southern Counties University
- MSc Computer Science, December 2014
- University of Technology, Kingston, Jamaica
- BSc Computing & Information Technology, November 2012

Key Skills

- Programming
- Programming Languages: C, C++, Java, VB.Net
- Database Programming: SQL
- Website Design
- Design Languages/Tools: HTML, CSS, JavaScript, Dreamweaver
- Problem Solving and Leadership
- Honed an analytical, logical and determined approach to problem solving and applied this as group leader for my final year (undergraduate) research project.
- Team Player
- Demonstrated the ability to work effectively within a team while developing a point-of-sale system over the course of three terms.
- Communication
- Demonstrated excellent written and oral communication skills through reports and presentations while pursuing my degrees, and as Public Relations Officer for the University of Technology's Association of Student Computer Engineers (UTASCE).

Continued

JYATITI MOKUBE **Page 2**

Work Experience

January 2013–December 2014

- Southern Counties University
- Graduate Research Assistant, School of Computing
- Developed a haptic application to demonstrate human–computer interaction using Python and H3D API.
- Developed an application to organize text documents using the Self-Organizing Map algorithm and MATLAB.

July–November 2012

- Cable & Wireless Jamaica Ltd, Kingston, Jamaica
- Internet Helpdesk Analyst
- Assisted customers with installing and troubleshooting modems and internet service-related issues via telephone.

July–August 2010

- National Commercial Bank Ja. Ltd, Kingston, Jamaica
- Change Management Team Member
- Generated process diagrams and documentation for systems under development using MS Visio, MS Word and MS Excel.

Awards/Honours

- Foundation Award for Academic Excellence & Outstanding Character　March 2012
- Nominated School of Computing student of the year　March 2012
- Recognized by Jamaica Gleaner as top student in School of Computing & IT　February 2012
- Nominated for Derrick Dunn (community service) Award　March 2011

Languages

- French (fluent), Italian (basic)

Extracurricular Activities

- Singing, acting, chess, reading
- Member of Association for Computing Machinery, ASU student branch

References

- Available upon request.

After

JYATITI MOKUBE
1 Any Street
Anytown AT1 0AA
00000 000000
jyatiti@anyaddress.co.uk

Talented, analytical and dedicated Software Engineer with strong academic background in object-orientated analysis and design, comfortable with a variety of technologies, and interested in learning new ones.

SUMMARY OF QUALIFICATIONS

- Excellent academic record. MSc Computer Science; BSc Computing & Information Technology.
- Familiarity with the software development lifecycle, from identifying requirements to design, implementation, integration and testing.
- Familiarity with agile software development processes.
- Strong technical skills in Java development and Object-Oriented Analysis and Design (OOA/D).
- Strong understanding of multiple programming languages, including C, C++, JavaScript, Visual Basic and HTML.
- Familiar with CVS version control software.
- Excellent communications skills with an aptitude for building strong working relationships with teammates.
- Proven background leading teams in stressful, deadline-orientated environments.

TECHNICAL SKILLS

Languages:	Java, JavaScript, C, C++, Visual Basic, HTML, SQL, VB.Net, ASP.Net, CSS
Software:	Eclipse, NetBeans, JBuilder, Microsoft Visual Studio, Microsoft Office Suite (Word, PowerPoint, Excel, Access), MATLAB
Databases:	MySQL, Oracle
Operating Systems:	Windows (NT/2000/XP Professional)
Servers:	Apache Server

EDUCATION

MSc in Computer Science, Southern Counties University

- Completed a thesis in the area of Computer Security (Digital Forensics: Forensic Analysis of an iPod Shuffle)

BSc in Computing & IT, University of Technology, Kingston, Jamaica, November 2012

LANGUAGES

Fluent in English, French and Italian

Continued

Page 2

PROFESSIONAL EXPERIENCE
Southern Counties University 2013–2014
Graduate Research Assistant, School of Computing

- Developed a haptic application to demonstrate human–computer interaction using Python and H3D API.

- Developed an application to organize text documents using the Self-Organizing Map algorithm and MATLAB.

Cable & Wireless Jamaica Ltd, Kingston, Jamaica   2012–2014
Internet Helpdesk Analyst

- Assisted customers with installing and troubleshooting modems and internet service-related issues via telephone.

National Commercial Bank Ja. Ltd, Kingston, Jamaica   2010
Change Management Team Member

- Generated process diagrams and documentation for systems under development using MS Visio, MS Word and MS Excel.

AWARDS/HONOURS

- Foundation Award for Academic Excellence & Outstanding Character 2012

- Nominated School of Computing student of the year 2012

- Recognized by Jamaica Gleaner as top student in School of Computing & IT 2012

- Nominated for Derrick Dunn (community service) Award 2011

PROFESSIONAL AFFILIATIONS

Association for Computing Machinery (ACM)

REFERENCES

Available upon request.

What was the result of this CV revamp? She started using the new CV and almost immediately got an interview and the offer of a job.

The target-job-focused CV opened doors, positioned her professionally, told her what the employer would want to talk about, and was a powerful spokesperson after she left. The end result was a great start to a new career.

Here is another example: the original CV, the third version, followed by the final (eighth) version, which generated eight interviews in the first week.

First CV:

Nancy Smith

1 Any Street

Anywhere AA1 1AA

55555 555555

nancysmith@anyaddress.co.uk

Public Relations Experience

Nancy Smith has more than 13 years of public relations experience, primarily focused on high-tech and start-up companies. An Olympic gold medallist in swimming, Smith also spent 12 years serving as a freelance commentator for sports/news outlets including Sky and ESPN.

Smith & Company Public Relations, *Founder and Director* **2010–present**

Provide the professional work of a large public relations agency along with the personal service available from a smaller company. Develop and execute PR campaigns that meet the specialized needs of each client. Programmes and services include corporate and product positioning, ongoing PR strategy and tactics, leadership branding, media training, speaker placement and ongoing media contact. Clients have included: *ABC Ltd*, *DEF.com*, *GHJ Associates*.

NW Public Relations, *Co-Founder and Director* **2008–2010**

Established a PR firm that helped high-tech companies accomplish objectives by managing leadership positioning, strategic branding and publicity. Clients included:

- *RST Systems* – Project work included managing all annual Sales Conference communications for the Company Secretary of Service Provider group. Helped launch Smith's new fiscal year strategy, objectives and goals to his 1,000+ employees.
- *XYZ Technologies* – Successfully positioned the start-up as an industry leader using the market's widespread use of XYZ's industry-standard networking software. Rapidly expanded the company's leadership position by garnering positive coverage in all targeted publications.

RST Systems, *Marketing Manager* **2007–2008**

Directed internal marketing activities for the Product after RST acquired LMN and its technology. Shortly after the acquisition, RST reorganized LMN and later licensed the Product trademark to OPQ.

LMN Technology Corporation, *Public Relations Manager* **2005–2007**

Designed and executed all company and product strategy. Placed hundreds of stories with news and feature media including the Today Show, The Game Programme's Y2K special hosted by Jon Smith, The Wall Street Journal, The Times and News Company. Within 18 months of launching LMN's PR, the company was acquired by RST Systems.

XYZ Public Relations, *Account Manager; Senior Account Executive; Account Executive* **2003–2005**

Designed and managed all PR strategy and activities for start-up and unknown software, internet and networking companies. Managed teams of up to 10 PR professionals. Promoted annually for delivering results for the following clients:

- *LMN Technology Corporation* – Repositioned LMN from fledgling company to a leader in the internet appliance space. Introduced the new management team, the Product and the back-end software. Garnered positive coverage in hundreds of media outlets including The Wall Street Journal, The Times and UK Today. LMN was acquired by RST Systems within 18 months of the PR campaign.

- *TX Digital Systems* – Accelerated TX and its CEO out of obscurity and into a position of undisputed leadership. Successfully positioned CEO as an industry expert with ongoing speaker placement and quotes in all of TX's top publications. Placed CEO on the magazine cover of the company's topmost publication. TX was acquired by XO after the two-year PR campaign.

- *UVW* – Transformed unknown company into a 'player' in the internet advertising arena. Placed hundreds of stories in both business and industry media including The Wall Street Journal, CNNfn and AdWeek. UVW was acquired by a major software company after an 18-month PR campaign.

- *The Internet Store* – Launched this obscure company to the press, landing continual coverage in all top internet and business publications including The Times and Internet World. Within a year of the campaign, the company was acquired by TW, now TWN commerce.

Other Relevant Experience

Motivational Speaker/Guest Celebrity   **1996–present**

Coach audiences at corporations, business forums, schools and functions on how to effectively set and achieve goals, using the road to the Olympics as a model. Travel the country making guest appearances at events, functions and conferences. Past or present clients include: XYZ, Hopwoods, Speed X and others.

Television Commentator   **1995–2007**

- Provided expert commentary for swimming events, including the Olympics for Sky.

- Provided half-time interviews and feature packages for the first Heat.

- Work included Sky, ESPN, Sportscover, SportsChannel, TN Sports, SportSouth and others.

The College Conference, Associate Commissioner   **1998–2000**

- Managed all aspects of Conference television and marketing packages.

- Increased marketing revenue by 33 per cent in the first year.

International Swimming Association, Assistant Director   **1996–1998**

- Helped drive fund-raising efforts for new projects.

- Served as one of three spokespeople for the Association, delivering speeches at community events.

- Successfully managed and completed all fund-raising aspects for the Association.

- Developed community affairs programmes.

Awards and Honours

- Two Olympic gold medals (1990 Los Angeles, United States), and a silver and bronze (1994 Seoul, Korea).

- Twice All Counties UK Champion.

- 26-time Southern Counties.

- Wikipedia: http://en.wikipedia.org/wiki/NancySmith

Education

University of the South, BA Journalism   **1996**

Third CV:

Nancy Smith, Account Supervisor

1 Any Street, Anywhere AA1 1AA • nancysmith@anyaddress.co.uk
• Tel: 55555 555555 Mobile: 000000 0000

Performance Profile

High-tech public relations professional with 11 years' experience in a variety of sectors including software, internet, networking and consumer electronics. Substantial experience in PR campaigns that lead to company acquisitions. Expertise in all aspects of strategic and tactical communications, from developing and managing PR campaigns, multiple accounts and results-oriented teams, to writing materials and placing stories. Twenty years' experience as a motivational speaker and 12 as a freelance TV commentator. Twice Olympic gold medallist.

Core Competencies

High-Tech Public Relations • Strategic Communications • Counsel Executives • Manage Teams • Manage Budgets • Multiple Accounts • Multiple Projects • Leadership Positioning • PR Messaging • Client Satisfaction • Media Training • Media Relations • Pitch Media • Craft Stories • Place Stories • PR Tactics • Press Releases • Collateral Materials • Research • Edit • Manage Budgets • Manage Teams • Mentor • Strong Writing Skills • Detail Orientated • Organizational Skills • Motivated • Team Player • New Business

Strategic Public Relations Leadership

Position companies as both industry leaders and sound investments. The following four companies were acquired within two years of commencing the PR campaigns: LMN Technologies (acquired by RST), TX Digital Systems (acquired by XO), UVW (acquired by AMSC), and The Internet Store (acquired by TW, now TWN Commerce).

Executive Communications Manager

Develop executive communications. Created positioning for the Company Secretary, and launched it to his 1,000+ employees at the RST Sales Conference. Refined Smith's public speaking delivery and style.

Media Coverage

Pro-actively place stories. Examples of past placements include: World News Tonight, Sky, The Today Show, Associated Press, The Sun, The Globe, Business Week, News Company, Financial Times, Forbes, Fortune Magazine, Inc, MSNBC.com, The Times, Mercury News, Business Journal, The Chronicle, UK Today, Wired, Wall Street Journal, AdWeek, CommsDesign, Computer Reseller News, Computer Retail Week, Computer Shopper, Computer World, CRN, CNET, EE Times, Embedded.com, Internet.com, InformationWeek, Internet Telephony Magazine, Light Reading, Network World, Phone+, PC Magazine, Red Herring, TMCnet, VoIP News, VON and ZDNet, Dataquest, Forrester Research, Frost and Sullivan, Jupiter Communications and London Group.

PROFESSIONAL EXPERIENCE

Smith & Associates Public Relations, Anywhere   **2013–present**

Develop and deliver strategic communications that meet the specific needs of each client. Drive all PR strategy and tactics, messaging, media training, media relations, budget management, story creation and placement. Examples of past or present clients include A&T Networks (also a former LMN, CS, Hopwell client), Central.com (eHealthInsurance.com founder), and PJ Aviation.

Continued

Page 2

Co-Founder and Director, NW Public Relations, Redwood   2008–2010
PR firm that partnered high-tech clients to meet their corporate objectives. In charge of developing and managing all strategic and tactical aspects of public relations including thought leadership, leadership branding, press materials, stories, media relations and publicity.
- CS Systems – Acting Executive Communications Manager to the Managing Director.
- NH Technologies – Company's first PR consultant. Repositioned obscure company, impaired by trademark dilution, into an industry leader. (Acquired by UA Technologies in 2008.)

Marketing Manager, RST Network Systems, Barwell, Manchester   2007–2008
Directed internal, cross-functional marketing activities for the Product® after CS acquired LMN and its technology. Shortly after the acquisition, CS dissolved the Managed Appliances Business Unit (MASBU) and later licensed the Product trademark to OPQ.

Public Relations Manager, LMN Technology Corporation, Redwood   2005–2007
Company's first PR manager. Advised CEO and Head of Marketing on all aspects of PR. Developed and implemented ongoing PR campaign, strategies and tactics.
- Established Product Reviews programme, garnering hundreds of additional positive stories.
- Managed and inspired cross-functional teams of marketing, operations and customer service.

Account Supervisor, Senior Account Executive, Account Executive, XYZ Advertising & Public Relations (Acquired by FSMH in 2000), London   2002–2005
Promoted annually for successful track record of positioning unknown start-up companies into industry leaders. Designed and managed all PR strategy and activities for start-up, software, internet and networking companies. Managed teams of up to 10 PR professionals.
- Accelerated TX and its CEO out of obscurity and into undisputed leadership. Continually landed top speaking placements and media coverage.
- Transformed the unknown UVW into a highly publicized leader in the internet advertising arena. Placed hundreds of stories in both business and industry media.
- Designed and managed LMN Technology's repositioning from fledgling company to a leader in the internet appliance space.
- Launched newcomer The Internet Store, landing continual coverage in all top internet and business publications.

OTHER RELEVANT EXPERIENCE

Motivational Speaker
Representative clients: XYZ, Hopwoods, Speed X   1996–present
- Coach audiences on how to use the Olympic model to set and achieve goals, and succeed in business and life.

Television Sports Commentator
Swimming analyst for Sky, ESPN, Sportscover, SportsChannel, TN Sports and others   1995–2000
- Covered the Barcelona Olympics. Half-time reporter for games.

AWARDS & ACHIEVEMENTS
Four Olympic swimming medals: two gold, one silver, one bronze
- Southern Counties and UK Swimming Champion.

EDUCATION
University of the South
- BA in Journalism.

Final CV:

Nancy Smith

1 Any Street
Anywhere AA1 1AA

Home 55555 555555
Mobile 5555555 5555
nancysmith@yahoo.com

Group Manager • Account Director • PR Manager

Performance Profile

High-tech public relations professional with 13 years' experience in the software, internet, networking, consumer electronics and wireless industries. Substantial experience in PR and strategic communications campaigns that lead to company acquisitions. Experienced in all aspects of strategic and tactical communications from developing and managing multiple campaigns, accounts and results-orientated teams to developing and placing stories. Seasoned motivational speaker and freelance TV commentator. Twice Olympic gold medalist.

Core Competencies

High-Tech Public Relations	Media Training	Acquisition Positioning
Strategic Communications	Multiple Projects	Pitch Media
Executive Communications	Story Placement	Market Research
PR Messaging & Tactics	Counsel Executives	Build & Lead Teams
Story Telling	Strong Editing Skills	Mentor
Collateral Materials	New Business Development	Client Satisfaction
Leadership Branding	Team Management	Organizational Skills
Analyst Relations	Budget Management	Thought Leadership
Media Relations	Account Management	PR
Craft & Place Stories	Project Management	Social Media
Strong Writing Skills	Detail Orientated	

Strategic Public Relations Leadership

Orchestrated PR campaigns that positioned companies as both industry leaders and sound investments. Developed and directed PR campaigns for four companies that were subsequently acquired within two years of the campaigns: *LMN Technologies* (creator of the first Product®, acquired by *ABC Network*), *TX Digital Systems* (acquired by *XO*), *UVW* (acquired by *AMSC*), and *The Internet Store* (acquired by *TW*). Proven client satisfaction demonstrated in repeat business and account growth: over a span of 10 years, contracted by former *LMN* executives to serve as communications consultant for *LMN Technologies*, *ABC Network Systems* and *AP Networks*.

Executive Communications Management

Executive Communications Manager for the Company Secretary of the *Service Provider Sales, ABC Network Systems*. Developed communication messaging, strategy and platform skills for CEO, Company Secretary and executives.

Continued

Nancy Smith   **Page 2**

Media Coverage

News Tonight, Sky, The Today Show, Associated Press, The Sun, The Globe, Business Times, Business Week, CNN.com, Fast Company, Financial Times, Forbes, Fortune Magazine, Inc., MSNBC.com, The Times, Mercury News, SF Chronicle, UK Today, Wired, Wall Street Journal, AdWeek, CommsDesign, Computer Reseller News, Computer Retail Week, Computer Shopper, Computer World, CRN, CNET, EE Times, Embedded Systems Design, Internet.com, InfoWorld, InformationWeek, Internet Telephony, LightReading, Network World, Phone+, PC Magazine, Red Herring, TMCnet, VoIP News, VON and ZDNet, Dataquest, Forrester Research, Frost and Sullivan, Jupiter Communications, London Group.

—— **Professional Experience** ——

Director   **2010–Present**

Smith & Associates Public Relations, Anywhere

Develop and deliver strategic communications. Drive all PR strategy and tactics, messaging, media training, media relations, budget management, story creation and placement for technology clients.

- Representative clients include *A&T Networks* (former *LMN* and *XLink client*), *Central.com* (founded by *eCompany.com* founder), and *PJ Aviation*.

Director   **2008–2010**

NW Public Relations, Redwood

Developed and implemented all strategic and tactical aspects of public relations for technology clients, including thought leadership, leadership branding, story creation and telling, media materials, stories, media relations and publicity.

- *RST Network Systems* – Executive Communications Manager to Company Secretary at *RST Network*, a highly pursued public speaker.

- *NH Technologies* – Company's first PR consultant. Repositioned obscure company, impaired by trademark dilution, into an industry leader by leveraging market's widespread knowledge and use of *NH*'s industry-standard networking software.

Marketing Manager   **2007–2008**

RST Network Systems, Barwell, Manchester

Directed internal, cross-functional marketing for Product, following RST Network acquisition of *LMN* and its technology.

- Shortly after acquisition, RST Network dissolved *Managed Appliances Business Unit (MASBU)*.

Continued

Nancy Smith **Page 3**

Public Relations Manager **2005–2007**

LMN Technology Corporation, Redwood

Advised CEO and Head of Marketing on all aspects of PR. Developed and implemented all strategies, tactics and stories.

- Revamped the start-up's teetering image that was ruining *Product* sales. After two press tours, garnered hundreds of additional stories in all top trade and consumer media with the *Product Reviews* programme. Catapulted company into a leadership position in the internet appliance industry, setting it up for acquisition. *Product* is now a household name.

- Managed and inspired cross-functional teams of marketing, operations and customer service to work outside their job responsibilities to deliver excellent service to hundreds of editors beta testing the *Product 2.0*.

Account Supervisor; Senior Account Executive; Account Executive **2002–2005**

XYZ Advertising & Public Relations (Acquired by FSMH in 2000), London

Promoted annually for successful track record of positioning unknown companies as both industry leaders and solid investments/acquisitions. Designed and managed all PR strategy and activities for start-up, software, internet and networking companies. Managed teams of up to 10 PR professionals.

- Repositioned, rebranded, relaunched, and reintroduced *LMN*, the *Product 1.0* and *2.0*, positioning them collectively as leading the nascent internet appliance space.

- Accelerated *TX* and its CEO out of obscurity and into undisputed leadership through media placement and top speaking engagements.

- Transformed unknown *UVW* into a highly publicized leader in the internet advertising arena. Placed hundreds of stories in both business and industry media.

- Launched *The Internet Store*, landing continual coverage in all top internet and business publications.

—— **Complementary Experience** ——

Motivational Speaker **1996–Present**

Coach audiences on how to use the Olympic model to set and achieve goals, and succeed in business and life. Representative clients: XYZ, Hopwoods, Speed X.

Television Sports Commentator **1995–2000**

Swimming analyst for Sky, ESPN, Sportscover, SportsChannel, TN Sports and others. Covered the Barcelona Olympics.

Awards & Achievements

Winner – Two Olympic swimming gold medals plus one silver and one bronze.

Southern Counties and UK swimming champion.

EDUCATION – University of the South; BA Journalism.

3
The basic ingredients

Your CV is the most important document you possess.
How well it comes out depends on what goes in. So if you want a great CV, you need a logical way to gather the right information to tell that story.

When in the previous chapter you got inside your customer's head, you gained a clear understanding for the story your CV needs to tell. Now with the requirements of your target job in front of you, work backwards through your professional life, methodically pulling out the skills and experiences that will help your CV tell the story of someone who can do this target job.

Examine your work history through the lens of your target job

Examine your work history through the lens of your survey, and gather all the information with the greatest relevance to your target job. This is the raw material for the story your CV will tell and for the way you define who you are as a professional: your professional identity. The more notes you have, the better. Even if some of the information doesn't make it into your CV, it will still have immense value preparing you for the interviews your CV will generate and the insights it will give you into yourself as a professional.

Fifty per cent of the success of any project is in the preparation

Here's the information-gathering questionnaire we use for our professional CV-writing service. It will help you gather all the information about your professional life in one place.

Half the success of any project depends on the preparation. The work you do here is also going to have a real impact on your career and the quality of your life for years to come. So bite the bullet and do it.

CV questionnaire

Name (exactly as wanted on CV): _____

Address: _____

Town: _____ County: _____ Postcode: _____

Home Phone: _____ Mobile: _____

E-mail: _____

Are you willing to relocate?   Yes ( )   No ( )

Are you willing to travel?   Yes ( )   No ( )

Please answer the following questions as completely and accurately as possible. Not all questions may apply to you. If they do not apply, mark them N/A.

Position/career objective: list top three job title choices in order of preference

If the titles are for related positions (*eg 1 – Sales; 2 – Marketing; 3 – Business Development*) your CV can be developed to reflect the cross-functional target(s). If the goals are not related (*eg 1 – Rocket Scientist; 2 – Pastry Chef; 3 – Landscape Designer*), the CV will be written to fit your first selection and we will discuss creating additional versions of your CV.

1. _____

2. _____

3. _____

Desired Industry _____

Is this a career change for you? Yes ( ) No ( )

Purpose of CV (eg job change, career change, promotion, business development/marketing tool)

_____

Summarize your experience in a couple of sentences. *Do not provide details of positions here – We just want a sentence or two about your background.* (For example: I have been in the accounting field for 12 years and received three promotions to the current position, which I've held for two years.)

_____

_____

_____

What are some terms (keywords) specific to your line of work? (If you're not sure, you can find these as words that show up consistently on job postings.)

_____

_____

What are your key strengths that you want to highlight on your CV? What makes you stand out from your competitors? Drill down to the essence of what differentiates you.

_____

_____

Current Salary: _____   Expected Salary: _____

Education

List all degrees, certificates, diplomas, dates received, school or college, and location of school or college. Begin with the most recent and work backwards.

Name of School/College/Univ: _____

City/Town: _____

Qualifications Obtained (ie GCSE, BSc, BA, MBA, PhD) _____

Year Completed _____

Extracurricular Activities (include leadership, sports, study abroad, etc):

_____

Name of School/College/Univ: _____

City/Town: _____

Qualifications Obtained (ie BSc, BA, MBA, PhD) _____

Year Completed _____

Extracurricular Activities (include leadership, sports, etc, study abroad, etc):

_____

Professional development (training courses/seminars/ workshops, etc)

Ongoing professional education signals commitment to success. If you attended numerous courses, list the most recent and/or relevant to your career and indicate that additional course information is available. Those courses rendered obsolete by technology and the passage of time can be ignored.

Course Name: _____

Completion Date: _____ Duration: _____

Qualification Obtained: _____ Location of Training: _____

Course Name: _____

Completion Date: _____ Duration: _____

Qualification Obtained: _____ Location of Training: _____

Course Name: _____

Completion Date: _____ Duration: _____

Qualification Obtained: _____ Location of Training: _____

Professional certification:

_____

Professional licences:

_____

Armed Services (include branch of service, locations, position, rank achieved, years of service, honourable discharge, key accomplishments, special recognition, awards, etc)

_____

Professional organizations/affiliations

Active membership in a professional association is a key tool for career success.

Name of Organization: _____

Positions Held: _____

Name of Organization: _____

Positions Held: _____

Publications/presentations: title/periodical/location/date (begin each on a new line)

Patents and copyrights

You can also include here your work on projects that resulted in copyrights and patents, so long as you make clear your real contribution.

Computer skills (include hardware, operating systems, software, internet, e-mail, etc)

Maybe it's just MS Word and Excel or maybe it runs to languages and protocols. Nobody today gets ahead without technological adeptness. Capture your fluency here and update regularly; that alphabet soup of technology just might help your CV in database searches.

Hardware:

Operating Systems:

Software Applications:

Other if relevant:

Foreign languages (indicate level of fluency and if verbal/written)

_____

Global experience/cultural diversity awareness

In our global economy any exposure here is relevant, and it doesn't have to be professional in nature. If you've travelled extensively or you grew up in a different country, that can be a big plus. Just name the countries not the circumstances.

Company Awards/Recognition (indicate where and when received):

_____

Community/Volunteer Activities (name of organization, years involved, positions held):

_____

_____

Hobbies/interests

How do you fill your out-of-work hours? Your CV can include those activities that say something positive about the professional you. For example, in sales and marketing just about all group activities show a desirable mindset. Playing bridge, for example, might argue strong analytical skills, and the senior exec who still plays competitive lacrosse and runs marathons is crazy not to let the world know.

_____

_____

_____

_____

_____

_____

Action verbs

In describing your work experience in each position you have held, use the action verbs that best characterize your daily work, duties, responsibilities and level of authority. Select from the following list or use other 'action verbs' when completing the sections:

accepted	conducted	executed	lectured
accomplished	consolidated	expanded	led
achieved	contained	expedited	maintained
acted	contracted	explained	managed
adapted	contributed	extracted	marketed
addressed	controlled	fabricated	mediated
administered	coordinated	facilitated	moderated
advanced	corresponded	familiarized	monitored
advised	counselled	fashioned	motivated
allocated	created	focused	negotiated
analysed	critiqued	forecasted	operated
appraised	cut	formulated	organized
approved	decreased	founded	originated
arranged	defined	generated	overhauled
assembled	delegated	guided	oversaw
assigned	demonstrated	headed	performed
assisted	designed	identified	persuaded
attained	developed	illustrated	planned
audited	devised	implemented	prepared
authored	diagnosed	improved	presented
automated	directed	increased	prioritized
balanced	dispatched	influenced	processed
budgeted	distinguished	informed	produced
built	diversified	initiated	programmed
calculated	drafted	innovated	projected
catalogued	edited	inspected	promoted
chaired	educated	installed	proposed
clarified	eliminated	instigated	provided
classified	emended	instituted	publicized
coached	enabled	instructed	published
collected	encouraged	integrated	purchased
compiled	engineered	interpreted	recommended
completed	enlisted	interviewed	reconciled
composed	established	introduced	recorded
computed	evaluated	invented	recruited
conceptualized	examined	launched	reduced

referred	retrieved	solved	taught
regulated	revamped	specified	trained
rehabilitated	revitalized	stimulated	translated
remodelled	saved	streamlined	travelled
repaired	scheduled	strengthened	trimmed
represented	schooled	summarized	upgraded
researched	screened	supervised	validated
resolved	set	surveyed	worked
restored	shaped	systemized	wrote
restructured	solidified	tabulated	

Accomplishments/achievements/successes

When completing the next few pages of the questionnaire, refer to the following questions to refresh your memory regarding your professional accomplishments and achievements. Remember: people hire results and look at past performance as an indication of the value you offer. Consider the various positions you've held and come up with four to six of the strongest contributions you made in each position. Ask yourself how your current employer is better off now than when the company hired you.

1   Did you increase sales/productivity/volume? Provide the percentage or amount.

2   Did you generate new business or increase the client base? How? What were the circumstances?

3   Did you forge affiliations, partnerships or strategic alliances that improved company success? With whom and what were the results?

4   Did you save your company money? If so, how and by how much?

5   Did you design and/or institute any new system or process? If so, what were the results?

6   Did you meet an impossible deadline through extra effort? If so what difference did this make to your company?

7   Did you bring in a major project under budget? If so, how did you make this happen? What was the budget? What were you responsible for saving in terms of time and/or money?

8 Did you suggest and/or help launch a new product or programme? If so, did you take the lead or provide support? How successful was the effort? What were the results?

9 Did you assume new responsibilities that weren't part of your job? Were they assigned or did you do so proactively? Why were you selected?

10 Did you introduce any new or more effective systems, processes or techniques for increasing productivity? What was the result?

11 Did you improve communication in your firm? If so, with whom and what was the outcome?

12 How did your company benefit from your performance?

13 Did you complete any special projects? What were they and what was the result?

When describing your accomplishments/achievements use the following three-step CAR format:

C = Challenge (what challenge did you face or what problem did you resolve?)

A = Action (what action did you take?)

R = Results (what was the result of the action you took? What was the value to the company?)

Professional experience

You're ready to assemble the information about your work history and experience. Begin with your present employer/project. Include self-employment, contract, and volunteer or unpaid work if it applies to your career target. Be sure to list different positions at the same company as separate jobs. Repeat the section below for all the professional positions you've held:

Name of company: _____

Location: _____

Dates of employment: _____

Your actual job title: _____

Your functional/working job title if different from actual title: _____

Title of person you report to _____

Number of people you supervise: _____

Their titles or functions: _____

_____

Briefly describe the size of the organization (volume produced; revenues; number of employees; local, national, or international; etc) _____

_____

_____

What is it that they do, make or sell? _____

_____

Where do they rank in their industry in terms of their competitors? _____

_____

_____

What were you employed to do? Briefly describe your duties, responsibilities and level of authority. Use numbers and percentages, quantify budgets, state with whom you interacted, etc. Provide two or three brief sentences about your overall area of responsibility and list them in order of importance. Refer back to the list of action verbs to help you brainstorm.

Example:

Selected to re-engineer and revitalize this £65 million business unit with accountability for 32 offices across the UK and Europe. Established strategic vision and developed operational infrastructure. Managed Supply Chain, Logistics/Distribution, Forecasting, System Integration, Project Management, Contracts Administration and Third-Party Site Operations.

Or more simply:

Drove production for the world's largest fabrication company, with 258 employees working in multiple shifts.

Briefly describe three to five of your accomplishments in this position. Use the achievements that best support your career target and describe them in a brief statement. Give facts and figures. How did your accomplishment contribute to the company?

_____

_____

_____

_____

_____

Take your time: you are laying the foundation for career success

When completing the exercises in this chapter it may be tempting to rush through them or to look for shortcuts, but remember that you are assembling the information that will be the bricks and mortar of your CV, the most financially important document you own. You need it to be as complete and well thought out as possible.

4

Building your professional identity

Long-term success, rewarding work without redundancies and professional growth to the degree that fits your goals are much easier to achieve when you are credible and visible within your profession.

Creating a professional identity as part of an overall career management strategy will help you to achieve this credibility and visibility because it gives *you* focus and motivation, and gives *others* an easy way to identity you.

Establishing a professional identity takes time; it doesn't happen overnight. But the greater the effort you put into building credibility and visibility, the quicker you progress in your department, your company and, ultimately, your profession.

Think of your professional identity as the announcement to the professional community of how you want to be seen in your chosen field, and recognize your CV as the primary tool for disseminating the message. It's your CV that captures your capabilities and behavioural profile, and in the process creates a clear image of a unique, consummate professional.

Components of a desirable professional identity

You create an identifiable professional identity by first identifying those skills and behaviours that make you different and desirable. In other words, your professional identity is the conscious positioning in your CV, of your best professional qualities. In order to do this well it helps to understand what employers believe are the most desirable professional qualities.

They can be broken down into three sections:

1 technical skills;

2 transferable skills;

3 professional values.

Technical skills

The technical skills of your current profession are the technical competencies that give you the ability to do your job, the skills needed to complete a task and the know-how to use them productively and proficiently. These technical skills are mandatory if you want a job in your profession. Technical skills vary from profession to profession, so many of your current technical skills will only be transferable within your current profession. Staying current with the skills of your chosen profession is going to be an integral part of your ongoing professional growth and stability. That's why the continuing education on your CV can be an important tool for developing your professional identity.

Transferable skills

Transferable skills are the skills that apply to *all* professions – the set of skills that underlines your ability to execute the *technical skills* of your job effectively, whatever your job might be. They are the foundation of all the professional success you will experience in this or any other career that you may pursue over the years.

Communication skills

Every professional job today requires communication skills; promotions and professional success are impossible without them.

The primary communication skills are:

- **Verbal skills** – what you say and how you say it.

- **Listening skills** – listening to understand, rather than just waiting for your turn to talk.

- **Writing skills** – writing clearly and concisely. Written communication is essential for any professional career. It creates a lasting impression of who you are, and it's an important expression of your professional identity.

- **Technological communication skills** – understanding and being able to use the most up-to-date methods of communication, including computers, smart phones and social media. Technology has changed the way we communicate, and your ability to navigate the new communication media can and will affect your professional success.

Teamworking skills

The professional world revolves around the complex challenges of making money, and such challenges require teams of people to provide ongoing solutions. This in turn requires you to work efficiently with others who have totally different responsibilities, backgrounds, objectives and areas of expertise.

Critical thinking skills

Critical thinking, analytical or problem-solving skills, allow the successful professional to think through and clearly define a challenge and its desired solutions, and then to evaluate and implement the best solution for that challenge from all available options. Remember, a company employs someone because it has a problem that needs solving.

Time management and organization

The ability to manage time and organize activities increases productivity. The people who do this, often thought of as high achievers and goal-orientated because they get so much done, are just people who learned how to organize themselves and consequently work with more purpose. The result is that they can multitask and seriously outperform their peers.

Leadership

When you are credible, when people believe in your competence and believe you have everyone's success as your goal, they will follow you; *you* accept responsibility but *others* get the credit. When your actions inspire others to think more, learn more, do more and become more, you are on your way to becoming a leader.

Creativity

There's a difference between creativity and just having ideas. Creativity enables the development of ideas with the strategic and tactical know-how that brings them to life.

In a professional context, creativity is the generation of new ideas related to a specific situation, challenge or goal.

Professional values

Professional values are an interconnected set of core beliefs that enable professionals to determine what is appropriate for any given situation. Highly prized by employers, this value system is integral to the successful delivery of technical and transferable skills.

Successful professionals embody these values every day in all they do. They will open doors of opportunity for you from the day you start your first job to the day you retire.

- **Motivation and energy:** motivation expresses itself in a commitment to the job, an eagerness to learn and grow professionally, and a willingness to take the rough with the smooth. Motivation is invariably expressed by the *energy* demonstrated through a person's work. The motivated employee always gives that extra effort to get the job done and to get it done well.

- **Commitment and reliability:** these qualities embody a dedication to your profession and your job, an understanding of the role your job plays in the company's success, and the empowerment that comes from knowing how you contribute to the greater good. Your dedication will also express itself in your *reliability*: Showing up is half the battle; the other half is your performance on the job. This requires following up your actions and not relying on anyone else to ensure the job is done.

- **Determination:** this value marks a resilient professional who doesn't get worn down and doesn't back off when a problem or situation gets tough. It's a value that characterizes the individual who chooses to be part of the solution rather than part of the problem.

- **Pride and integrity:** pride in yourself as a professional means always making sure the job is done to the best of your ability, paying attention to the details and to time and cost constraints. Integrity means taking responsibility for your actions, both good and bad. It also means treating others, within and outside the company, with respect.

- **Productivity:** always work towards enhanced productivity through efficiencies of time, resources, money and effort.

- **Economy:** most problems have two solutions, and the expensive one isn't always the better. Ideas of efficiency and economy should engage your creative mind in ways that others would not consider.

- **Procedures:** you should recognize the need for procedures and understand that they are implemented only after careful thought. Understand and always follow the chain of command. Don't implement your own 'improved' procedures or organize others to do so.

Identifying your competitive difference

The people who hire you need to differentiate you from the other candidates. The following questions will help you identify the factors that help to make you unique. Each of these is a component of your professional identity that you can integrate into your CV.

- Which of the transferable skills, behaviours and values best captures the essence of the professional you?

- Which of the transferable skills, behaviours and values have you marked for further professional development?

- What qualities or characteristics do you share with top performers in your department/profession?

- What have you achieved with these qualities?

- What makes you different from others with whom you have worked?

- What are the four traits that best define you as a professional and how does each help your performance?

- How does each help your co-workers?

- How does each help your department and boss?

- How does each help your company?

- Why do you stand out in your job/profession? (If you realize you don't stand out and you want to, examine why the people you admire stand out and use them as a model for development.)

- How are you better than others doing the same job? Can you quantify this difference?

- What excites you most about your professional responsibilities?

- What are your achievements in these areas?

- What do your peers say about you?

- What does management say about you?

- What do your subordinates say about you?

- What are your top four professional skills and what have you achieved with them?

- What are your top four leadership skills and what have you achieved with them?

- What do you believe are the three key requirements of your job?

- What gives you greatest satisfaction in the work you do?

- What value does this combination of skills, behaviours, values and achievements bring to employers in your target market?

When you identify these transferable skills, learned behaviours and core values they become part of your professional identity:

- They can appear in your CV: in your opening or closing statements, performance profile or performance/career highlights sections or in the body of your CV.

- They will inform the substance of your answers to questions at job interviews.

- When you identify a transferable skill/learned behaviour you *do not* possess, it should immediately become part of your professional development programme.

Positioning your skills

Understanding the transferable skills and values you possess and how they differentiate you from others is an important step in defining your professional identity. The impact these skills and values have on your work can be used in your CV, in your covering letters, and as illustrative answers to questions in interviews.

If development and application of these skills is central to establishing a valid professional identity, then part of promoting your identity is the need to position them in your CV and at interviews. As you read through these skills and values, you'll see, for example, 'communication', and think, 'Yes, I have good communication skills'. When this happens, come up with examples of how your communication skills played an important role in the successful completion of an assignment.

Reading about 'time management and organization', you might say, 'Now *there's* something I have to work on!' In this instance you have identified a key behaviour that needs improvement, and you can immediately set about a personal development programme.

Integrating your professional identity into your CV

Your professional identity is communicated throughout your CV especially with the opening and closing statements. The first place you establish a professional identity is with your target job title where you consciously decide on the job that best allows you to package your skills. The opening statement that follows gives the reader a focus on your CV's purpose and goal. It says in effect, 'These are the benefits my presence on your payroll will bring to your team and your company.'

Notice how the following statements focus on the benefits brought to the job, but do not take up space identifying the specifics of how this was done:

- Senior operations/plant management professional: Dedicated to continuous improvement ~ Start-up & turnaround operations ~ Mergers & change management ~ Process & productivity optimization ~ Logistics & supply chain.

- Mechanical/design/structural engineer: Delivering high volume of complex structural and design projects for global companies in manufacturing/construction/power generation.

- Account management/client communications manager: Reliably achieving performance improvement and compliance within Financial Services Industry.

Closing brand statement

You can also achieve a powerful effect with a final comment that relates to your professional identity:

I understand customer service to be the company's face to the world and treat every customer interaction as critical to our success; leadership by example and conscientious performance management underlies my department's consistent customer satisfaction ratings.

Benefits of a defined professional identity

Understanding the skills and attributes needed for professional success might be your most recognizable benefit. Your professional identity is also extremely valuable for your long-term success. Knowing who you are, what you offer and how you want to be perceived will differentiate you from others. And because you understand yourself and can communicate this understanding you will have a professional presence.

In this new, insecure world of work, it makes sense to maintain visibility within your profession. It is nothing more than intelligent market positioning. The professional identity built into your new CV is the profile you should keep posted on your professional networking sites. This increases your credibility and visibility within your profession as well as the recruitment industry, making you more desirable as an employee and increasing your options.

5
Choose your format

First impressions are important. You have the right and the obligation to package your professional experience to its greatest benefit.

In this chapter you'll find out how you can put your CV together to present yourself in the best possible way, creating a compelling, professional document that highlights your unique professional identity.

We'll look at:

- Choosing a CV template: chronological, functional or a combination of the two

- Customizing the template to suit your specific needs

- Filling in and editing the template to create the best impression.

Choosing a CV template

Everyone has different work experience: you may have worked for just one employer throughout your career or have worked for five companies in 10 years; you may have changed careers entirely, or you may have maintained a predictable career path, changing jobs but staying within one profession or industry.

The format you choose for your CV depends on what your unique background brings to the target job. There are three broadly defined CV formats but their goals are the same:

1 to maximize your performance in the CV databases;

2 to demonstrate your grasp of the job's requirements;

3 to create a professional identity for someone who lives and breathes this work;

4 to showcase relevant achievements, attributes and expertise to best advantage;

5 to minimize any weaknesses.

The three major formats for presenting your CV are: chronological, functional and combination. Your particular circumstances will determine the right format for you.

The chronological CV

The chronological CV is the most widely accepted format. It is what most of us think of when we think of CVs, a chronological listing of job titles and responsibilities. It starts with your current or most recent employment, then works backwards to your first job.

This format is good for demonstrating your growth in a single profession. It is suitable for anyone with practical work experience who hasn't suffered prolonged periods of unemployment. It is not always the best choice if you are just out of education or if you are changing careers, where it might draw attention to a lack of specific, relevant experience.

The distinguishing characteristic of the chronological CV is the way it ties your job responsibilities and achievements to specific employers, job titles and dates.

This is the simplest CV to create.

The chronological CV (page 1)

PARAG GUPTA

1 Any Street • Anytown AA1 1AA • 55555 555555 • parag.gupta@technical.com

SYSTEMS ENGINEER:

Motivated and driven IT Professional offering 9+ years of hands-on experience in designing, implementing and enhancing systems to automate business operations. Demonstrated ability to develop high-performance systems, applications, databases and interfaces.

- Part of TL9000 CND audit interviews that helped Technical get TL9000 certified, which is significant in Telecom industry. Skilled trainer and proven ability to lead many successful projects, like TSS, EMX and TOL.
- Strategically manage time and expediently resolve problems for optimal productivity, improvement and profitability; able to direct multiple tasks effectively.
- Strong technical background with a solid history of delivering outstanding customer service.
- Highly effective liaison and communication skills proven by effective interaction with management, users, team members and vendors.

Technical Skills

Operating Systems:	Unix, Windows (2000, XP, 7), DOS
Languages:	C, C++, Java, Pascal, Assembly Languages (Z8000, 808x, DSP)
Methodologies:	TL9000, Digital Six Sigma
Software:	MS Office, Adobe FrameMaker, MATLAB
RDBMS:	DOORS, Oracle 7.x
Protocols:	TCP/IP, SS7 ISUP, A1, ANSI, TL1, SNMP
Tools:	Teamplay, ClearCase, ClearQuest, M-Gate keeper, Exceed, Visio, DocExpress, Compass
Other:	CDMA Telecom Standards – 3GPP2 (Including TIA/EIA-2001, TIA/EIA-41, TIA/EIA-664), ITU-T, AMPS

Professional Experience

Technical, Main Network Division, Portsmouth **Jan 2006–Present**

Principal Staff Engineer • Products Systems Engineering • Nov 2011–Present

- Known as 'go-to' person for CDMA call processing and billing functional areas.
- Created customer requirements documents for Technical SoftSwitch (TSS) and SMS Gateway products. All deliverables done on/ahead schedule with high quality.
- Solely accountable for authoring and allocation, customer reviews, supporting fellow system engineers, development and test, and customer documentation teams.
- Support Product Management in RFPs, customer feature prioritization, impact statements and budgetary estimates.
- Mentored junior engineers and one innovation disclosure [patent] submitted in 2014.
- Resolved deployed customer/internal requirements issues and contributed to Virtual Zero Defect quality goal.
- TOL process champion and part of CND focus group that contributed to reducing CRUD backlog (NPR) by 25% and cycle time (FRT) by 40%.
- Recognized as the TL9000 expert. Triage representative for switching and messaging products.
- Achieved 'CND Quality Award' for contribution to quality improvement, May 2014.
- Senior Staff Engineer • MSS Systems Engineering • May 2009–Oct 2011.
- Led a team of 12 engineers for three major software releases of TSS product included around 80 features/enhancements to create T-Gate SE deliverables.
- Led a team of 12 engineers for three major software releases of TSS product included around 80 features/enhancements to create T-Gate SE deliverables.

Continued

The chronological CV (page 2)

PARAG GUPTA   Page 2 of 2

- Mentored newer engineers to get up to speed on TSS product.
- Created requirements for TSS product, 30 features/enhancements contributing to five major software releases. Recognized as overall product expert with specific focus on call processing and billing.
- Played integral role in successfully implementing proprietary commercial TSS billing system.
- Supported PdM organization by creating ROMs, technical support for RFPs (Vivo, Sprint, TELUS, TM, Tata, Inquam, Alaska, Reliance, Pakistan, PBTL, Mauritius, Telefonica, Brasicel and Angola).
- Proactively identified functional areas of improvement for requirements coverage, contributed to resolving several faults, improved customer documentation, and provided reference for future releases as well as other customers.
- Received 'Above and Beyond Performance Award' Oct 2010.

Senior Software Engineer • EMX Development • Aug 2007–Apr 2009

- Successfully led and coordinated the cross-functional development teams, 30 engineers, to meet the scheduled design, code and test completion dates ensuring Feature T-Gates are met.
- Feature Technical Lead for Concurrent Voice/Data Services feature, the largest revenue-generating feature for KDDI customer.
- Feature Lead for Paging Channel SMS feature. Created requirements and design; led implementation phase of five engineers' teams supported product, network and release testing; and created customer reference documentation.
- Performed the role of functional area lead for Trunk Manager and A1 interface functional areas. Provided two-day technical workshops for internal/customer knowledge sharing and functional area transition from Caltel.
- Provided customer site testing and FOA (First Office Application) support for major EMX releases and off-hours CNRC (Customer Networks Resolution Centre) support.
- Received 'Bravo Award' May 2008, Sep 2008, Jan 2009.

Software Engineer • EMX Development • Jan 2006–Jul 2007

- Developed design and code for SMS feature as a Trunk Manager functional area lead for the largest FA impacted by the feature. Supported product, network and release testing.
- Contributed to customer release documentation. Supported feature-level SMS testing at various internal labs and customer sites resulting in successful deployment at customer sites.
- Designed and coded phases for wiretap and virtual circuits feature development, initial assessment of internal and customer EMX PRs (problem reports) to route/classify issues and providing problem assessments for many of these PRs.
- Created an implementation process to serve as reference for new hires.
- Provided CNRC support during the Y2K transition.
- Received 'Above and Beyond Performance Award' Jan 2007, Dec 2007 and 'Certificate of Outstanding Achievement' Jun 2006.

Education:

MSc in Computer Engineering • University of London •2005
BSc(Hons) Electronic Engineering • Technology and Science Institute, India •2003

Significant Trainings Include

- Open Source Software • WiMAX • Agile Management for Software Engineering
- WSG Requirements Process • Product Security

The functional CV

The functional CV format focuses on the professional skills you bring to a specific target job, rather than when, where or how you acquired them. It de-emphasizes employers and employment dates by putting them on the second page, which gets less attention than your lead page.

The functional format is useful for:

- mature professionals with a storehouse of expertise pursuing second careers;

- entry-level professionals whose skimpy experience might not justify a chronological CV;

- career changers who want to focus on skills because their experience was developed in a different professional context;

- people returning to the workplace after a long absence.

Although functional CVs are more freeform than chronological ones, they should share certain structural features:

- Target job title: for any CV to be effective it must be written with a specific target job in mind, and this is especially true for a functional CV. Because it focuses so strongly on skills and the ability to contribute in a particular direction, rather than a directly relevant work history, you really must have an employment objective clearly in mind.

- Performance profile/performance summary or career summary: your target job should be followed by a short paragraph that captures your professional capabilities as they address the requirements of the target job.

- Core competencies: a core competencies section in your functional CV will help its performance in databases; the use of critical keywords early on shows that you have the essential skills for the job.

- Performance highlights: based on your target job, this is where you identify the skills, behaviours and accomplishments that make you suitable for the job.

- Dates: if your employment history lacks continuity, a functional CV allows you to de-emphasize dates somewhat, but an absence of employment dates altogether will just draw attention to a potential problem. See Chapter 6 for more about how to handle employment dates.

The functional CV (page 1)

Charles Chalmers
1 Any Street, Anytown AA1 1AA • 55555 555555 • fineartist@anyisp.co.uk
Senior Curator

Performance Profile

My professional life is focused on art and all it embraces: drawing, painting, sculpture, photography, cinema, video, audio, performance and digital art, art history and criticism; my personal life is similarly committed. Recently relocated to Bristol, I intend to make a contribution to the south-west arts community that harnesses my knowledge, enthusiasm and sensibilities.

Core Competencies

Photographer ~ editor ~ drawing ~ painting ~ sculpture ~ photography ~ cinema ~ video ~ audio ~ performance and digital art ~ art history and criticism ~ global artist networks ~ first-rank private collectors ~ social networking-themed, resourced, sequenced shows ~ outreach & community involvement ~ education & outreach ~ installation-hang, light and label-media kits ~ artist materials ~ Photoshop-art-staff management ~ curriculum development ~ art handlers-maintenance ~ printers ~ catering ~ graphics ~ portfolio prep-int/ext shows ~ theatre sets ~ streamed video gallery tours

Performance Highlights

ART HISTORY

Thorough knowledge of art history from caves of Lascaux through current artists such as Bruce Nauman, Jessica Stockholder and Luc Tuymans. Film history from Lumière Brothers to Almodovar. Current with key critical art and film theory. Ongoing workshops and lectures on the likes of Matthew Barney, Louise Bourgeoise and Andy Goldsworthy.

RESEARCH NEW ARTISTS

Connected to cutting-edge art and artists through involvement with the art communities and galleries and the faculty, students and student networks of Central Saint Martins, Goldsmiths College, The Central School of Art & Design, and now UWE. Twenty years of gallery openings and networking with artists at Tate and Tate Modern, ICA, British Film Institute, International Centre for Photography workshops and lectures.

SOURCING ART WORK

Through local artists, regional and global artist networks, intercultural artist exchanges, community groups, private collectors, personal and family networks, and internet calls for submissions.

ART AND THE COMMUNITY

Conception and launch of themed, resourced and sequenced shows that invigorate campus and community involvement. Reconfigure existing art spaces to create dynamic dialogue with visitors. Education and outreach programmes.

Continued

The functional CV (page 2)

CHARLES CHALMERS   Page 2 of 2

ART INSTALLATION
Maintain fluidity of gallery space in preparing exhibitions with recognition of size/time considerations for the art, to ensure a sympathetic environment for the presented works. Hang, light and label shows in sequences that create dialogue between the works.

PUBLIC RELATIONS MATERIALS
Energizing invitations, comprehensive press kits, illustrated press releases and artist binder materials. Sensitive to placing art in historical/cultural context. Photoshop.

Management experience

Fourteen years' art-staff management experience, including curriculum development. Responsible for art instructors, art handlers, maintenance crews, and working with printers, catering and graphic arts staff.

Professional experience

1999–2010 Head of Visual Arts, The Greenway School
Duties: Curriculum development, portfolio preparation, internal and external monthly shows, theatre sets, monthly video news show, taught art history and all the studio arts, managed staff of three.

1994–2009 President Art Workshops
Duties: Private art studio and art history curriculums, staff of four. Private groups to London museums and gallery tours.

1985–1994 Freelance artist, photographer and editor
Highlights from the sublime to the ridiculous include: Taught photography at Trinity School, London; editor of Informat, insurance industry trade magazine; assistant to Audrey Logan, documentary filmmaker and director.

Education

BA Central Saint Martins School of Art, 1988
Awards: ****** ***** Prize for film criticism
Taught undergraduate Intro to Film, under ****** ***** and ****** ******.

Memberships

Tate Gallery, RWA, Ashmolean Museum, Metropolitan Museum of Art, ICA.

Recent exhibitions

2009. Centre Gallery, Southampton
2010. Friel Gallery, Portsmouth
2011. Fuller Museum, Exeter
2007, 2012. Zeitgeist Gallery, Cambridge

Features of a functional CV

The example functional CV shown here is for someone applying for a job as a gallery or museum curator whose only prior experience is as an art teacher.

- Despite his lack of experience in the target job, he has all the relevant skills the position requires and his first page covers everything that a good gallery or museum curator needs to know.

- It is quite clear that this person really understands the work of a curator. The first time this CV was used, it resulted in an interview and a job offer.

- The fact that this person had been head of the art department of a private school rather than a curator was never an issue, because he so clearly understood the demands of the target job and was able to demonstrate on his CV that he had exactly the credentials needed.

- A Core Competencies section could be added to increase database visibility.

The combination CV

This format is fast becoming the CV of choice in a database-dominated world. It has all the flexibility and strength that comes from combining both the chronological and functional formats:

- It allows maximum flexibility to demonstrate your grasp of the job and its requirements.

- It encourages greater data density and detailed information, which improves database retrieval.

- It offers more flexibility and scope for establishing a professional identity.

It should include the following structural features:

- Target job title (here's the job I want).

- Performance profile/performance summary (here's a snapshot of what I can do).

- Core competencies (here are the professional skills that help me to do my job well).

- Technology/technical competencies (optional: here are the technical skills that help me to do my job well).

- Performance highlights (optional: outstanding achievements).

- Professional experience (when and where everything happened).

The combination CV (page 1)

John William Wisher, MBA
1 Any Street
Anytown AA1 1AA

jwisher@ameritech.net   55555 555555

Expert leadership in cost-effective supply chain, vendor and project management within organizations.

EXECUTIVE PROFILE

A visionary, forward-thinking SUPPLY CHAIN AND LOGISTICS LEADER offering 20+ years of progressive growth and outstanding success streamlining operations across a wide range of industries. Excellent negotiation and relationship management skills with ability to inspire teams to outperform expectations. Proven record of delivering a synchronized supply chain approach through strategic models closely mirroring business plan to dramatically optimize ROI and manage risk.

Supply Chain Strategy: – Successfully led over 500 supply chain management initiatives across a wide spectrum of businesses, negotiating agreements from £5K to £27 million. Implemented technology solutions and streamlined processes to reduce redundancies and staffing hours, improving both efficiency and productivity. Industries include: industrial manufacturing, consumer goods, government and defence, healthcare, high tech and retail.

Industry Knowledge: – Extensive knowledge base developed from hands-on industry experience. Began career in dock operations with experience in Hub and Package Operations, multi-site retail operations management, to custom supply chain strategy development over 21-year career with DHL.

Supply Chain Process Costing: – Built several information packets on total cost of ownership (TCO) and facilitated negotiations to identify and confirm opportunities. Worked to increase awareness among stakeholders on efficiencies and cost-saving measures ROI. Delivered £3.75 million total cost savings to client base over three-year period.

Operations Reorganization: – Designed and implemented new sales force alignment and reporting structure; increased daily sales calls by 20%, reduced travel mileage 23%, and head count by nine; total annual cost savings of £920K.

Logistics: – Experienced across all modes of transportation: ocean, air freight, mail services and small package. Perform complex analysis to develop strategy based on cost and delivery requirements.

Project Management: – Implemented complete £1.2 million redesign of 11 new DHL customer centres. Managed vendor and lease negotiations, developed budgets, training and sales structure. All 11 centres up and operational on time and on budget.

Cost and Process Improvements

- Implemented complete warehouse redesign for a large optical distributor. Optimized warehouse operations through engineering a new warehouse design, integrating and automating technology, and synchronization of goods movement through ocean, air, ground and mail services. Reduced transportation expense by 15%, increased production levels by 25%, reduced inventory by 15% and staffing by 20%.
- Built custom supply chain for a nationally recognized golf club manufacturer. Improved service levels by 30%, reduced damage by 45%, and integrated technology to support shipping process automation, reducing billing function staffing hours 50%.

Trust-Based Leadership

Vendor/Client Negotiations

Cross-Functional Collaboration

Supply Chain Mapping

Financial Logistics Analysis

Contingency Planning

Risk Management

Competitive Analysis

Haz Mat Compliance

Inventory Planning, Control & Distribution

Recruiting/Training/Development

Project Management

Organizational Change Management

Distributive Computing

Budget Management

Labour Relations

Continued

The combination CV (page 2)

John William Wisher, MBA   Page 2 of 3

PROFESSIONAL BACKGROUND

DHL Parcel Service   1991–Present

World's largest package-delivery company and global leader in supply chain services, offering an extensive range of options for synchronizing the movement of goods, information and funds. Serves more than 200 countries worldwide.

DIRECTOR/AREA MANAGER – SUPPLY CHAIN SALES, 2010–Present

Promoted to lead and develop a cross-functional sales force of 18 in consultative supply chain management services to Northern-area businesses. Directs development of integrated supply chain management solutions across all modes of transportation, closely mirroring client business plans. Mentors team in Demand Responsive Model, a proven methodology to quickly align internal and external resources with changing market demands, situational requirements and mission critical conditions. Manages £100 million P&L.

Accomplishments:
- Implements over 100 multi-million-pound supply chain integrations per year with 14% annual growth on 8% plan.
- Develops future organizational leaders; four staff members promoted through effective mentoring and development.
- Choreographed a supply chain movement from Northern Europe for a global fast-food chain to deliver 300k cartons to 15k locations all on the same day. Utilized modes of ocean, air and ground services, allowing for a national release synchronized to all locations on the same release date.
- Designed and implemented an automated reverse logistics programme for a nationally recognized health food/supplement distributor. Automated returns process to reduce touches and costly staffing hours. Eliminated front-end phone contact using technology and web automation.

MARKETING MANAGER   2009–2010

Fast tracked to streamline sales processes, increasing performance. Performed analysis of sales territory, historical data, operations alignment, reporting structure and sales trends to devise solutions. Managed and coached area managers in business-plan development and execution of sales strategies. Delivered staff development in cost-reduction strategies and compliance requirements. Accountable for £500 million P&L.

Accomplishments:
- Drove £500 million+ in local market sales. Grew revenues 2009/2010 revenues 12% and 7% respectively.

RETAIL CHANNEL/OPERATIONS MANAGER   2007–2009

Charged with turning around this underperforming business unit. Managed development and implementation of new retail strategy across Northern UK. Rebranded XYZ Customer Centres and the XYZ Store. Performed vendor negotiations and collaborated with nine regions to support additional implementations.

Accomplishments:
- Developed key revenue-generating initiatives across multiple channels. Attained 65% growth in discretionary sales. Several strategies adopted across the national organization.
- Re-engineered inventory for over 1,000 dropoff locations, reduced lease expenses by 45% and inventory levels by 40% through weekly measurement, inventory level development by SKU, order process automation and order consolidation.
- Implemented new retail sales associate structure in 1,100 locations; scored highest national service levels by mystery shoppers.
- Selected as corporate team member on Mail Etc acquisition integration.

Continued

The combination CV (page 3)

John William Wisher, MBA   Page 3 of 3

PROJECT MANAGER   2006–2007

Selected to support several underperforming business areas. Managed key segments of district business initiatives and compliance measures for 1,000 dropoff locations. Reported on status to corporate management. Supervised office staff of 16. Negotiated vendor and lease agreements.

Accomplishments:
- Rolled out and managed ongoing Haz Mat compliance programme for all locations.
- Generated £6 million in sales through cross-functional lead programme and increased participation from 20% to 100%.
- Attained union workforce sponsorship of support-growth programme through careful negotiations and persuasion.

SENIOR ACCOUNT MANAGER   2004–2006

Delivered £2.8 million in growth on £1.1 million plan, rated 3rd of 53 managers in revenue generation

ACCOUNT MANAGER   2002–2003

Top producer out of 53; £1.3 million sales on £500K plan.

SERVICE PROVIDER   1999–2001

Top producer out of 53; £1.3 million sales on £500K plan.

SUPERVISOR OF PACKAGE OPERATIONS   1999

Managed 65 full-time service providers. Performed post-routine analysis, operating strategy development, compliance, payroll, service failure recovery and new technology implementation. Met 100% DOT and Haz Mat compliance. Reduced post-delivery staffing time by 50% and missed pickups by 65%.

SUPERVISOR OF HUB OPERATIONS   1993–1999

Managed up to 100 employees and staff processing 75K pieces per day involving 40+ outbound bays. Performed complex staff scheduling and maintained low turnover rates. Designed new management reporting format, reducing administrative time by 20% and improved load quality by 30%.

OPERATIONS DOCK WORKER AND TRAINING LEAD   1991–1992

EDUCATION
MBA
London University

BA, Business, Supply Chain Management
Elmhurst College, Elmhurst

Additional Specialized Courses:
- Supply Chain Mapping, 20 Hours
- Financial Logistics Analysis (FLOGAT), 10 Hours
- Hazardous Materials, 20 Hours
- Labour Relations, 30 Hours
- Managers Leadership School, 100 Hours
- Managing from the Heart, 30 Hours

Choose a template

If you haven't already, now is a good time to start choosing a CV template. Go to the CV section, Chapter 10, to find examples suitable for your needs.

It is common to look for CV templates that reflect someone in your profession. This is *wrong*! CV templates have never been designed with particular professions or jobs in mind. There is no magically ordained format for CVs by profession. It doesn't matter at all if an accountant chooses the CV template of a geologist.

Choose your template based on its ability to accommodate your story in a visually appealing way.

6

The simplest, smartest, fastest way to write your CV

I've been writing about CVs for 25 years and writing them for longer, longer than most. No one likes writing a CV, but you have to trust me when I tell you that there is no easier way than the way I am showing you. That shortcut you're thinking of? It won't work. If it did we'd be talking about it.

This is the most streamlined way I know to give you a premium, powerful CV for a professional job in the shortest time with the least hassle.

Five steps to a great CV

Your CV is a concise sales document that gives a snapshot of your professional life in a couple of pages. A great finished product usually takes five steps:

1 A first draft to capture all the essentials on a basic CV template.

2 A second draft made up from gradually improving versions developed as you tweak words and phrases; add and subtract; cut, move and paste until you cannot possibly improve it further.

3 A third draft to integrate your defined professional identity throughout the CV.

4 A fourth draft, where you paste your work into different templates and choose the one(s) best for you.

5 A final draft of your formatted CV, where you complete the editing and polishing process.

Putting together your first draft

With your target job survey and your completed CV Questionnaire from the previous chapter, you know what the customer wants and what you have to offer. All that remains is to assemble the pieces in a way that tells your story effectively.

To help you do this, I've created a CV *Layout Template*. It is not intended as a template for your finished CV, just a gathering place for all the components of your finished document in a CV-like format. By using it you'll become familiar with all the CV building blocks, and when the time comes to decide on a layout and template, everything will be ready to cut and paste.

CV layout template (page 1)

(Name)
Address • Telephone & Mobile phone • e-mail address

Target Job Title
Pharmaceutical Sales

Experienced professional in pharmaceutical software sales with a verifiable record of achievement in major pharmaceutical companies

A target job title, perhaps followed by an optional professional statement, as shown here, helps database visibility and gives focus to the reader. A one-sentence professional statement suggests the value you bring to the job.

Performance Profile / Career Summary

A maximum of five lines of text can be followed by a second paragraph or short list of bullet points. Your intent is to capture your ability to do the target job – take the most common requirements from your target job survey and rewrite as your performance profile. This will help your CV's database visibility and will create immediate resonance with the recruiter. Always note bilingual skills here – we live in a global economy.

Core Competencies

This should be a bulleted ~ list ~ of all the keywords ~ you identified In your survey ~ this list can be ~ as long as ~ you like ~ a Core Competency section ~ increases database visibility ~ and for the reader ~ gives them immediate focus ~ 'Oh she can talk about this and this and this' and each word you use here ~ can be repeated in the context ~ of the jobs where ~ it was applied

Technical Competencies

[An optional category depending on your experience]

Performance Highlights

[An optional category depending on your experience]

Professional Experience

Company name & location
Job title • employment dates

Continued

CV layout template (page 2)

Name * Telephone & Mobile phone • e-mail address * **Page number**

Company name & location
Job title • employment dates

Company name & location
Job title • employment dates

Education

(May come at front of CV if these are critical professional credentials, especially relevant or highlighting an important strength.)

Licences/Professional Accreditations

(May come at front of CV if these are critical credentials, especially relevant or highlighting an important strength.)

Ongoing Professional Education

Professional Organizations/Affiliations

Publications, Patents, Public Speaking

Languages

Extra Curricular Interests

(If they relate to the job.)

Closing Professional Statement (optional)

I believe that leadership by example and conscientious performance management underlies my department's consistent customer satisfaction ratings.

References Available on Request

(Employers assume that your references are available so only end your CV with this if there is space.)

The template section by section

Your personal details

- *Name*. There's no need for Mr, Mrs, Ms or Miss. However, if you have a title such as Dr, then you could use that if its relevant.

- *Address*. Condense this into one line if space is an issue.

- *Telephone numbers*. Home phone and mobile but not your work number.

- *E-mail*. Don't use your work e-mail address. Companies can and do monitor e-mail use. Make sure the address you use reflects your professionalism.

Use subheads to guide the reader

Using headlines and subheads in your CV helps the reader absorb your message. Look at these headlines and the way they guide a tired and bored reader through your CV:

Target Job Title
(Here's the job I'm after.)

Performance Profile
(This is a snapshot of what I can do.)

Core Competencies
(Here are all the key professional skills that help me do my job well.)

Technical Competencies
(Optional: here are all the technical skills that help me do my job well.)

Performance Highlights
(Optional: Outstanding achievements.)

Professional Experience
(Where and when everything happened.)

In little more than half a page these headlines help the reader get fast access to what you have to offer. These headlines have tested extremely well with headhunters and HR managers because of the clarity and understanding they deliver.

Target job title

A target job title explains what the CV is about. Identify your target job title by taking all the title variations you collected in your survey and decide on a job title that works for you. You can always change it if you find a better one. Examples:

- Certified Occupational Health Nurse Specialist;
- Global Operations Executive;
- Agricultural/Environmental Manager;
- Horticultural Buying – International Experience.

Professional statement

A short personal statement following the target job title introduces the value you bring to the job. More on this shortly with an example that blends the target job title and the professional statement.

Performance profile

The essence of every manager's job is performance management, and they spend a portion of every year thinking about and giving performance reviews. For this reason, this powerful headline will resonate with every manager. Take the major skills and experience from your target job survey and turn them into a performance profile that demonstrates your grasp of the job and your customer's priorities:

1 Write three to six bulleted statements about your skills and experience that capture the most common requirements identified in your target job survey.

2 Combine this information into just three to five short sentences that clearly show what you bring to the target job.

3 See that, wherever possible, you use the same words that employers are using to describe their jobs.

4 Dense blocks of text are hard on the eyes. If you have more than five lines, break the text into two paragraphs.

The aim of your performance profile is to show that you possess exactly the skills employers are seeking. It's a powerful way to open your CV, both for its impact with the CV search engines and because it gives the reader a clear, immediate summary of what you bring to the table.

Example:

PERFORMANCE PROFILE

Strategic communications professional with nine years' experience developing effective, high-impact and cost-efficient media outreach plans for consumer, business and policy audiences in media, entertainment and technology practice areas. Experienced in managing corporate and crisis communications. Goal and deadline orientated with five years' experience managing internal and external communications team members. Adept at working with multiple teams and stakeholders.

Professional core competencies

A section including core competencies or professional competencies in your CV helps you in three ways:

1 It ensures your CV contains all the keywords that will help it get pulled out of the CV databases for human review.

2 These keywords act as headlines and are a time-saving device, quickly identifying that you possess the skills needed for the job.

3 The section reminds you to use as many of the words as you can in the Professional Experience part of your CV, showing the context in which they were used.

Employers appreciate a Core Competency section as a summary of your skills. Each keyword or phrase flags up a skill area and possible topic of conversation.

There's no need to use definite or indefinite articles or conjunctions, just list the skills, such as 'Financial modelling' or 'Project Management'.

Here's an example from a PR professional:

- High-Tech Public Relations
- Strategic Communications
- PR Messaging & Tactics
- Press Releases
- Collateral Materials
- Media Relations
- Leadership
- Branding
- Media Training
- Media Pitch & Relations Story
- Strong Writing Skills
- Executive Counselling
- Acquisition Positioning

- New Business Development
- Team Management
- Budget Management
- Account Management
- Project Management
- Detail Orientated
- Research
- Team Building & Leadership
- Mentoring
- Client Management
- Organizational Skills
- Investment Positioning

An example for a technologist, demonstrating a different layout:

– Core Competencies –

Strategic Planning ~ Full-Cycle Project Management ~ Technical & Application Standards ~ IT Governance Process ~ Technical Vision & Leadership ~ Architecture Roadmaps ~ Technical Specifications & Project Design Best Practices ~ Team Building & Leadership ~ Standards & Process Development

---

If you work in technology or you have developed a range of technology competencies, you might choose to add a separate Technology Competencies section.

Here's an example:

Technology Competencies

Hardware:	Sun Servers; HP-UX; AIX; p-Series, z-Series; Windows Server
Operating Systems:	Sun Solaris; AIX; HP-UX; Linux; z/OS; OS/400
Languages:	C / C++; COBOL; Visual Basic; Java; Unix Korn Shell Scripting; Perl; Assembler; SQL*Plus; RPG
Databases:	Oracle; DB2; SQL Server; Microsoft Access; Informix
Applications:	MQSeries; Tuxedo; CICS; Microsoft Project, Word, Excel, Outlook, PowerPoint, SharePoint, and Visio; HP Service Desk; Provision; Telelogic DOORS; Change Synergy; Rational System Architect; Rational System Developer; Visual Studio; CA Clarity; Livelink Other: Cobit 4.1

Adding to professional competencies

Your CV is a living document, and its content may well change as your job search – and professional development projects – progresses. Whenever you come across keywords in job postings that reflect your capabilities, but which are not in your CV, it is time to add them. If nowhere else, at least put them in the Professional Competencies section.

Use keywords often

1 Give the most important of your professional competencies first in the Performance Profile/Performance Summary section of your CV.

2 Include a complete list of your skills in the Professional Competencies section. It is the perfect spot to list the technical acronyms and professional jargon that demonstrate the range of your professional skills, especially if they won't fit into the Professional Experience section of your CV.

3 A Professional Competencies section should remind you to use as many of the keywords as you can in the Professional Experience part of your CV, where usage will show the context in which those skills were developed and applied.

This strategy will make your CV data-dense for improved database performance, while also demonstrating that you have the relevant skills and putting them in context for the recruiter in a *visually accessible* manner. Yes, it will make your CV longer; just understand it has a much better chance of being pulled from the CV databases, and because its content is completely relevant to the needs of the job, you will get a better response rate.

Performance highlights/career highlights

In completing the CV questionnaire you gathered evidence of achievements and contributions in your work and quantified them whenever you could. Choose two to four of these (depending on the depth of your experience) and capture them in confident statements using action verbs.

PERFORMANCE HIGHLIGHTS

35 per cent increase in on-time delivery + 20 per cent reduction in client complaints

Effective operations management demands understanding every department's unique problems and timelines. Building these considerations into daily activities helped:

- Finance & Supply Chain, which saved £55,000 in the last three quarters.
- To increase productivity, with a 35 per cent increase in on-time delivery.

These on-time delivery increases were achieved with improved communications, connecting purchasing, supply chain, customers, and customer service, which:

- delivered 20 per cent reduction in client complaints.

Professional experience

Company names

Each job needs to be identified with an employer. There is no need to include specific contact information, although it can be useful to include the location.

When working for a multidivisional company, you may want to add the division, Computer Memory Division, for example.

Here is how you might combine a job title, company name and location:

Design Engineer

XYZ Industries, Ltd, Computer Memory Division, Manchester

Employed professionals are justified in omitting clear identification of their current employer. Instead of the employer's name you might substitute:

- A National Retail Chain

- A Leading Software Developer

- A Major Commercial Bank

A company name can be followed by a brief description of the business:

ABC Travel plc, Dover   **1997 to present**

£500 Million Company – One of Largest Travel and Tourism Development/Sales Companies in UK. In Rapid Growth and International Expansion

Employment dates

A CV without employment dates does worse than a CV that has them – and those dates need to be accurate because they can be checked. With a steady work history and no employment gaps, you can be very specific:

January 2004–July 2008

If you had an employment gap of six months in, say, 2008, you can disguise this:

MBO Ltd   **2006–2008**
XYZ plc   **2008–present**

I am *not* suggesting that you should lie about your work history, and you must be prepared to answer honestly and without hesitation if you are asked.

Responsibilities and achievements

Each section of the CV represents another opportunity to communicate your unique achievements and contributions, so replace timeworn descriptions in the Professional Experience section with strong action statements:

- **Before:** responsible for identifying and developing new accounts.

- **After:** drove advances in market share and revitalized stalled business by persistently networking and pursuing forgotten market areas – lost sales, smaller, untapped businesses, prospects overlooked by the competition.

This section where you address your responsibilities and achievements in each job, as they relate to your customer – the employer's needs – is the meat of your CV. When working on this part, constantly remind yourself of the details that employers most likely want to read about, and the keywords that will help your CV stand out in database searches.

The responsibilities and contributions you identify here are those that best relate to the needs of the target job. This can be illustrated by showing you part of a CV that came to my desk recently. It is that of a professional who listed her title and duties for one job like this:

> *Motivated a sales staff of six, recruited, trained, managed. Hired to improve sales. Sales Manager increased sales.*

The writer mistakenly listed everything in the reverse order of importance. She was not focused on the importance *to a future employer*, who above all will want to hire someone who can increase sales. Let's look at what subsequent restructuring achieved:

> *Employed to turn around stagnant sales force.* (Demonstrates her skills and responsibilities.)

> *Successfully recruited, trained, managed and motivated a consulting staff of six. Result: 22 per cent sales gain over first year.* (Shows what she subsequently did with the sales staff, and just how well she did it.)

Notice how this is clearly focused on the essentials of any sales manager's job: to increase income for the company.

By making these changes, her responsibilities and achievements become more important in the light of the problems they solved. Be sure to match your CV to employers' needs and to the priorities of the job.

Achievements

Business has very limited interests, they can be reduced to a single phrase: making a profit. This is done in three ways:

1 by saving money for the company;

2 by increasing productivity, which in turn saves money and provides the opportunity to make more money in the time saved;

3 by simply earning money for the company.

That does not mean that you should address only those points in your CV and ignore valuable contributions that cannot be quantified. But it does mean that you should *try to quantify your achievements wherever you can*.

Pick two to four accomplishments for each job title and edit them down to bite-size chunks:

> *Responsible for new and used car sales. Earned 'Salesman of the Year' awards, 2006 and 2007. Record holder: Most Cars Sold in One Year.*

Here's another example from a fundraiser's CV:

- *Created an annual giving programme to raise operating funds. Raised £2 million.*
- *Targeted, cultivated and solicited sources including individuals, corporations, foundations and government agencies. Raised £1,650,000.*
- *Raised funds for development of the Performing Arts School facility, capital expense, and music and dance programmes. Raised £6,356,000.*

You can cite achievements as part of a sentence/paragraph or as bullets:

> *COLLECTIONS:*
> *Developed excellent rapport with customers while significantly shortening payout terms. Turned impending loss into profit. Personally salvaged and increased sales with two multimillion-pound accounts by providing remedial action for their sales/financial problems.*

COLLECTIONS:
Developed excellent rapport with customers while significantly shortening payout terms:
- *Evaluated sales performance; offered suggestions for financing/merchandising, turned impending loss into profit.*
- *Salvaged two multimillion-pound problem accounts by providing remedial action for their sales/financial problems. Subsequently increased sales.*

Whenever you can, keep each paragraph to a maximum of four or five lines. This ensures that the finished product has plenty of white space so that it is easy on the reader's eyes. If necessary, split one paragraph into two.

Education

Educational history is normally placed wherever it helps your case the most. The exact positioning will vary according to the length of your professional experience and the importance of your academic achievements to the job and your profession.

If you are recently out of school or university with little practical experience, your educational credentials might constitute your primary asset and should appear near the beginning of the CV.

After two or three years in the professional world, your academic credentials become less important and move to the end of your CV. The exceptions are in professions where academic qualifications dominate – medicine and law, for example. The highest level of academic attainment always comes first.

Ongoing professional education

Being in ongoing education looks good on a CV; and all other things being equal, when say, a BSc is required:

BSc Accounting. (Result anticipated Sept 2016)

This can help you overcome an otherwise mandatory requirement.

Identify all relevant professional training courses and seminars you've attended. It speaks of your professional competency and demonstrates your commitment to your profession. It also shows that an employer thought you worthy of the investment.

Technology is rapidly changing the nature of all work, so if you aren't learning new skills every year, you are being paid for an increasingly obsolescent skill set. Ongoing professional development is a smart career management strategy.

Accreditations, professional licences and civil service grades

If these are mandatory requirements in your profession, you must feature them clearly. If you are close to gaining a particular accreditation or licence you should identify it:

Passed all parts of C.P.A. exam, September 2015 (expected certification March 2016)

Professional associations

Membership of associations and societies related to your work demonstrates strong professional commitment, and offers great networking opportunities. If you are not currently a member of one of your industry's professional associations, give serious consideration to joining.

Publications, patents and public speaking

These three capabilities are rare and make powerful statements about creativity, organization, determination and follow-through. They tell the reader that you invest considerable personal time and effort in your career and are therefore a cut above the competition:

'Radical Treatments for Chronic Pain.' 2002. Journal of Medicine.
'Pain: Is It Imagined or Real?' 2000. Science & Health Magazine.

Languages

With the current state of communications technology, all companies can have an international presence. Consequently you should always cite your language abilities:

Fluent in Spanish and French   *Read and write Serbo-Croatian*
Read German   *Understand conversational Mandarin*

If you are targeting companies that have an international presence, I suggest you cite your linguistic abilities at the end of your Performance Profile.

Armed forces

Always list any military experience. It demonstrates, amongst other things, your determination, teamwork, goal orientation, and understanding of policies and procedures.

Summer and part-time employment

This should only be included if you are just entering the workforce or re-entering it after a substantial absence. The entry-level person can feel comfortable listing dates, places and times. The returnee should include the skills gained but minimize the part-time aspect of the experience.

References

Never list the names of referees on a CV: interviewers very rarely check them before meeting and developing a strong interest in you – it's too time-consuming.

Employers assume that your references are available, so 'References available upon request' may not be absolutely necessary, although those four extra words don't do any harm.

However, if you have to cut a line anywhere this should be one of the first to go.

While we're on the subject, if you have ever worked under a different surname, you must take this into account when giving your references. A recently divorced woman I know lost a potential job offer because she was using her maiden name on her CV and at the interview. Three prior employers denied ever having heard of her.

Personal interests

A study showed that executives with team sports on their CVs averaged £3,000 a year more than their more sedentary counterparts. If you participate in team sports, determination activities (running, climbing, bicycling) and 'strategy activities' (bridge or chess), consider including them along with any other activities that could contribute to your chances of being hired.

If you are a recent entrant into the workplace, your meaningful extracurricular activities are of greater importance. Include your position on the school newspaper or the student council, memberships of clubs, anything that demonstrates your potential as a productive employee. As your career progresses, however, prospective employers care less about your school life and more about your work life, so once you are two or three years into your career these involvements should be replaced by similar activities in the adult world.

What never goes in

Some information just doesn't belong in CVs. Make the mistake of including it and, at best, your CV loses power, while at worst, you fail to land the interview.

- Qualifying factors such as availability, willingness or unwillingness to relocate, commute or travel. These can be saved until you are offered the job.

- Salary. If you are asked specifically for salary details, address them in your covering letter and give a salary range rather than an exact figure.

- Photograph.

- Marital status.

- Age, race, religion.

- Health, physical description.

- Reasons for leaving.

- Heading such as Curriculum Vitae, CV, Resume. It is already clear what it is.

7

How to give your CV impact

First impressions are important. Editing polishes your content and helps it deliver a greater impact.

Your CV needs to be visually accessible, for reasons that will become clear shortly. You also need to make sure that the words you use make sense, read intelligently and pack a punch by addressing the reader's – your customer's – needs.

You can assume that anyone who reads your CV has a vacancy to fill and is numb from reading CVs. Understanding exactly what this feels like will help you craft a finished CV that is readily accessible to the tired eyes and distracted minds of employers.

Imagine for a moment you are a recruiter. You have just completed a CV database search and have 20 CVs to read. As an example of this, turn to the sample section of this book and try to read 20 CVs without a break.

After about 15 minutes, you'll lose the ability to concentrate. You'll realize why your focus on relevant content and a clear layout are critical for getting your CV read and understood – and why those headlines are so appreciated.

Customize the templates you choose

While CV layouts are based on common sense, you are still free to customize the layout. As a rule of thumb, the most relevant information should always come first. For example, when you have no experience, your degree is front and centre. As your experience increases, your education becomes less important. This is why you usually see education at the end of a CV, unless your target profession's particular demands require it to be emphasized. There are some professions – medicine, education and the law, for example – where academic and professional accreditations tend to be kept at the front of the CV. Bear this in mind if you work in one of these professions.

You can customize the template to suit your needs. For example, you might decide that by moving languages, special training or other information typically found at the end of the CV to the first page, this increases the strength of your argument. If that makes sense, go ahead and do it.

Filling in the template

Go through your chosen template and transfer the information you developed earlier and, almost immediately, you have a document that is beginning to look like a finished product. But you're not finished yet. Not by any means.

Tighten up sentences

Sentences gain power with action verbs. For example, a woman with 10 years of clerical experience had written in her original CV:

I learned to use a new database.

After she thought about what was really involved, she gave this sentence more punch:

I analysed and determined the need for a comprehensive upgrade of database, archival and retrieval systems. Responsible for selection and installation of cloud-based archival systems. Within one year, I had an integrated company-wide archival system working.

Notice how verbs tell the reader what she did and how she did it.

Now, while the content is clearly more powerful, the sentences still need tightening.

Tight sentences have bigger impact

Aim for simplicity and clarity:

- shorten sentences by cutting unnecessary words;
- make two sentences out of one.

Vary the length of sentences when you can. You can start with a short phrase and follow with a colon:

- followed by bullets of information;
- each one supporting the original phrase.

So, the example above might read:

Analysed and determined need for comprehensive upgrade of database, archival and retrieval systems:

- *Responsible for hardware and software selection.*
- *Responsible for selection and installation of cloud-based archival systems.*
- *Responsible for compatible hardware and software upgrades.*
- *Trained users from managing partner through to administrators.*
- *Achieved full upgrade, integration and compliance in six months.*

Notice that by dropping personal pronouns and articles the result is easier to read. It also suggests a professional who understands the importance of getting to the relevant information quickly.

Big words or little words?

The goal of your CV is to communicate quickly and efficiently, so just as you use short sentences, you should also use common words. They are easy to understand and communicate clearly and quickly. Remember:

- Short words in short sentences.
- Use them to make short, gripping paragraphs.
- Short words in short sentences in short paragraphs help tired eyes.

CV length

The rule used to be one page for every 10 years of experience, and never more than two pages. However, *the length of your CV is less important than its relevance to the target job*. Ideally the first half to two-thirds of the first page of your CV should be tightly focused on a specific target job and include a target job title, performance profile, core competency and, perhaps, career highlight sections. Do this and any reader can quickly see that you are suitable for the job.

Given the increasing complexity of jobs, the length and depth of your experience, and the need for data-dense CVs, if it takes three pages rather than two to tell your full story, then do so. Just make sure that everything you've included is relevant.

Does my CV tell the full story?

When your CV is complete, begin to polish by asking yourself the following questions:

- Are all statements relevant to the target job?
- Where have I repeated myself?
- Can I cut out any paragraphs?
- Can I cut out any sentences?
- Can I condense two sentences into one?
- Can I cut out any words?
- Can I cut out any pronouns?

Remember: if in doubt, cut it out – leave nothing but the focused story and action words!

Proofread your final draft

Once your CV is as tight and focused as you can make it – and you can easily go back to it a dozen times, improving it a little at each pass – take a break from it for 24 hours to clear your mind, then come back and proofread your work.

Checklist

Contact information

- Are your name, address, phone numbers and e-mail address correct?

- Is your contact information on every page?

- Is the e-mail address hyperlinked, so that a reader of your CV can read it on their computer and reach out to you instantly?

Target job title

- Do you have a target job title that echoes the job titles you collected when surveying the target job?

- Is this followed by a short one-sentence professional statement that captures the essence of your professional identity?

Performance profile

- Does it give a concise synopsis of the professional you as it relates to the target job?

- Does the language reflect that of typical advertisements for this job?

- Is it prioritized in the same way employers are prioritizing their needs in this job?

- Is it no more than five lines long, so it can be read easily? If more, can you cut it into two paragraphs or use bullets?

- Does it include reference to the transferable skills and professional values that are critical to success? If they don't fit here, make sure they are in the Core Competencies section.

Core competencies

- Is all spelling and capitalization correct?

- Are there any other keywords you should add?

- Do you have experience in each of the areas you've listed?

- Can you illustrate your experience at the interview?

Career highlights

- If you included a Career/Performance Highlights section, do the entries support the central arguments of your CV?

Professional experience

- Is your most relevant work experience prioritized throughout the CV?

- Does it correspond to the employer's needs?

- Does it address the employer's priorities?

- Does it emphasize your relevant competencies, contributions and achievements?

- Is your work history in chronological order, with the most recent employment coming first?

- With a chronological or combination CV, does each company history start with details of your most senior position?

- Can you come up with a strong professional statement to end the CV? One that supports the focus and story you have told?

- Have you kept it punchy and focused by eliminating extraneous information?

- Have you included any volunteer, community service or extracurricular activities that can lend strength to your application?

Education

- Is education placed in the appropriate position?

- Is your highest educational attainment shown first?

- Have you included relevant professional courses?

Writing style

- Have you substituted short words for long words?

- Have you used one word where previously there were two?

- Is your *average* sentence no more than 20 words? Have you shortened any sentence of more than 25 words or broken it into two?

- Have you kept paragraphs under five lines?

- Do your sentences begin, wherever possible, with powerful action verbs and phrases?

Spelling and grammar

Incorrect spelling and poor grammar are guaranteed to annoy CV readers, besides drawing attention to your poor written communication skills. Spellcheckers are not infallible; check the spelling and grammar and then send your CV to the most literate person you know for their input.

You need some distance from your creative efforts in order to gain detachment and objectivity. When you think your CV is finished, leave it at least overnight before re-reading it. That way, you will be able to read it with fresh eyes and see the parts that need tweaking.

8

Getting the most from your CV

The way things are today, you will almost certainly need more than one CV for your job search, and you may need to repackage your background into three or four different delivery vehicles.

Customizing your CV for specific openings

Your CV is a living, breathing document, and the *primary* CV you so carefully developed is never really finished. It evolves throughout your job search as you learn more about the skills and experience your marketplace needs, and how to express your possession of them in ways most accessible to your customers.

Most importantly, it evolves every time you customize that CV in response to a particular job posting. Before sending your CV, evaluate it against the job description, and tweak it *so that it clearly reflects the stated needs of that job*.

You will notice that the *transferable skills* we talk about (communication, critical thinking, multitasking, teamwork, etc) crop up frequently in job postings:

'Work closely with' means you are a team player working for the good of the team and the goals to which you are collectively committed.

'Communication skills' means you listen and can take direction in all circumstances. It also refers to verbal and written skills, dress, body language, your social skills and emotional maturity.

'Multitasking' does not mean you rush heedlessly from one emergency to the next but that you carefully plan your activities based on sound time management and organizational skills.

'Problem-solving skills' means you think through the likely effects of your actions before taking them, and that you know your area of expertise well enough to identify, prevent and solve the problems it generates on a daily basis.

Tweak your CV for *keyword* resonance

Match the job posting against your CV to ensure that the words you use to describe your skills match the words the employer is using.

Think how the job posting requirement of, say, 'work closely with others', applies to the actual job. For example, an accountant might, on hearing 'work closely with others', think about problem accounts and working with sales and non-paying customers, as well as working laterally and upward within the accounting department.

When you think through your work experience and discover achievements that match the stated needs of an employer, you can draw attention to this close match in either your CV or a covering letter.

Keywords in a cover letter

In a cover letter, keywords might appear as the company statement in quotation marks followed by an achievement in that area:

'Analytical/critical thinking/problem-solving skills'
- Thorough knowledge of the issues that impact productivity in Operations have resulted in a 35 per cent increase in on-time delivery.

'Work closely with' and 'communication skills'
- Improvements in on-time delivery also made possible by improved communications with stakeholders: Purchasing, Supply Chain, Customer and Customer Service; which also delivered a 20 per cent reduction in client complaints.

'Multitasking'
- Effective operations management demands understanding every department's critical functions and timelines. Building these considerations into daily activities helped Finance & Supply Chain save £55,000 in the last three quarters.

Keywords in a CV

In a CV, you might decide to highlight such highly relevant achievements with a *Performance Highlights* or a *Career Highlights* section, coming right after the *Professional Competencies* section.

This section will comprise a short sequence of bulleted statements, each addressing one of the company's stated requirements, emphasizing the fit between the employer's needs and your capabilities.

However, space might be at more of a premium in your CV than in your cover letter, and so use the achievements without the quotes:

PERFORMANCE HIGHLIGHTS

35 per cent increase in on-time delivery + 20 per cent reduction in client complaints

Effective operations management demands understanding every department's unique problems and timelines. Building these considerations into daily activities helped:

- Finance & Supply Chain, saved £55,000 in the last three quarters.
- Increased productivity, with a 35 per cent increase in on-time delivery.

These on-time delivery increases were achieved with improved communications, connecting Purchasing, Supply Chain, Customers and Customer Service:

- Delivered 20 per cent reduction in client complaints.

A job-targeted CV for that other job

With just a few years' experience in the professional world, most people reach a point where they have experience that qualifies them for more than one job. Build your *primary CV* around the job for which the odds are shortest, but that doesn't mean there aren't other jobs you can do and want to pursue.

After your primary CV is completed, it is fairly easy to create a CV for any additional job you want to pursue. You already have a template to start with; plus the dates, layout, chronology, contact information, and possibly the employers, are all going to remain the same. There's a methodology, as I'm about to show you, that helps you refocus and edit your primary CV into a CV for that second or third target job.

1 Save a duplicate copy of your primary CV, under the new target job title. Although the job is different, a great deal of the information and layout will remain the same.

2 Complete a target job description exercise on the new target job.

3 On the copy of your CV, edit out irrelevant details and replace them with the information that is more relevant to the new target job.

4 Edit and polish, and you have a customized CV for that second or third target job.

A social networking profile/CV

Social networking has exploded on the internet over the last few years, and using this approach in a job search has proved successful for many people. Its impact has been further increased because recruiters see professional networking sites like LinkedIn as the perfect venue to find candidates.

There are two reasons for using a social networking site: to find people and to be found. In both instances, you will need to create a profile of who you are. When you reach out to potential networking contacts, they are likely to check out your profile before responding. When recruiters and others are in turn looking for someone like you, the quality of that profile determines:

- Whether you will be found amongst those 100 million-plus users

- Whether the recruiter follows through with a contact

Use the information from your carefully prepared primary CV to fill in the sections in your profile, including those well-researched keywords for maximum impact.

A profile will generally have more room than a CV so you can be more expansive, adding additional information and details, but remember to keep it focused and relevant.

A CV for promotion

We tend to think of our CV as a tool to get a new job at another company, and forget that we can use it to get a promotion where we already are.

You need a job-targeted CV for pursuing internal promotions because:

- No one is paying as much attention to you as you would like.

- It shows an employer you are serious about growth.

- It's a powerful way to get yourself viewed in a different light.

- It puts you on a par with external candidates who will have job-targeted CVs.

- It puts you ahead of these candidates, because you are a known quantity.

- When you have the required skills, it's much easier to get promoted from within.

Promotions come to those who earn them, not as a reward for watching the clock for three years. Think through what's needed for your next step up the ladder, build the skills to earn that promotion, then create a CV that positions you for the job. It's smart, strategic thinking.

Your promotion campaign starts with determining a specific target job for the next step and then understanding the requirements for someone holding that job title.

Collect job postings for that next step and deconstruct the specific requirements. Once you have a crystal-clear idea of what is needed to succeed in the target job:

- Identify areas for skill development.

- Determine how you will develop these skills.

- Volunteer for assignments that build these skills and give you practical experience that can become part of your CV.

Once your skills have reached 70 per cent of those required for the new job, you can start building a CV targeted on that promotion.

Your CV online

From a company's perspective, internet recruitment serves a dual purpose: personnel openings are cost-effectively advertised to attract candidates, and the technologically challenged applicants screen themselves out.

How can the internet benefit your job search? It allows you to:

- research your industry and identify companies;

- create customized documents and communicate with potential employers and recruiters almost instantly;

- find job openings through job banks and employers' job sites;

- have potential employers find you, whether you are currently looking for a position or just maintaining visibility for career growth opportunities;

- use database and networking sites to identify names and titles;

- pick up useful job search and career management advice.

You can post your CV on the internet so that companies and recruiters can find you; you can surf for job openings and you'll have access to more information about prospective employers, making you a better-informed candidate. The internet offers you access to millions of job openings and thousands of companies and recruiters. The internet allows you three primary methods of CV distribution:

1 Responding to recruitment ads – job postings.

2 Posting your CV on job sites and databanks.

3 E-mailing your CV directly to companies and recruitment agencies.

The electronic CV

Companies increasingly store even the paper CVs they receive in databases, so you need to create a CV that can be stored where Human Resources people and recruiters can have quick access to it.

Because of competition and the growth of the internet, CV scanning and searching capabilities are now available to virtually all companies. When an employer needs to sort through CVs for job candidates, they type in a job title, are presented with a list of keywords, and choose those most relevant to the job being filled. The software program searches in the company's database looking for documents containing any of the selected keywords, which is why the more keywords your CV matches the better your chances of having it read, because the program not only looks for CVs that contain those keywords, it also ranks the generated list and puts the most keyword-heavy CVs at the top.

Make your CV scannable

When a company transforms your paper CV to an electronic format, they scan or digitize it to create a file with a picture of your CV. Here are some general rules to ensure that your print CV is scannable:

- Avoid paper with a dark or even medium colour, a coloured border, heavy watermark or graining – plain white paper is best.

- Be circumspect about adding borders around a document or around a section of text in the CV. The software could identify it as a single character and omit the entire content of that section.

- Do not use columns – when scanned, the order of words will be out of sequence and that could hurt the effectiveness of your keyword sections.

- Do not use fonts smaller than 10 point; 12 point is ideal. If the employer experiences difficulty in scanning your CV you will not receive a polite phone call asking you to resubmit.

Sending your CV

There are three different ways you can send your CV electronically:

1 formatted, usually as a Microsoft Word document;

2 ASCII or plain text;

3 web-based/HTML.

You may not need all three, but you will definitely need at least the first two. Here are descriptions of all three:

1 *Formatted CV:* this CV is sent via e-mail as an attachment; it is usually your CV as created in a word-processing document, the same as the one you print out. Sending it as an attachment saves all the formatting of the document, so the recipient gets a CV that is exactly the same as your printed one. When sending CVs, without prior contact to determine that the recipient expects the attachment, however, paste your CV into the body of your e-mail with a note that a copy is also attached. Many companies will not open attachments from people they do not know, for fear of viruses. Rather than writing out your entire CV again, you can convert your existing formatted version into an ASCII version.

2 *Plain text or ASCII:* this is the simplest version of the three; an ASCII CV looks like the average e-mail you receive and is used when you need to send your CV in the main body of your e-mail rather than as an attachment. ASCII CVs are also important because this is the only format that any computer, whether PC or Mac, can read, so software compatibility needn't be considered.

3 *Web or HTML CV:* a web CV is not a 'must have' for everyone but there are some advantages; for example, you can include audio and video clips, music and pictures. If you are in a creative profession and would typically have a portfolio, a web CV can allow access to your work samples. Likewise if you are a web-page design professional, then use the internet to show your creative abilities.

How to convert your formatted CV to ASCII

Converting your CV into an ASCII version is simple.

Job search folders

Create a section within your 'My Documents' folder and then create a series of folders within that to hold your 'CVs', 'Cover Letters', 'Job Descriptions', etc.

Open your CV using your word-processing program. Copy the entire document by choosing 'select all' from the 'edit' pull-down menu, then by choosing 'copy' from the 'edit' pull-down menu or Ctrl+C for Windows.

Converting your CV

Open a new document. Set the margins to 1.5 inches on both right and left sides, which equates to about 60 characters per line depending on type size and font. The number of characters in each line must be limited because e-mail screens are restricted to that viewing width.

Setting margins

Paste the CV you just copied into this new document: choose 'paste' from the 'edit' pull-down menu, or Ctrl+V for Windows. Initially, the document will look very similar to your previous CV, but we will modify it further.

Go to the 'edit' pull-down menu and choose 'select all' – you are going to change the font type and size. Choose 'font' from the 'format' pull-down menu and change the font type to Times New Roman or Courier. Change the size to 12 point.

Changing the font

Save this new document using the 'save as' command. Select the document as 'text only', and rename the document. Let's call it 'Text CV 1' and put it in a new folder.

You will get a message box saying that you will change your formatting and asking if you want to continue. Answer 'yes'. An ASCII CV strips out formatting that could make your document difficult to read. Notice that the file name of the CV no longer ends with .doc; it now ends in .txt, meaning text-based document.

The document has lost many of its features, spacing is also altered and any tabs, tables or columns used in your formatted version have disappeared or look strange. Make your document readable by removing empty spaces and tabs.

A text-only CV

You will need to use ALL CAPS for section headers and to replace things that were in bold or underlined. Likewise, all your bullet points will be gone and you will have to adjust the spacing to create a new type of emphasis, or use characters on your keyboard such as '*'. Remember that the goal is to get your CV downloaded into the databases of potential employers and then retrieved by the software. A better-looking paper CV can be sent after this first contact with the employer.

A properly edited text CV

Before you send your CV, proofread it carefully. Send cover letters and CV attachments to yourself and to a friend or a family member and ask them for printouts to ensure that what you intended to send is actually what was received. Often this exercise will help you find problems incurred during the conversion process.

Posting your CV, and tricks to online questionnaires

Job sites have evolved tremendously over the last few years. There are literally thousands of job boards on the internet, from mega sites to very focused sites that cater to a specific location or profession.

Most of the larger sites offer free job delivery and CV posting services. You just select a few criteria, and job listings matching your specifications are automatically sent to your inbox. With the CV banks, your CV goes into a database for employers and recruiters to search by keywords; when there is a match you will be notified. If you are already employed, these sites allow you to stay on top of your career by keeping abreast of available opportunities.

If you are currently in a full-blown job search, spend plenty of time browsing. Keep your search criteria broad-based; you might even eliminate salary or geographical requirements when you begin. This enables you to uncover the maximum number of companies and recruiters in your industry. Even if the specific job opening isn't a great match, you'll be able to check your CV against the requirements being advertised and the keywords being used to describe them; additionally, you'll become aware of these companies for future reference.

Internet CV posting allows an employer to find you while you are sleeping, playing or working – it never sleeps. It sounds great and it works – if you understand the rules of the game.

Not all job sites and CV banks work the same way. On some sites, you simply e-mail your CV. On other sites, you'll have to complete a profile or questionnaire.

These sites are usually free for job hunters. The job sites work with prospective employers to develop better screening tools, since the employers are the paying clients. By making job seekers fill out very specific profiles and questionnaires, employers have more specific data with which to screen.

When filling out a profile or questionnaire, keep these two things in mind:

1 What is my audience? Who will be reading this?

2 What are they really asking me?

Let's take a closer look at the Monster.co.uk CV builder and at what you can do to make it work to your benefit.

Setting up a new account at Monster.co.uk

Once on the site, follow the buttons for new users, and set up your free 'My Monster Account'.

You can either upload your existing CV or create one using your Monster profile.

One of the nice features of Monster.co.uk is that it allows you to maintain more than one CV/profile; this is particularly useful when you have a broad background and can do a number of different jobs. Use this opportunity! Make some of your profiles very specific, and make others very broad in order to increase your visibility.

The Monster CV builder is typical in that it breaks up the CV into a number of specific topics such as Career Objective, Target Job, Target Location, Salary, Work Status, Skills, References, and Education. You can edit and update these fields as often as you want; just click on 'view my profile'.

A Monster.co.uk online CV

The 'Objective' field, Monster tells us, holds up to 2,000 characters. Following the site's examples by writing a two- or three-sentence objective would be wasting an opportunity to inundate employers with favourable keywords. Remember, it is not just the keyword itself that is counted by the software; the number of times it is repeated counts too. So, from your CV, pick keywords that highlight your skills, experience, qualifications and technical knowledge. Describe past successes that will attract the attention of database search software and, consequently, prospective employers.

One of the very first screens you will be asked to complete includes your 'Desired Job Title'. The site offers examples to help you but their advice is not in your best interest. Remember, the employer pays the job sites and they are trying to help the employer screen you out. Monster advises you to list a specific title and, in the

'Professional Overview' field, to write a short professional profile and list your career goals.

If you want to increase your visibility, then you need to think beyond these questions. This is all about keywords. As the 'Title' field holds up to 60 characters, you have the opportunity to add more detail besides your actual title. The best way to make use of that space is to list any special skills or qualifications you have. As well as using your keywords in your summary, you can also add as many 'Job Occupations' as are relevant to you, and as many skills in the 'Skills Section' as you want.

As you continue to complete your profile, you will come to a section that breaks down your 'target job'. The important thing to notice is that you are not always limited to one answer. For your desired job type, you may be able to select *Employee and Temporary/Contract/Project*, and even *Intern* if you want. Test the site to see if you can select more than one answer – never assume you are limited.

Choosing a target job

You will also be asked about your salary requirements. Although the salary question is sandwiched between 'required' fields, it is not itself required. So you can, and should, leave it blank. In instances where you are forced to answer the question, answer in terms of a range as you would in an interview situation.

The next question on this screen allows you 500 characters to describe your ideal job. This is an opportunity to use keywords to describe the kind of job in which you can succeed. Remember that the more keywords that appear in your profile, the higher on the list it will appear; and the more likely it is to be read by a human being.

Now the relocation question – make sure that this is a required field. If it isn't, don't answer it. If it is, keep your answer broad. Any company only interested in local applicants will use the address on your CV as the search parameter.

Here's the rule: you can always say 'no', but you can't say 'yes' unless you've been asked. For the right job, the right opportunity and the right money, we all might move to Timbuktu.

You are most likely to come across online questionnaires and profiles when:

- registering with a job site;
- posting on a job site;
- applying for a job within a company;
- registering with a recruitment firm.

In each case, consider who is asking you the questions and why. They are trying to screen you in or out, so consider your responses carefully. Always read the instructions, avoid questions on salary and relocation if possible, and add as many keywords as you can. Proofread and spellcheck everything you enter, and only post to sites that allow editing and updating.

Sending your CV directly to companies and recruiters

The third way to distribute your CV via the internet involves direct contact with companies and recruiters. There are a number of ways to use the internet to help you locate companies and recruitment firms and the appropriate executives within them. Once you are aware of a company in your industry or a recruitment firm that makes placements within your profession, why not make contact?

You can look at job postings simply as a way of identifying companies so that you can apply to them directly, whether or not you have seen a relevant job advertised. Visit the company websites and browse there. Send a cover letter and your CV to specific individuals or the HR department. Add this contact information to your database for future job-search efforts.

There are many database sites that exist to help develop corporate intelligence, allowing you to search entire industries and develop long lists of companies and their executives.

A second use for this data is accumulating e-mail addresses. Write a cover letter suitable for a mass distribution, and 'blast' your CV out there yourself. By using the bcc (blind copy) feature on your e-mail software, you can e-mail 100 letters at a time. To my mind, though, just blasting CVs and cover letters to companies doesn't provide a worthwhile return. The only situation where this is viable is mass e-mailing the headhunting community.

Internet job search strategies

The following list is a brief overview of strategies for internet-based CV distribution:

- *The blitz* – you need a job ASAP; you have no concern for confidentiality and want maximum exposure and results. Post your CV on a selection of job sites, professional association and profession specific sites. 'Blast out' CVs to all the companies and recruiters on the database you have accumulated from your research.

- *Focused attack* – a more focused version of the blitz. Use a couple of the major job boards, specialty sites, associations and specific company sites. It can work well for those pursuing multiple potential career paths, or for those interested in a career/industry change. If you are still employed but have informed your employer that you are looking for a change, then this is the perfect strategy for you.

- *Stealth mode* – there are two types of job seekers fitting this strategy. The first is the employed seeker who understands the value of keeping an eye on the job market. Only post confidential CVs, and only use sites that deliver jobs to you. The second type of job seeker using this strategy is one who has identified his or her dream company or dream job. You are employed, and are using the internet to monitor sites, send them confidential CVs, research executive bios, association members and other information, and to find an open door.

No single strategy is a sure-fire way to find a suitable job. Always use an integrated approach employing all your online and offline resources.

9
Ready to launch

Here are some powerful strategies to make your CV simultaneously information-dense and visually accessible to tired, distracted recruiters and hiring managers.

You are in the home stretch, giving your CV the final polish before releasing it to a very discriminating public. It has to be:

- Job-focused and data-dense to beat the competition in the CV database wars.

- Typographically clean, and visually accessible to accommodate the recruiters' initial scan.

- Headline-rich and textually concise to deliver a compelling message.

Make this happen and your CV will get serious attention.

The importance of immediate impact

Your CV will get from 5 to 40 seconds of initial scan, and the more accessible it is to the tired and distracted eyes of managers, the closer the attention it will receive. You'll improve its chances if you:

1 *Make it readable.* Stop worrying about page count. In CVs, as in everything, *form follows function*; use the space you need to tell the story you need to tell.

Don't use 9- and 10-point fonts that only a 20-year-old can read, in order to cram everything on one or two pages. (Tip: 20-year-olds are almost never in a position to hire you.) Use 11- and 12-point fonts that are easier on adult eyes.

2 *Check your headlines*. They help a reader maintain focus. The first page of your CV needs to start off strong, and there is no better way of doing this than with headlines that help accessibility and comprehension:

Target job title
(What the CV is about.)

Performance profile/performance summary
(A snapshot of what I can do.)

Professional competencies
(The key professional skills that help me do my job well.)

Technology competencies
(Optional: the technical skills that help me do my job well.)

Performance highlights
(Optional: my outstanding achievements as they relate to the job.)

Professional experience
(Where and when everything happened.)

3 *Check professional competencies and technical competencies*. These are the hard skills that enable you to do what you do. Each word or phrase should act as a beacon of capability and topic for discussion.

4 *Performance/career highlights*. This is an optional section, if your experience has the achievements to support it.

A first page with these headlines and job-focused content in readable fonts will draw in the reader.

Fonts and font sizes

You can use one font throughout your CV, and never use more than two: one for headlines and the other for the body copy. The most popular fonts for business communication are Arial and Times or Times New Roman. They probably look boring because you are so used to seeing them, but you see them so much because they are clear and very readable.

Some other appropriate fonts are:

Good for headlines:
Arial
Times/Times New Roman
Century Gothic
Verdana
Gill Sans
Lucida Sans

Good for body copy:
Arial
Times/Times New Roman
Garamond
Georgia
Goudy Old Style

Each of the above is in 12-point font, but you can see that the nature of each font is unique and the actual size of each will vary – some might look better in 11pt.

Avoid 'script' fonts that look similar to handwriting. While they look attractive to the occasional reader, they are harder on the eyes. You can do plenty to liven up the visual impact of the page and create emphasis with **bold**, *italic*, ***bold italic***, underlining, the size of words and highlighting, used judiciously.

Avoid typos like the plague!

A couple of years ago I helped an executive in the £100k-per-year range. He was having problems getting interviews. The first paragraph of his CV stated that he had 'superior communication skills'. Unfortunately, the rest of the sentence contained a spelling error! Fortunately, we caught it. In an age of spellcheckers, this sloppiness isn't acceptable at any level.

A word of caution: the spellchecker can't catch everything. For example, spellcheck won't catch the common mistyping of 'form' for 'from' because 'form' is a word. Similarly, your spellchecker can't discern *too* from *to* and *two*, *your* from *you're*, or *it's* from *its*.

The printed CV

Even in the age of e-mail and databases, you will need print versions of your CV. For example, you should always take printed copies to your interviews: this guarantees that each interviewer has your background laid out in the way you want it. Check the printed copy for:

- layout and balance;

- typos and grammatical errors;

- punctuation and capitalization;

- page alignment errors;

- that everything has been underlined, capitalized, bolded, italicized and indented exactly as you intended.

Appearance checklist

Let the CV rest overnight or longer, then review it with fresh eyes:

- What is your immediate reaction to it? Is it clear who and what this document is about? Does it clearly address the needs of your target job?

- Does the copy under each of your headlines tell a convincing story?

- Does the first page of the CV identify you as someone clearly capable of delivering the job's requirements?

- Have you used only one side of the page?

- Are your fonts readable, in the 11- to 12-point range?

- Does the layout accommodate the reader's needs, rather than concerns about CV length?

- Are your paragraphs no more than five lines long? Are your sentences fewer than 20 words long?

- Are your sentences short on personal pronouns and long on action verbs?

- Is there plenty of white space around important areas, such as Target Job Title and Professional Competencies? Plenty of space helps readability.

The final product

The paper version of your CV should be printed on standard A4 paper. Paper comes in different weights and textures; good CV-quality paper has a weight designation of between 80 grammes and 100 grammes. Lighter paper feels flimsy and curls; heavier paper is unwieldy.

As for paper colour, white, pale grey and cream are the prime choices. They are straightforward, no-nonsense colours that denote professionalism.

Cover letter stationery should have the same contact information as your CV and should *always* match the colour and weight of the paper used. Again, it's part of the professional branding that underlies all the little things you pay attention to in a job search.

Set up a letterhead for your cover letter stationery, using the same fonts you used on the CV. The coordinated paper size, colour, weight and fonts will give a cohesive look.

Cover letters increase your impact

A job search is all about getting into conversation with people in a position to hire you. Because a letter introducing your CV enables you to highlight your message and your professional identity, it dramatically increases your odds of an interview.

When an e-mail or envelope is opened, your cover letter is the first thing the reader sees. A cover letter personalizes your application in ways that are unachievable by the more impersonal nature of your CV. It sets the stage for the reader to see your CV, and therefore you, as something and someone special. It can create common ground between you and the reader and demonstrate that you are well qualified and suitable for *this* job with *this* company.

With the internet at your fingertips there are countless ways to identify the people who can help. Use search engines to find something to show your knowledge of the company and perhaps the name of executives you can approach.

Try keyword searches for your target company, execute general web searches and news searches.

When you find relevant intelligence you can use it as an opener for your letter or e-mail:

- Refer to the article and its relevance in your letter.

- In an e-mail, paste the article and attach it.

- In a traditional letter, enclose a copy of the article.

Your professional identity in written communication

The professional identity you've established will be transmitted through the materials you send out to employers:

- Getting your CV directly in front of a manager makes you special.

- Introducing your CV with a covering letter that establishes a connection between you and the reader makes you special.

- Ensuring that your paper is good quality and that fonts are legible and coordinated make you special.

- Writing a message that is clear and succinct makes you special.

- Differentiating your behaviour and actions from others will make you stand out as someone special.

- If your written communication looks good, carries a succinct, relevant message, and makes that message readily accessible, showing a professional with a clear sense of self, you are on your way to establishing a viable professional identity.

- Following up your interviews with letters that continue to present you as a consummate professional confirms your professional identity and makes you special.

Cover letter rules

There are four steps for creating a productive cover letter, and the underlying rules of effective communication embodied in these four steps can be applied to any memo or business letter you ever write.

Step one

First, grab your reader's *attention*. You do this with the appearance of your letter: the type is large and legible enough for others to read, it is free of misspellings and it is well laid out so that it is easy on the eye; and, if that letter is going by mail rather than e-mail, use quality stationery and matching envelopes.

Example:

[YOUR ADDRESS/LETTERHEAD
AND TELEPHONE NUMBER]

[DATE]

[ADDRESSEE ADDRESS]
[SALUTATION]

Recently I have been researching the leading local companies in data communications. My search has been for companies that are respected in the field, and who provide ongoing training programmes. The name of DataLink Products keeps coming up as a top company.

I am an experienced voice and data communications specialist with a substantial background in IBM environments. If you have an opening for someone in this area you will see that my CV demonstrates a person of unusual dedication, efficiency and drive.

My experience and achievements include:

- The complete redesign of a data communications network, projected to increase efficiency company-wide by some 12 per cent.
- The installation and troubleshooting of a Defender II call-back security system for a dial-up network.

I enclose a copy of my CV, and look forward to examining any of the ways you feel my background and skills would benefit DataLink Products. While I prefer not to use my employer's time taking personal calls at work, with discretion you can reach me on 020 8123 4567 to initiate contact.

Yours sincerely,

[SIGNATURE]
[TYPED NAME]

Step two

Generate interest with the content. Address the letter to someone by name and explain what you have to offer: the first sentence grabs attention, the rest of the paragraph introduces your suitability. The secret is to introduce yourself with conviction.

As we've already discussed, a little research can get your letter off to a fast start. For example:

- 'I came across the enclosed article in Newsweek magazine and thought it might interest you. It encouraged me to do a little research on your company. I am now convinced of two things: you are the kind of people I want to be associated with, and I have the kind of qualifications you can use.'

- 'I have been following the performance of your fund in *Mutual Funds Newsletter*. The record over the last three years shows strong portfolio management. Considering my experience with one of your competitors, I know I could make significant contributions.'

- 'Recently, I have been researching the local _____ industry. My search has been for companies that are respected in the field and that provide ongoing training programmes. The name _____ keeps coming up as a top company.'

- 'Within the next few weeks I will be moving from London to Edinburgh. Having researched the companies in my field in my new home town, I know that you are the people I want to talk to.'

- 'What is state of the art in _____ changes so rapidly that it is tough for most professionals to keep up. I am the exception. I am eager to bring my experience to bear for your company.'

Step three

Turn that *interest* into *desire*. First, make a bridge that ties you to a job category or work area. Start with phrases like:

- I am writing because...

- My reason for contacting you is...

- ... should this be the case, you may be interested to know...

- If you are seeking a _____ , you will be interested to know...

- I would like to talk to you about your personnel needs and my ability to contribute to your department's goals.

- If you have an opening for someone in this area, you will see that my CV demonstrates a person of unusual dedication, efficiency and drive.

Then call attention to your merits with a short paragraph that highlights one or two of your special contributions or achievements:

- I have an economics background (LSE) and a strong analytical approach to market fluctuations. This combination has enabled me to consistently pick the new technology flotations that are the backbone of the growth-oriented mutual fund.

Include any qualifications, contributions and attributes that present you as someone with professional commitment and talent to offer. If an advertisement (or telephone conversation with a potential employer) revealed an aspect of a particular job not addressed in your CV, it can easily be included in the cover letter. For example:

- I notice from your advertisement that audio and video training experience would be a plus. In addition to the qualifications stated in my enclosed CV, I have over five years' experience writing and producing sales and management training materials in both these media.

Step four

Turn *desire* into *action*. You want to make the reader dash straight to your CV, then call you in for an interview. You achieve this with brevity; whet the reader's appetite, but leave them asking for more.

Make it clear that you want to talk. Just as you worked to create a strong opening, make sure your closing carries the same conviction. It is the reader's last impression of you, so make it strong.

Useful phrases include:

- I look forward to discussing our mutual interests further.

- It would be a pleasure to give you more information about my qualifications and experience.

- I will be in your area around the 20th, and will call you prior to that date to see if we can arrange a meeting.

- The chance to meet you would be a privilege and a pleasure. To this end I will call you on the 20th.

- I look forward to speaking to you further and will call in the next few days to see when our schedules will permit a face-to-face meeting.

- May I suggest a personal meeting where you can have the opportunity to examine the person behind the CV?

- I look forward to exploring any of the ways you feel my background and skills would benefit your organization.

- With my training and hands-on experience, I know I can contribute to your company, and want to speak to you about it in person. When can we meet?

- You can reach me on 020 8123 4567 to arrange an interview. I know that the time invested in meeting me will be amply repaid.

- Thank you for your time and consideration. I hope to hear from you shortly.

- May I call you for an interview in the next few days?

Writing the cover letter

Keep your sentences short – and your paragraphs concise and to the point. Paragraphs can often be a single sentence, and should never be longer than five lines. This makes the page more inviting, by providing adequate white space to ease eye strain.

Short words work best; think in terms of sending a telegram, where every word must work its hardest. Use the action verbs and phrases that breathe life into your work.

Here is an example of a letter in reply to an advertised vacancy:

Dear Ms Pena,

I have always followed the performance of your fund in *Mutual Funds Newsletter*.

Recently, your notice regarding a Market Analyst in Investors Daily caught my eye – and your company name caught my attention – because your record over the last three years shows exceptional portfolio management. With my experience with one of your competitors, I know I could make significant contributions.

I would like to talk to you about your personnel needs and how I would be able to contribute to your department's goals.

An experienced market analyst, I have an economics background and a strong analytical approach to market fluctuations. This combination has enabled me to pick the new technology flotations that are the backbone of the growth-oriented mutual fund.

For example, I first recommended Fidelity Magellan six years ago. More recently, my clients have been strongly invested in Pacific Horizon Growth (in the high-risk category), and Fidelity Growth and Income (for the cautious investor).

Those following my advice over the last six years have owned shares in funds that consistently outperformed the market.

I know that CVs help you sort out the probables from the possibles, but they are no way to judge the personal calibre of an individual. I would like to meet you and demonstrate that, along with the credentials, I have the personality that makes for a successful team player.

Yours sincerely

Jane Swift

Jane Swift

Here is an example of a cover letter sent as a result of a conversation:

Dear Ms _____ ,

I am writing in response to our telephone conversation on Friday the 10th regarding a new- and used-car sales management position.

With a successful track record in both new- and used-car sales, and as a sales manager, I believe I am ideally suited for the position we discussed. My exposure to the different levels of the sales process (I started at the bottom and worked my way up) has enabled me to meet the challenges and display the leadership you require.

I am a competitive person professionally. Having exercised the talents and skills required to exceed goals and set records as a Sales Manager, I believe in measuring performance by results.

I would appreciate a meeting where I could discuss in more detail my sales and management philosophy, and capabilities. Please call me at your earliest convenience to arrange a personal meeting.

Sincerely yours,

James Sharpe

James Sharpe

Finally, here is an example of the somewhat different cover letter that you would send to a corporate headhunter:

Dear Mr _____ ,

As you may be aware, the management structure at XYZ Ltd will be reorganized in the near future. While I am enthusiastic about the future of the company under its new leadership, I have elected to make this an opportunity for change and professional growth.

My many years of experience lends itself to a management position in any medium-sized service firm, but I am open to other opportunities. Although I would prefer to remain in Liverpool, I would be amenable to relocation if the opportunity warrants it. I am currently earning £65,000 a year.

I have taken the liberty of enclosing my CV for your review. Should you be conducting a search for someone with my background – at the present time or in the near future – I would greatly appreciate your consideration. I would be happy to discuss my background more fully with you on the phone or in a personal interview.

Yours sincerely,

James Sharpe

James Sharpe

The executive briefing

The executive briefing is an effective form of cover letter. It gets right to the point and makes life easy for the reader.

An executive briefing ensures that each CV you send out addresses the job's specific needs and that every interviewer is fully aware of that. It provides a comprehensive picture of a thorough professional, plus a personalized, fast and easy-to-read synopsis that details exactly how you can help with an employer's needs.

It also allows you to bring your work history right up to date should a great opportunity catch you with an out-of-date CV. It can even demonstrate your suitability for a job that might not specifically be targeted by your CV as it stands. In both cases, you can fire off an executive briefing with your existing CV to signal your interest immediately, then follow-up with a more tailored CV in due course.

The executive briefing looks like this:

From: top10acct@aol.com
Subject: Re: Accounting Manager
Date: 18 February 2005 10:05:44 PM EST
To: rlstein@McCoy.com

Dear Ms Stein,

I have nine years' accounting experience and am responding to your recent posting for an Accounting Manager on Careerbuilder. Please allow me to highlight my skills as they relate to your stated requirements.

Your Requirements	My Experience
Accounting degree, 4 years exp	Obtained a C.A. degree in 2000 and have over four years' experience as an Accounting Manager.
Excellent people skills and leadership	Effectively managed a staff of 24, ability to motivate staff including supervisors.
Strong administrative and analytical skills	Assisted in the development of a base reference skills library with Microsoft Excel for 400 clients.
Good communication skills	Trained new supervisors and staff via daily coaching sessions, communication meetings and technical skill sessions.

My CV, pasted below and attached in MSWord, will flesh out my general background. I hope this executive briefing helps you to use your time effectively today. I hope we can talk soon.

Yours sincerely,

Joe Black

An executive briefing ensures that each CV you send out addresses the job's specific needs and that every interviewer is fully aware of that. It provides a comprehensive picture of a thorough professional, plus a personalized, fast and easy-to-read synopsis that details exactly how you can help with an employer's needs.

10
The CVs...

I have included CVs from a wide range of jobs so you will probably find a CV telling a similar story to yours. However, *these CV layouts are not designed for specific professions or job titles; they are designed to tell a person's professional story*. So when you see a CV layout that works for you, use it; don't be restrained because the example is of someone in another profession.

Registered nurse

Healthcare

CHANTILE FAUSETT
1 Any Road, Anytown, Anyshire AX0 0AA • 020 8123 4567 • ERNurse@med.net

REGISTERED NURSE
ER...Shock/Trauma...Immediate Care...Triage

Performance Profile

- Two years' experience as a Registered Nurse in ER, Shock/Trauma, Immediate Care and Triage units.
- Hardworking and energetic; adapt easily to change, stressful environments and flexible work schedules.
- Maintain strong observation, assessment and intervention skills essential to providing competent patient care.
- Advocate for patients/family rights; effectively communicate a patient's needs and concerns to medical team.

Education

Western Community College, Brentwood, Essex
Currently enrolled in Graduate Medical Programme with a concentration in Nursing, 2010–Present
Coursework: Anatomy and Physiology, Chemistry, Psychology, Sociology, Statistics

Diploma in Nursing 2011
North Brentwood School of Nursing, Brentwood, Essex
Clinical Skills Upgrade Programme 2012

Licences & Certifications

Registered Clinical Nurse Assistant, 2011
Basic EKG and Phlebotomy

Professional Experience
Registered Nurse, North Brentwood Hospital, Brentwood, Essex   4/09–Present

- Work with a team of nurses and physicians throughout Emergency Room, Shock/Trauma, Immediate Care and Triage departments for Brentwood Hospital, one of the only Level 1 Trauma hospitals in Essex.
- Care for up to 200 patients per shift within a 29-bed Emergency Room Unit, and for patients in a 7-bed Trauma Unit; assist with intubating of patients, life support systems and general post mortem procedures.
- Provide direct patient care in areas of vital signs, phlebotomy, EKGs, treatment of surgical wounds, gynaecological examinations, Activities of Daily Living, and patient transportation within the hospital.
- Prepare patients for transfer to all critical care units, demonstrating quick thinking skills and ability to multitask while remaining focused and calm under pressure.
- Under the direction of the staff nurse, perform initial assessments of patients upon admission within a fast-paced Triage unit, and establish a Plan-of-Care for all patients.
- Assist orthopaedic physicians with splinting, casting, positioning and set up of tractions.
- Closely monitor and report changes in patients' conditions and malfunctioning of medical equipment.

Prior positions: Hospital Attendant; Pharmacist Assistant   Evening/Night Shifts
Pharmacist Assistant, One Way Pharmacy, West Islip, Essex   6/07–10/08
Customer Service Representative, Safeway Transportation, Islip, Essex   5/07–6/08

Registered nurse

Cheryl used this CV to land her first RN position straight out of college.

Healthcare

Cheryl Bloom, RN
1 Any Road, Anytown, Ayrshire AX0 0AA • 020 8123 4567

Registered Nurse

- Strongly motivated graduate with experience in hospital, sub-acute and other healthcare settings.
- Clinical skills combine with dedication to excellent patient care, compassion and professionalism to integrate patients' medical and emotional care.
- Able to relate to patients quickly and work effectively with physicians, peers and other healthcare professionals. Conscientious, team-orientated and eager to learn.

Education, Licensure and Certification

BSc in Nursing, 2010
Chenneworth College, Croton, Northamptonshire

Registered Nurse, 2011

Basic Life Support with Automatic External Defibrillator, British Heart Association
COR, British Heart Association
Certified Nursing Assistant, 2008

Additional: Maths and Science courses, Flynn Community College

Core Skills

- Physical Assessments
- Vital Signs/Blood Glucose
- Catheter Insertion
- Finger Sticks
- Patient & Family Education

- Dispensing Medications/Intravenous Therapy
- Documentation/Care Maps
- Nasopharangeal & Oral Suctioning
- Application of Dressings/Wound Care
- Cast Care/Pin Care/Traction Care/Tracheotomy Care

Clinical Training

Acquired hands-on clinical experience and knowledge in nursing procedures while completing several rotations at the following facilities. Experience with patients ranging from paediatric to geriatric.

Medical–Surgical	Rockport General Hospital
OB/GYN	Melville Memorial Hospital
Paediatric	Montessori School
Gerontology	Evergreen Health Care Centre, Mediplex, Kimberley Hall, Northampton

Professional experience

Patient Care Technician – Jackson Memorial Hospital, Croton   **2008–present**
Provide post-operative care to patients on an 80-bed Medical-Surgical Unit. Diverse responsibilities include: monitoring vital signs, blood glucose and tube intake/output, collecting specimens, assisting with personal hygiene and feeding, and recording patient status. Transport patients to medical procedures and operating portable electrocardiogram. Educate patients and family members on home care.

Prior Employment

Waitress, Calinda's Restaurant, Preston   2003–2008
Earned reputation for dependability, accuracy and delivering superior customer service by providing well-timed, professional service. Demonstrated skills in communication, organization and problem solving, as well as ability to work efficiently in a fast-paced environment. Gained computer skills.

Registered nurse

Kate-Lynne Kennedy, RN

REGISTERED NURSE

1 Any Street
Anytown, Ayrshire AX0 0AA

Tel: 020 8123 4567

Healthcare

PERFORMANCE PROFILE

Recent RN graduate with over 10 years' experience in healthcare and nursing profession. Comprehensive knowledge of nursing procedures and committed to delivering quality patient care. Successful in managing time and prioritizing tasks. Communicate well with staff, family and patients. Punctual, reliable and able to be counted on in a crisis.

Awarded scholarship from the Long-Term Care Federation for continued studies in nursing.

EDUCATION

Bachelor of Science in Nursing, May, 2012
University of South London, School of Nursing

CPR, The British Heart Association, 2002

PROFESSIONAL EXPERIENCE

Mendelsohn House – London   2006–2009

Charge Nurse
Provided quality patient care in a 200-bed residential nursing facility. Supervised Certified Nursing Assistants, Rehabilitation Aides, and assisted in training new licensed staff. Performed patient assessments, developed care plans, and coordinated with other disciplines including: physical therapy, occupational therapy, dietary, activities, and consult with psychologists, pharmacists and social workers regularly. Distributed medications, as indicated by physicians; order and document labs by lab cards.

- Supervised night-shift as the one licensed nurse on duty.
- Provided patient care in unit, observing patients' progress with medication, treatment and rehabilitation; revised shift documentation, ensuring accuracy and completeness of forms and monthly summaries.
- Resolved pharmacy problems relating to delays and reimbursement issues and ensured compliance with documentation requirements.
- Received rarely issued management recognition award for excellence in nursing, flexibility and willingness to work varied shifts to accommodate scheduling needs.

UNITY HEALTHCARE – Mountain View, Cardiff   2004–2006

Nurse
Provided outsourced nursing care in various settings: Medsurg, Detox, Special Needs School, Long-term Care, Group Home, Adult Care.

CITY INFIRMARY, Birmingham   1998–2004

Charge Nurse (2002–2004); *Certified Nurses' Aide*   (1998–2002)
Supervised staff of six CNAs, and one Rehabilitation Aide, in providing nursing care for two floors, 35 patients each. Monitored blood glucose, labs, therapeutic drug levels and equipment; performed assessments, treatments and documentation. Organized staff/patient assignments and patient care.

Trauma Coordinator

Healthcare

Pat Richardson

1 Any Street   12345 67890
Anytown, AX0, 0AA   prichardson@email.com

TRAUMA COORDINATOR
Bilingual Registered Staff Nurse

Performance Profile/Performance Summary

13+ years' experience with principles, methods and procedures of ER and trauma care. Currently in charge of 40 nurses in 43-bed emergency room and Emergency Department. Dedicated, resourceful, background in training, mentoring and support. Experience in coordinating and executing outreach programmes. *Fluent Polish*.

Core Competencies

⁃ Extreme Trauma	⁃ ER	⁃ Training & Development
⁃ Scheduling	⁃ Community Outreach	⁃ Trauma Procedure Standards
⁃ JCAHO	⁃ Data Analysis	⁃ Emergency Medical Processes
⁃ Programme Development	⁃ Conflict Resolution	⁃ DOH Regulation
⁃ Quality Assurance	⁃ Public speaking	⁃ Systems & Procedures

Education & Credentials

BSc Nursing   Anticipated Feb 2015
London University
Associate Degree in Science   2003
Eastern University

Certifications
ACLS, BLS, PALS, TNCC, ENPC
Member, Emergency Nurse Association

PROFESSIONAL EXPERIENCE

CITY MEDICAL CENTRE – Luton   2007–Present

Registered Staff Nurse
43-bed Emergency Room (over 40 nurses at any given time), perform Relief Charge Nurse duties at least once per week. Match patients with nurses at various levels and direct ambulances to different stations.

➤ Senior nurse within unit, serve as official mentor for organization

➤ Trainer for new graduates

➤ Resolution specialist to address conflicts between staff members

➤ Nurse Staff Counsel for the Emergency Department over the past two years

Continued

Pat Richardson   123145 67890   prichardson@email.com   Page 2

Healthcare

Contributions & Achievements

Implementing strategies for upholding high level of morale within understaffed, stressful situations while maintaining optimal emergency and trauma care.

➢ Assisted unit in ensuring fulfilment of standards for DOH, as well as improving quality assurance and safety objectives.

➢ Coordinated successful, well-received Injury Prevention Outreach Programme.
Health Fairs and work with local fire and rescue departments to disseminate information regarding fireworks safety measures.

➢ Served as key member of Student Advocacy Subcommittee, ensuring proper training for high school, nursing and EMT students. Took on educator role with students circulating through ER, contributing to improved capabilities.

➢ Earned 'Excellent' ratings on performance evaluations and received acknowledgement from multiple patients for high level of care and personal attention. Used bilingual background to serve Polish-speaking community.

Eastern Centre, Rotherham   2001–2007

Registered Staff Nurse

Performed various nursing duties, including those of Emergency Room.

Participated in extreme trauma cases.

Affiliations
Member, Emergency Nurse Association

➢ Currently serve as Injury Prevention chairperson

➢ Attended National ENA Convention for the past three years

Nurse

Healthcare

Sarah Vincent
1 Any Street, Anytown, AX0 0AA
Phone: 020 8123 4567 E-mail: svincent@email.com

NURSING PROFESSIONAL
Registered Nurse
Legal Nurse Consultant

EDUCATION

BSc (Hons) Nursing Studies – Current
Kaplan College, West Somerset

Advanced Diploma in Nursing – 2005
St Petersburg Community College, Wilts.

CERTIFICATIONS/TRAINING

Advanced Cardiac Life Support (ACLS)
Paediatric Advanced Life Support (PALS)
EMT-Tactical, Counter-Narcotics Tactical Operations
Introduction to Chemical, Biological & Radiological Defence

Associate in Science in EMS Management – 2000
EMT and Paramedic Certification Programme
St Petersburg Community College, Wilts.

PROFESSIONAL EXPERIENCE

Registered Nurse – Emergency Room, Radiology Specialist
MEASE HOSPITAL, Cardiff
Current
General nursing duties within a critical care setting.

SWAT Paramedic
MEASE HOSPITAL, Cardiff
1998 to 2008
Directed field medical patient care and supervision.

Medical Assistant, 2nd Class,
NAVAL RESERVE, Plymouth
1999 to 2007
Provided field medical patient care and coordinated urinalysis,
immunization and annual medical/dental screening programmes.

Emergency Medical Services to Lab Supervisor
HILLSBOROUGH COMMUNITY COLLEGE, Hillsborough
2004 to 2007
Monitored and assessed student progress.

PROFESSIONAL PROFILE

Competent and knowledgeable medical professional with more than 10 years of increasingly responsible experience. Effective critical thinking, problem solving and interpersonal skills.

EXPERTISE

Legal Nurse Consultant
- Direct initial client assessments to identify potential liability
- Organize and review medical charts and records
- Review surgeons and expert witness depositions

Nursing Expertise
- Direct patient care and advocacy
- Triage
- Intubation and airway management
- Medication administration
- Cardiac monitoring and EKG rhythm interpretation
- Conscious sedation
- Counselling and education
- Chart review quality assurance

Trauma specialist

Richard is leaving the Navy, where he gained a great deal of experience in trauma treatment and crisis management.

Healthcare

RICHARD P ISAACS, RN, BSN
1 Any Street
Anytown, AXO OAA
55555 555555
richi@email.com

···

DISASTER RESPONSE • ACUTE & CRITICAL PATIENT CARE • MEDICAL/SURGICAL CARE
Pediatrics / Geriatrics / Post-Surgical / Nuclear & Biological Hazards

PERFORMANCE SUMMARY

Health care professional with over eight years' intensive experience in fast-paced military hospital environments. Demonstrated capacity to provide direct patient care and effectively supervise support staff in a variety of clinical settings. Specialized training in dealing with nuclear and biological exposure, as well as experience treating patients with infectious diseases including typhoid, meningitis, AIDS and other contagions. Proven capacity to function well in crisis situations, plus excellent ability to relate to patients from diverse cultural backgrounds and various age groups.

···

CORE COMPETENCIES

RN	BSN	Medical	Surgical	ICU
Outpatient	Terminal	Oncology	Acute	Infectious Disease
Telemetry	Burns	Cardiac	BLS/ACLS	Mass Casualty
Typhoid	Tuberculosis	Meningitis	Field Hospital	Shipboard Hospital
AIDS	PALS I	IVCS	Pediatrics	Geriatrics
Incarceration	Humanitarian	Anesthesia	Biological Hazard	Nuclear Hazard
Care	Response	Recovery	Response	Response

PRIMARY CLINICAL EXPERIENCE:

LIEUTENANT, ROYAL NAVY (2008 – Present)
UK Naval Hospital; Gibraltar
Patients encompass infants through to geriatrics, with conditions including a broad range of infectious diseases and physical injuries.

Staff Nurse / Charge Nurse – Adult & Pediatric Care   **May 2012 – Present**
- Provide bedside care to patients; administer medications and implement physician orders.
- Confer with physicians and other care team members on treatment plans for various patients.
- Address the needs of patients in isolation with typhoid, meningitis and other contagious diseases.
- Train and provide leadership for staff of seven RNs and LPNs in Charge Nurse role.
- Participate in field exercises to maintain readiness for combat deployment in support of Marine units.

Key Accomplishment:
Restructured medical supplies inventory and wrote new Standard Operating Procedures (SOPs) to improve departmental efficiencies.

Staff Nurse / Division Officer – Post-Anaesthesia Care Unit   **May 2011 – May 2012**
- Served needs of post-operative patients, addressing special concerns of post-anaesthesia recovery.
- Otherwise supported surgical teams in treating patients with a broad range of medical conditions.

Healthcare

Richard P Isaacs, RN
Page Two

PRIMARY CLINICAL EXPERIENCE *(continued)*:

Naval Hospital; Plymouth
Patient base included military dependents and retirees, as well as active military personnel, including several 'VIP' patients.

Staff Nurse – Medical / Telemetry Acute Care Unit   **Apr 2008 – Apr 2011**
- Addressed acute care needs of medical patients, including oncology and infectious disease patients.
- Cared for patients in isolation wards with tuberculosis, AIDS and other contagious diseases.
- Monitored cardiac activity of patients using state-of-the-art telemetry technology.

Accomplishment:
Selected to serve as part of Humanitarian Relief Response Team.

STOCKPORT GENERAL HOSPITAL; Cheshire
Facility providing full range of medical services.
Staff Nurse / Charge Nurse – Medical / Surgical Unit   **2005 – 2008**
- Provided direct patient care including telemetry monitoring.
- Served needs of incarcerated individuals in conjunction with police service.

ADDITIONAL CLINICAL EXPERIENCE:
EXPOSERVE MEDICAL SERVICES; Yorks
Per Diem Registered Nurse – York Children's Centre   **2008 – 2011**
- Served the needs of paediatric patients in a clinical outpatient setting.

HEARTLAND NURSING SERVICES; Riverhead, Yorks
Per Diem Registered Nurse   **2007 – 2008**
- Cared for burn victims, cardiac patients, post-surgical patients, ICU patients and the terminally ill.

EDUCATION:
NORTH YORKSHIRE UNIVERSITY
Master of Science, Community Service
Anticipated May, 2015
NORTH YORKSHIRE UNIVERSITY
BSc (Hons), Nursing   **May 2006**
WALES UNIVERSITY
Associate of Science, Hotel & Restaurant Management   **June 1991**

CERTIFICATIONS / SPECIALIZED TRAINING:
Registered Nurse
Advanced Cardiac Life Support (ACLS); Basic Life Support (BLS)
Pediatric Advanced Life Support (PALS I)
Intravenous Conscious Sedation (IVCS)
Nuclear & Biological Hazard Medical Training
Mass Casualty Training; Field Hospital Training; Shipboard Hospital Training
Suturing; Chest Tube Insertion

References Provided On Request

Hospital nurse

Stephanie recently completed a special programme allowing LPNs to earn RN status by completing just two terms of college. She is looking to make the leap to an RN position in a hospital.

Healthcare

Stephanie A Monaco

1 Any Street, • Anytown AX0 0AA • 020 8123 4567 • sam@email.com

PROFESSIONAL PROFILE:
Graduate Nurse with over 12 years' healthcare experience. Includes patient care in long-term care facilities and private homes. Experience dealing with a broad range of medical conditions: ventilator-dependent, dialysis, cardiac rehabilitation, post-operative orthopaedic, emphysema, heart failure and Alzheimer patients. Outstanding interpersonal skills: strong patient rapport, excellent ability to relate to patient families, and capacity to interact with nurses, physicians and other providers. Demonstrated leadership skills: directed activities of nursing aides and fulfilled other supervisory functions.

PROFESSIONAL EXPERIENCE

Staff Nurse, Strong Memorial Hospital; Rochester, Kent   **Jan 2011–Present**

- Provide direct patient care for two to five patients in a critical care step-down unit.
- Address patients' respiratory needs, including ventilator care.
- Implement treatment plans consistent with directions of physicians and RNs.

Team Leader, The Hemlock Hills Living Centre; Mendon, Wilts   **2007–2010**

(An Affiliate of Highland Hospital & Strong Health)

- Accountable for day-to-day care of up to 50 residents in a long-term care setting.
- Supervised and delegated duties to six Certified Nursing Aides.
- Addressed treatment needs of Alzheimer, kidney dialysis and cardiac/orthopaedic rehab patients.
- Conferred with physicians, therapists and other providers to develop and implement care plans.
- Assessed residents on a daily basis and reported changes to physicians and/or nurse practitioners.
- Interacted with families of residents to discuss care plans and otherwise address any concerns.
- Assisted Registered Nurse in fulfilling 'Charge Nurse' duties on a recurring basis.

page 1 of 2

Stephanie A Monaco
page 2 of 2

Nurse's Aide (Private Duty), The Collins Family/William R Jeffords; Rochester, Kent
2002–2007
- Addressed daily living needs of geriatric patients in their homes.
- Under direction of RNs and physicians, administered medications for heart failure and hypertension.
- Assisted clients with nutrition, ambulation and daily exercise regimes.
- Conferred with nurses, physicians and family members to discuss care plans and other issues.

Personal Care Assistant (Private Duty), Emerline VanderGelder; Rochester, Kent   **1991–1992**
- Fulfilled the daily living needs of patient with emphysema and congestive heart failure.

EDUCATION:
Associate of Applied Science, Nursing   **May 2010**
Monroe Community College; Rochester, Kent
Enrolled in Advanced Standing Two Term Option

BSc Nursing Practice   **2007**
Isabella Graham Hart School of Practical Nursing; Rochester, Kent
Clinical Rotations at The County Hospital

CERTIFICATIONS:
Registered Nurse/CPR Certified/Basic Life Support (BLS)/Telemetry Certified

References Available Upon Request

Ophthalmic doctor's assistant/technician

Career change: this former sales representative attained her ophthalmic certification and then obtained successful employment in her new field.

Healthcare

THERESA R KEEBLER
55555 555555 • 1 Any Street, Anytown AA1 1AA

OPHTHALMIC DOCTOR'S ASSISTANT / TECHNICIAN
Building organizational value by assisting with diagnostic and treatment-orientated procedures

Technical Skills:
Precise Refracting/Work Up
Scribing
Goniometry
Sterile Techniques

Procedures & Treatments:
Chalazion Surgery
Glaucoma Treatments
Conjunctivitis
Diabetes Monitoring
Retinopathy of Prematurity
Macular Degeneration
Strabismus
Cataracts
Palsy
NLD Obstruction
Blepharplasty

Equipment:
A Scans
Lasers
Tonometry
Slit Lamp
Lensonetry
Keratometer
Visual Fields
Topography

PERFORMANCE SUMMARY

Personable and capable professional experienced in conducting diagnostic tests; measuring and recording vision; testing eye muscle function; inserting, removing and caring for contact lenses; and applying eye dressings. Competently assist physicians during surgery, maintain optical and surgical instruments, and administer eye medications. Extensive knowledge in ophthalmic medications dealing with glaucoma, cataract surgery and a wide variety of other diagnoses.

PROFESSIONAL EXPERIENCE

AUGUSTA EYE ASSOCIATES, Bristol – since 2010
Employed as a **Technician/Assistant** for a cornea specialist in a large ophthalmic practice. Performed histories, vision screenings, pupil exams and precise manifest refractions. Assisted with a variety of surgical procedures. Quickly build trust and rapport and streamline processes to ensure physician efficiency.

GUGGINO FAMILY EYE CENTRE, Bath – 2009 to 2010
Taught customer service techniques and promoted twice within two months to an **Ophthalmic Doctor's Assistant** for a paediatric neurology ophthalmologist performing scribing, taking histories, preparing patients for examination and educating patients on treatment procedures.

DAVEL COMMUNICATIONS, Bath – 2006 to 2008
Recruited as a **Regional Account Manager** and promoted within three months to **National Account Manager**. Contributed to the company doubling in size within 10 months; maintained a 100% satisfied customer retention rate.

CHILI'S BAR & GRILL, Neath – 2000 to 2005
Hired as a **Hostess** and quickly promoted to **Server**.

EDUCATION

Bachelor of Science, Organizational Communication – 2006
University of Wales

CERTIFICATION

Certified Ophthalmic Assistant (COA) – expected July 2015

Dental assistant

Burton wanted a position with a larger practice. The CV highlighted his extensive training and certifications as well as experience. It contains lots of information, in a great layout.

Healthcare

Burton Roberts, CDA

Dental Assistant • CDA, EFDA, CPR Certified

DENTAL ASSISTANT
Oral Surgery • Periodontics • Endodontics • Orthodontics

PERFORMANCE SUMMARY

Highly skilled, energetic and flexible dental professional with experience in 4-handed dentistry, radiology, sterilization, laboratory and office duties. Adept at earning patient's trust and confidence. Demonstrated initiative and commitment, and a proven asset to a growing practice.

CORE DENTAL SKILLS

- 4-Handed Dentistry
- Preventive Care
- Instrument Sterilization
- Diagnostic X-Rays

- Infection Control
- Oral Surgery/Extractions
- Emergency Treatment
- Prosthetics/Restorations

- Teeth Whitening
- Casts/Impressions
- Root Canals
- Patient Education

CHAIRSIDE EXPERIENCE

- Prepare tray setups for dental procedures. Obtain dental records prior to appointment.
- Prepare patients for procedures – ensure comfort and develop trust; calm distressed patients; instruct patients on postoperative and general oral health care; take and record medical and dental histories.
- Oversee cleanliness of operatories and instruments; ensure safe/sanitary conditions using autoclave, ultrasound and dry heat instrument sterilization.
- Assist dentist with extractions, fillings and sealants. Take casts and impressions for prosthetics/restorations.

LABORATORY EXPERIENCE

- Prepare materials for impressions and restorations.
- Pour models and make casts.
- Expose radiographs and process X-ray film.

Page 1 of 2

Burton Roberts
Page 2 of 2

Healthcare

OFFICE EXPERIENCE

- Greet patients; arrange and confirm appointments; keep treatment records.
- Order dental supplies and materials; maintain stock in accordance with monthly budgets.
- Develop and document office policies and procedures. Share best practices with staff.

PROFESSIONAL HISTORY

Chairside Assistant, Dr George Rose, Dublin　　　　　　　　　　January 2010–Present
Student Intern/Chairside Assistant, Dr Victoria Mercer, Dublin　September 2009–December 2009
Student Intern/Nitrous Oxide/Oxygen Administration, Dr John Mann, Belfast　　　　October 2009

EDUCATION AND PROFESSIONAL DEVELOPMENT

CPR Certification – Adult, Infant and Child, Red Cross, January 2010–January 2012
Tooth Bleaching, Home Study Educators (Continuing Education Recognition Programme) 2011
Certified Dental Assistant, Community College, 2010
Expanded Function Dental Assistant (EFDA), University of the South School of Dentistry, 2010
Schuster Centre for Professional Development, 2010
Radiology Certification, 2009
Nitrous Oxide/Oxygen Administration Certification, 2009
ADA Midwinter Dental Conventions, 2008–2011
Photocopier Technician Certification, 2001

BBA University of the South, May 1998

1 Any Street, Any town, AX0 0AA • 020 8123 4567 • burtrob@email.net

Medical assistant

Jennifer's actual paid experience was minimal and dated; her skills needed to be brought to the forefront.

Jennifer Martin
55555 555555
email@address.com
1234 Any Street
Anytown, AA1 1AA
MEDICAL ASSISTANT

CORE SKILLS

Triage	Injections	Patient Scheduling
Medical Terminology	Phlebotomy	Chart Updating
Patient Intake	Vital Signs	ICD and CPT Coding
Dosage Calculations	Infection Control	Insurance Claims
Sterilization Procedures	Urinalysis	Accounts Payable/Receivable
Blood Smears and Blood Tests	Hematocrit	Collections
Lab Equipment Operation	EKG	Data Entry

PROFESSIONAL EXPERIENCE

Patient Care
- Cared for in-home patients with complex, multi-symptom illnesses for three years
- Eased patient discomfort by conducting accurate assessment and drawing techniques
- Fostered healthy environment for diabetic patient through meal preparation, medication dispensing and glucose-level monitoring

Administrative
- Improved cash flow by recovering uncollected accounts in excess of £1 million
- Increased accuracy of patient files by designing and implementing new patient update sheet
- Exceeded daily quotas and minimized overhead expenses with effective scheduling and management of part-time employees

Computer Skills
- Microsoft Windows, Word, Excel and Works
- Corel Word Perfect
- Medical software including Medical Manager and Great Plains

EDUCATION

Western College, Exeter
Medical Assistant Certificate, 2004

Community High School, Anytown
A levels: Biology; Physics; Sociology

RELATED EMPLOYMENT HISTORY

Billing Specialist, Bookkeeper, Medical Assistant (various – Wiltshire and Somerset)	2004–2005
Medical Assistant (Internal Medical Office – Anytown)	2004
Long-term/Acute Care Provider (self-employed – Anytown)	2000–2003

Pharmacy operations

Healthcare

JESSICA BUSH

1 Any Street ♦ Anytown AX0 0AA ♦ 01234 567890 ♦
jbush@email.com

Pharmacy Operations

Performance Summary

Licensed pharmacist dedicated to pursuing the highest quality of pharmacist's care. 14+ years' experience in pharmacy and pharmacy practice settings, including retail, hospital, sales and long-term care. In-depth knowledge of all pharmaceutical operations, including drug distribution systems, drug utilization evaluation, equipment and delivery systems, emerging medications, and DOH pharmacy regulations.

- Calm, flexible and focused in deadline-driven, fast-paced and urgent environments.
- Accurate and detail-oriented with superior organizational skills.
- Services delivered with a sense of timeliness, accountability and integrity.
- Proven ability to quickly resolve problems and implement solutions while moving seamlessly from strategy to operations.
- Superb interpersonal skills, with ability to build and maintain strategic business/client relationships while interfacing positively with people of all levels and backgrounds.

Professional Competencies

✓ Customer Development/Service	✓ Negotiation
✓ Marketing & Sales	✓ Project Management
✓ Problem Resolution	✓ Reports
✓ Multi-site Management	✓ Long-Term Care
✓ Training/Development	✓ Technically Adept
✓ Innovation	✓ Financial Reporting
✓ Presentations	✓ Relationship Building
✓ Coaching	

Professional Experience

JustCare, Ltd, Avonmouth
　　　2010–Present
Regional provider of a broad array of pharmacy-related products to hospitals, outpatient surgery clinics and long-term care facilities.

Divisional Director of SW Operations　　　　　　　　　　　　　　　2012–Present
Responsible for operational management of all SW accounts, including pharmacies in 42 client facilities. Assist in division's multi-pharmacy budgeting process of £500 million in annual sales and approximately one million dispensed prescriptions.

- Cost savings of £250K annually with new stat delivery-reduction initiatives.
- Developed key performance indicator dashboard to conduct weekly and monthly reviews of site efficiency and service levels.

Continued

Healthcare

JESSICA BUSH   ♦ 01234 567890 ♦ jbush@email.com ♦   Page Two

- Identified and provided assistance and upgrades for underperforming pharmacies.
- Increased pharmacy performance: 8% increase in revenue, 4% increase in operating profit.
- Partner with Divisional Compliance Officer to identify regulatory goals and corresponding operational processes and best practices.
- Establish and execute operational best practices and standards and performance improvement plans to facilitate high-level, consistent patient care through provision of pharmaceuticals in challenged pharmacy sites.
- Research, evaluate and implement new technologies, including eMARs, CPOE, e-Prescribing and automation across 42 client sites.

JustCare Ltd, Glasgow
Regional Manager   2010–2012
Accountable for multi-site management of 37 client pharmacies and annualized revenue of £37 million.

- Managed 37 client pharmacies to ensure financial and operational success as well as compliance with DOH regulations.
- Assisted in consolidating subsidiary acquisition, capturing additional £37 million in annual revenue.
- Implemented hub/spoke model for pharmacies, resulting in efficiencies and significant cost reductions.
- Secured £5.5 million in annualized revenue as part of XYZ pharmacy acquisition.
- Key Account Manager for Healthcare Management, with eight long-term nursing facilities and annualized revenue of £4.2 million, plus five assisted living facilities for New Life Management with £2.2 million in annual revenue.

ABC, Birmingham
Sales Representative   2001–2010

- Managed finance and budgets to achieve company goals, and ensured regulatory compliance of pharmacies for annual inspection. Recruited, selected, trained and coached all personnel.
- Increased productivity by coordinating training, implementation and evaluation of IV programme – £40K.

DEF, Halton   1999–2001
Pharmacy Manager

DEF, Coniston   1997–1999
Pharmacy Manager

Education

BSC/MPharm, University of Birmingham

Professional Development

Corporate Finance
Microsoft Office Certificate

Professional Licenses

GPhC registered

Professional Organizations/Affiliations

Institute of Pharmacy Management
National Pharmacy Association

Pharmacy technician

OLIVIA S KOSTER, CPhT

PHARMACY TECHNICIAN

1 Any Street
Any Town AXO OHA
020 8123 4567

Healthcare

PROFILE

Focused and disciplined, with more than eight years' retail experience, reflecting:

- ability to read/understand/dispense prescriptions
- knowledge of drugs and drug strengths
- sound judgement, seeking professional assistance when needed
- outstanding communication/customer service skills
- awareness of legality issues
- experience with inventory control and stocking
- proficiency in computer operations/data entry

Well-developed communication skills, interacting effectively with people on all levels; speak English, French, Spanish and Hungarian.

Conscientious and detail-orientated with an earned reputation for dependability, integrity, efficiency and professionalism.

EXPERIENCE

2007–2015	ABC Pharmacy, 2/11–8/15	Wellingborough
	XYZ Pharmacy, 5/07–12/11	Wellingborough
	Senior Certified Pharmacy Technician	

Provided assistance to registered pharmacist and pharmacy customers, managing up to 700 prescriptions daily:

- Answered phones for orders and repeats; answered questions on pricing.
- Contacted physicians to verify prescriptions/repeats and address third-party issues; communicated with warehouse and wholesalers for inventory information; followed up with customers.
- Filled prescription under guidance of registered pharmacist; prepared labels using InterCom Plus system.
- Worked with customers at Drop Off Window, ensuring optimum customer service to generate repeat and referral business.
- Entered prescriptions into computer system's patient profiles and checked for drug allergies.
- Managed special orders; received and stocked inventory, maintaining appropriate documentation.
- Received outstanding ratings from Safeway Secret Shopper Programme.

EDUCATION

South West College

- Pharmacy Technician Liability Controlling Errors
- Civil Liability and the Evolving Role of Pharmacy Technician

XYZ Drug Stores
Pharmacy Technician Training – OJT

Scottsdale Community College   Scottsdale
NVQ level 3 Pharmacy Services

Healthcare

Pharmaceutical sales and service

Catherine was a bright sales and service specialist who was growing in her career responsibilities and accomplishments and wanted to move into more advanced management positions.

Catherine Atree
1 Any Street, Anytown AA1 1AA • 55555 555555 • catherineatree@email.com

PHARMACEUTICAL SALES

PERFORMANCE SUMMARY

High-energy sales professional with experience developing product awareness through building business relationships. Proven performer with track record of outperforming sales targets, delivering high levels of customer service and achieving successful sales results built on key strengths of:

- **Consultative Sales Skills** – experience and education involving custom pharmaceutical and consumer products
- **New Business Development / Territory Management** – prospecting and building a territory; identifying and capitalizing on opportunities, knowledge of sales cycles
- **Customer Retention / Relationship Building** – excellent communication (listening, speaking) and interpersonal skills
- **Goal Setting** – experience in setting and achieving both independent and team-driven targets

CORE SALES COMPETENCIES

➢ Consultative Sales	➢ New Business Development	➢ Territory Management
➢ Prospecting	➢ Market ID	➢ Sales Cycles
➢ Goal Setting	➢ Customer Retention	➢ Relationship Building
➢ Contractual Sales	➢ Customer Service	➢ Strategic Partners
➢ Product Launches	➢ Strategic Planning	➢ Market Share
➢ Sales Trainer	➢ Problem Solving	➢ Interpersonal Skills
➢ Product Presentation	➢ Corporate Liaison	➢ Collaborative Thinking
➢ Account Maintenance	➢ Cold Calls	➢ Formulary Status Promotion

PROFESSIONAL EXPERIENCE

ABC HEALTHCARE INCORPORATED; Coalport
Largest domestic contractual sales and marketing partner providing solutions to pharmaceutical and healthcare industries

Pharmaceutical Sales Specialist, 2008–current
Manage team-driven pharmaceutical sales responsibilities in Southeast area. Interact with physicians, nurses, physician assistants and medical professionals to represent a premier product line. Interact with other sales reps to do strategic planning, problem solving and collaborative thinking. Manage 35–40 weekly calls on physicians to increase market share in territory.

- Coordinated product launch for new acid reflux drug.
- Petitioned physicians to contact their HMOs and recommend formulary status; received formulary standing in January 2010.
- Member of market-leading Prosec sales team.
- Consistently over sales quota; won highest call activity contest. Regional sales leader for hypertensive drug.

Continued

Catherine Atree
Page 2 of 2

OFFICE MAX [2005–2008]; Oldham
Multibillion-pound global retailer of office supplies, furniture and technology
Business Development Specialist, 2006–2008

Promoted to develop new business while maintaining current business in competitive Southeastern and central area; focused on small to medium-size companies. Managed complete sales cycle from initial contact, through presentation and consultation, to close of sale. Acted as liaison between sales centre rep team and corporate office in London.

- Consistently maintained above-expected goal percentage in regional and corporate sales.
- Trained new reps in all areas of product presentation, solution selling, and customer service.

Sales Representative, 2000–2005

Managed sales and account maintenance with companies. Independently maintained relationships with company personnel to increase visibility and credibility. Developed leads through cold calls; met with customers to identify needs.

- Developed new customers; maintained high goal percentages; recruited to higher position.

EDUCATION & TRAINING
UNIVERSITY OF MANCHESTER

Bachelor of Science degree in Interdisciplinary Studies/Social Science with a focus in Health & Humanities; 2000
Vocational courses: Leadership Sales, Presentations Skills

References available on request

Healthcare

Medical sales representative

Healthcare

Jennifer J Rogers

1 Any Street
Anytown AX0 0AA

020 8123 4567
jrogersmed@email.com

Medical Sales Representative

Professional Profile

17-year proven track record in prospecting, consultative sales, new business development and account retention. Proficient in sales presentations, introducing and detailing products, conducting inservices with physicians and nursing staff. Strong customer and assessment abilities. Well-developed closing skills for large capital purchases. Experienced sales trainer. Highly motivated, enthusiastic and committed to professional excellence.

Achievements – percentage of plan by year

2014 – 183%	2011 – 105%	2008 – 90%	2005 –164%
2013 – 78%	2010 – 159%	2007 – 92%*	2004 – 110%
2012 – 100%	2000 – 138%	2006 – 111%	

*started new territory

Core Competencies

Medical Supplies	Capital Equipment	Instrumentation
Large Systems Deals	Large Capital Purchases	Prospecting
Consultative Sales	New Business Development	Account Retention
Sales Presentations	Introducing/Detailing	Physician/Nurse In-services
Needs Assessment	Sales Trainer	Field/Platform

Professional Experience

Experience includes the sales of medical supplies and capital equipment. As a Senior Monitoring Consultant, worked with sales representatives throughout the West to assist in the presentation and closing of large systems deals. Outstanding achievements include:

- securing multiple orders for patient monitoring systems in excess of £1 million;
- excellent product knowledge with quick learning abilities;
- excellent long-term customer relationships evidenced by strong repeat business.

Career Progression

ABC Monitoring • prior to 2008 known as XYZ Systems • Exeter

Senior Representative • *2012–Present*
Position achieved by recommendation of Sales Director and MD

Sales Trainer/Sales Representative • Northwest Region • *2010–Present*
Territory includes North West and Scotland

Medical Sales Representative • South East Region • *2005–2010*
Co-Medical
Medical Sales Representative • *2000–2005*
ABC Hospital Pharmacy Department • Nottingham
Technician Coordinator • *1995–2000*

Education & Awards

- Six Award Trips
- Multiple Sales Awards
- National Accounts Award Winner • *2010*
- Monitoring Consultant of the Year • *2009; 2010*

BSc Biological Sciences • Medical Assistant Programme, Nottingham University

Medical equipment sales

Erik is seeking to move from pharmaceutical sales to sales of medical equipment. The CV demonstrates a track record of accomplishments and outstanding sales and account development capabilities.

Healthcare

ERIK CLAYTON
erikclayton@email.com

1 Any Street
Anytown AA1 1AA

Home 212 555-1234
Mobile 212 555-4321

MEDICAL EQUIPMENT SALES

Top-producing sales professional with five years' progressive experience, including three years in pharmaceutical sales. Natural communicator with expertise in forging solid working relationships with professionals at all levels. Proven ability to identify and capitalize on market opportunities to drive revenues and capture market share. Strong closer who consistently exceeds targets in a consultative sales environment.

—Core Skills—

Sales & Marketing • Business Development • Account Development & Retention Client Relations
• Team Building & Leadership • Training & Educating Prospecting & Closing Negotiations
• Consensus Building Problem Solving • Presentations • Public Speaking

---

PROFESSIONAL EXPERIENCE

Sales Representative • 2008 to Present
INDUSTRY-LEADING PHARMACEUTICAL CO, York
Represent leading pharmaceutical company in consultative sales of select medications to GPs, Pharmacists, Pharmacy Technicians and Pharmacy Managers throughout the UK.
- Call on 250 accounts monthly; consistently exceed company targets.
- Increased product market share from 25% to 46%.
- Educated clients on launch of product, achieving 35% market share within three months.
- Selected by District Manager, out of 12 representatives, to anchor and train new hires.
- Placed 2nd in country for sales of main product out of 2,500 reps.
- Achieved 1st in district two consecutive years, 2010, 2011.
- Nominated for *Representative of the Year* award (2010).
- Nominated for company's most prestigious award (2009).

Account Executive • 2006 to 2008
COMPUTER MASTER, York
Gained valuable sales and client relations experience with £5 million computer sales company.
- Serviced existing accounts and developed new business, including several major companies.
- Increased territory gross sales by 20%.

EDUCATION

BSc Communications
YORK UNIVERSITY; 2006

Professional Development
Company Sponsored Sales Training; 2010
Team Train the Trainer (Company home office, one week); 2010

Computer Skills: Windows, Microsoft Word, PowerPoint

Medical technology sales

Healthcare

Jane Petroski

1 Any Street
Any Town AX0 0AA
020 8123 4567

MEDICAL INDUSTRY PROFESSIONAL
Training Specialist/Pharmaceutical Sales/Medical Software Support

Radiography Technology graduate integrating work and education to achieve career goal. Ability to communicate highly technical medical information to professionals, as well as to patients and their families. Persuasive public speaker delivering high-impact presentations to diverse audiences including board of instructors. Expert time manager with tenacity and perseverance to handle rejection without taking it personally. PC proficient in MS Office, Lotus and industry-specific software.

EDUCATION
BSc Diagnostic Radiography with Biology, University of the South, 2010
  Courses: Medical Terminology, Physics, Microbiology, Human Anatomy and Physiology

Radiography Placement, Chapman General Hospital, London
  Studied all Radiography modalities by rotating through areas of CV, Mammography, CAT Scan, Special Procedures, Ultrasound, Radiation Oncology, Diagnostic, Surgery, Nuclear Medicine and Patient Care. Observed procedures and participated in hands-on training; completed detailed patient histories.
  Established network of physician contacts by demonstrating exemplary performance and providing competency/reliability in the operating room and at clinical sites.

Bedford Community College, 2005
  A levels: A* Sociology, Psychology, Biology

CONTINUING PROFESSIONAL DEVELOPMENT
  Emergency and Triage Seminar, Chapman General Hospital, London, 10/06
  Trauma Seminar, Chapman General Hospital, London, 7/06
  Caring for Customer Service, A. D. Banker & Company (8-week course), Reading, Berks, 8/95

PROFESSIONAL EXPERIENCE
CHAPMAN GENERAL HOSPITAL, London   2/06 to Present
CAT Scan Technician (Part Time)
  Administer quality CAT Scans for outpatients and inpatients, plus emergency and trauma patients, while pinpointing immediate problems to provide patient care. Trained on operation of G.E. and Phillips machines, acquiring knowledge of physics principles. Assess and triage patients according to procedural priorities. Facilitate communication between doctors and patients. Interact with patients' families in crisis situations. Delegate tasks, as necessary, to maintain homeostasis. Dispense correct patient contrast and radiation dosage to prevent contraindications.
  React quickly and accurately in trauma situations using critical thinking and reasoning.

Continued on Page 2

Healthcare

Page 2, CV of Jane Petroski **020 8123 4567**

ADDITIONAL EXPERIENCE

Accounts Clerk, RYAN & FESTER, Bedford 6/2001 to 1/05
Performed general accounting functions for tax and litigation law firm.

Office Manager/Secretary, AUTO SUPPLY OUTLET, Bedford 4/2001 to 6/2001
Supported six outside account representatives, assisting with direct sales and customer service.

Accounts/Shipping/Line Manager, C&B EMBROIDERY, Bedford 11/99 to 4/2001
Supervised quality control and resolved problems as liaison between employees and owners.

Data Entry Clerk, XYZ BANK, Brighton 2/99 to 11/99
Rewarded several times for speed and accuracy with large return items.

Office Manager, ABC CONSTRUCTION, Brighton 11/96 to 9/98
Established business relationships with vendors and HSE.

Accounts Clerk, CPA FIRM LTD, Portsmouth 5/95 to 11/96
Assisted Department Supervisor in this CPA firm: performed A/P, A/R and data entry.

Customer Service Manager, BANKS & COMPANY LTD, Portsmouth 6/93 to 5/95
Delivered train-the-trainer presentations on customer service techniques.

EARLY POSITIONS
Accounts Assistant/Secretary to Owner, 3/93 to 6/93
Reproduction Department Head/Relief Receptionist, 6/92 to 3/93
Store Manager, 8/91 to 6/92
Dental Assistant, 6/90 to 8/91

PROFESSIONAL AFFILIATIONS/CERTIFICATIONS

Member: Society of Radiographers, 2 years
CPR and Advanced Lifesaving Certificates, 2007
Radiologic Science Club, Charitable Volunteer Coordinator, Member, 2 years

COMMUNITY INVOLVEMENT

Famine Relief: prepared and served dinner to families through community project, 2014.
Hope House: collected and delivered clothing and home products through community project, 2013.
Angel Tree: collected gifts for children of incarcerated parents through community project, 2013.

Biochemistry researcher

Young professional making first job change with a powerful and well-focused CV.

Healthcare

SOPHIA L MEYERS

1 Any Street
Anytown AA1 1AA

55555 555555
sophialmeyers@anyserver.co.uk

Talented young professional with skills and training in:
NEUROBIOLOGY AND BIOCHEMISTRY RESEARCH

Highly-accomplished, quick learner with an impressive **hands-on knowledge base** encompassing the entire spectrum of **neurobiological research**, with special expertise in Organic, Inorganic, Analytical, Solutions, Instrumental Analysis and Physical Chemistry. Regarded by peers and mentors as an overachiever who is **committed to excellence in this field**, as demonstrated by **outstanding academic achievement**. Demonstrate thorough and detailed research capabilities. *Experience and academic preparation include:*

- Molecular Theory
- Quantum Mechanical Modelling
- Mathematical Modelling
- Particle Location and Density
- DNA Analysis and Separation

- Reagent Preparations
- EDTA Titration Process
- Electron Neutron Diffraction
- Electrophoretic Techniques
- Thermodynamic Principles

- Ethology
- Blood Typing
- Diffusion Principles
- X-Ray Diffraction
- GCMS/MS

EDUCATION

MSc Neurobiology, City University ~ 2013 Biology and Biochemistry 2.1
BSc (Hons) City University ~ 2011

RELEVANT EXPERIENCE & EMPLOYMENT

Administrative Coordinator ~ Radiology Consultants ~ 5/2011 to present
MSc Neuroscience ~ City University ~ 8/2010 to 5/2011
Medication Care Manager ~ Sunrise Assisted Living, East Grinstead ~ 2/2008 to 7/2010

Clinical Trials: Administered a significant drug trial and established a dosage response curve for the identification of invertebrate behaviour using neuromodulators.

Medication Management: Completed training to confidently, legally and safely administer patient medication and effectively document their immediate reaction. Managed a staff of 10, ordered and controlled the administration of all narcotics.

Ethology: Performed pet care behavioural science medical procedures, including the administration of both local and general anaesthesia, catheters, IV and injectables. Confidently handle X-rays and assess behaviour modifications due to hormones, neuroreceptors and neurotransmitters.

Quality Assurance and Statistical Analysis: Delivered 3+ years in-depth reagent preparation and reaction writing capstone project culminating in and solidifying expertise in testing chemicals to determine molarity of any solution.

Spectroscopy: Trained in Chemical Detection Methods including UV detection, chromotrography and polarity, as well as finding unknown chemicals by running samples using search criteria.

Gamete Shedding/In Vitro Fertilization: Oversaw a developmental biology project devoted to the in vitro fertilization of insects, rats and invertebrates, whereby deliberate injection led to gamete shedding, fertilization of eggs in petri, and ultimately the reintroduction of eggs into animals.

PRESENTATIONS & CONFERENCES

Presented Topic: 'Octopomine vs. Serotonin as a Neuromodulator and Neurotransmitter'
Society for Neuroscience National Conference – 2010

MEMBERSHIPS, CERTIFICATIONS & AFFILIATIONS

Society of Neuroscience ~ Society for Analytical Inorganic and Organic Chemistry

Occupational therapist

A great combination-style CV for a recent master's degree graduate

Healthcare

EVELYN WILLIAMS   ewilliams@email.com

Value to your organization   1 Any Street
Anytown AX0 0AA
020 8123 4567

OCCUPATIONAL THERAPIST

- **Interpersonal skills** achieved by successfully communicating with physicians, patients, professors, co-workers, visitors, hospital personnel and other agencies.
- **Leadership skills** displayed by developing and directing groups related to stress management, substance abuse awareness, assertiveness training and self-awareness; volunteer assistant basketball coach.
- **Problem-solving skills** gleaned by determining and providing individualized care and rehab to patients with neurological, orthopaedic and generalized diagnoses in home and clinical settings, and by visualizing and preparing goals with functional outcomes to maximize patient independence level.
- **Organizational skills** as evidenced by the ability to manage and prioritize tasks in a fast-paced environment; co-organized EMU Reach Out 'Run for the Homeless'.

EDUCATION

EASTERN UNIVERSITY, Norwich
Master of Occupational Therapy, 2011

EASTERN UNIVERSITY, Norwich
Bachelor of Arts in Psychology, 2009

WORK EXPERIENCE

1/11–Present   **PRIVATE RESIDENCE**, Birmingham
Home Health Aide
8/09–12/10   **EVERGREEN CARE & REHABILITATION CENTRE**, Birmingham
Certified Nursing Assistant
9/08–8/09   **RAINBOW REHABILITATION CENTRE**, Chester
Rehab Assistant – Traumatic Brain Injury

CLINICAL/PRE-CLINICAL EXPERIENCE

3/09–6/09   **ST VINCENT MEDICAL CENTRE**, Chester
Physical Dysfunction, Inpatient Acute Care Setting
1/09–3/09   **HERITAGE HOSPITAL**, Cheltenham
Psychosocial Dysfunction, Inpatient Psychiatric Hospital
9/08–12/08   **McPHERSON HOME SERVICES**, Howell, Cheltenham
Occupational Therapy in Home-Based Community Setting
1/08–4/08   **INTENSIVE PSYCHIATRIC COMMUNITY CARE**, Gloucester
Intensive Clinical Case Management, Department of Health

ACTIVITIES & AFFILIATIONS

UK Occupational Therapy Association; EMU Stoic Society Member.

ADDITIONAL SKILLS

- First Aid • NeuroDevelopment Techniques • CPR • MMT
- Bloodborne Pathogens • ADL • Adaptive Equipment
- Pre-fabricated Splinting • Spanish • Microsoft Office XP

Occupational health services manager

Susan was successful in finding an Occupational Health Services management position in another industry after being a casualty of airline downsizing.

Healthcare

SUSAN BROWN, RN
Manchester
Mobile: 5555555 5555
Pager: 800-555-3642 PIN#1937761
E-mail: susanbrown@email.com

OCCUPATIONAL HEALTH SERVICES MANAGER

Certified Occupational Health Nurse Specialist / Certified Case Manager / Certified Occupational Hearing Conservationist / Case Management / HSE & DOT Compliance / Ergonomics / Workers' Compensation / Corporate Safety / Training / Customer Service / Problem Solving / Quality Assurance / Sales & Marketing
- 10 years' direct experience developing innovative occupational health programmes and establishing clinics.
- 14 years' experience in trauma centres and critical care units.
- Success in driving revenue stream and cost-saving initiatives through strong combination of business management and clinical skills.
- Registered Nurse.
- Proficient in Sign Language, Microsoft Office and Outlook.

PROFESSIONAL EXPERIENCE

Supervisor, Occupational Health Services, Southwest Air Lines, Manchester   2006–Present

Recruited to implement and manage Southwest's first onsite employee health clinic in eight years. Accountable for care of work-related and non-occupational injuries and illnesses for 5,000 airport employees (from baggage handlers to pilots). Coordinated care for another 1,500 employees in Rochdale and 1,000 employees at Gatwick. Hired and directly supervised 13 registered nurses. Managed £1 million budget. Assisted with the launch of new Southwest clinics in four other airports. Standardized policies and procedures and created training programmes.

Developed position to also encompass system-wide responsibilities, and established self as the resource for HSE-related matters, insourcing opportunities, ergonomic issues, and post-job offer testing programmes. Updated operational managers on daily events, occupational health programme progression, new programmes, ongoing testing, compliance achievement, drug testing programme, etc.

Achievements
- Overcame resistance and established first-ever Manchester airport onsite clinic as an integral part of operations. Planned the department design, oversaw the architect and contractors, hired and trained staff, and developed an orientation manual from scratch.
- Conceived and implemented matrix to document value of occupational health services to Southwest. Demonstrated an average of 55% ROI each month.
- Generated annual revenue of £120,000 by spearheading a drive to insource business from other airport companies, promoting the use of the Southwest clinic instead of an offsite clinic.
- Initiated joint venture with Comair and opened a lucrative satellite clinic in Manchester for Comair employees.
- Innovated a post-job offer functional testing programme to address the high percentage of injuries among new employees. Worked closely with Southwest Legal and Human Resources and researched vendors.
- Negotiated inpatient services volume discount with most utilized hospital system that will save £60,000+ per year.
- Developed an improved nurse orientation process and a charting quality assurance programme.

Continued

SUSAN BROWN, COHN-S/CM   **PAGE TWO**

Trainer, Manchester   2004–Present

Provided continuing education, with CEUs approved by Hampshire Board of Nurses, on Workplace Violence Guidelines for Health Care Workers, Nuts and Bolts of Occupational Health Nursing, HSE Compliance and the Occupational Health Nurse, and Workers' Compensation Fraud Prevention and Update.

Programme Supervisor, Allied Health Corporation, Boston, Lincs   2003–2006

Accountable for providing a broad range of quality services in a convenient, efficient and cost-effective manner for this 8,000-employee Hospital Based Occupational Health Services Programme dedicated to 'Business Health'. Supervised staff of 50 at 35 different companies.

- Managed successful start-up of eight freestanding occupational medicine walk-in clinics.
- Instrumental in winning £600,000 in new business through marketing the placement of clinics, doctors and/or nurses at company sites.

Manager, Occupational Health Services, Cumberland Farms, Cumbria   2000–2003

Managed department, workers' compensation benefits, HSE compliance issues, and health and wellness initiative for this multi-million-pound division of XYZ Industries with 1,000 employees.

- Decreased compensation costs by 66% over three years.

Occupational Health Nurse, Granite Industrial Constructors, Boston, Lincs   1999

Provided occupational health and case management services to this large construction company.

Previous experience working at several medical centres and a trauma centre providing direct emergency nurse care as a lead trauma nurse and charge nurse.

EDUCATION & TRAINING

BSc (Hons) Nursing, University of Durham   1988

Select Ongoing Professional Development (attended numerous occupational health and case management continuing education programmes):

- 28 hours towards Bachelor of Science, Nursing Practice, Manchester Community College
- Certification Programmes for Occupational Health Nurse Specialist, Certified Case Manager, and Occupational Hearing Conservationist
- 50 hours of HSE Training

PROFESSIONAL MEMBERSHIPS

- Member, Association of Occupation Health Nurses (AOHN) – 10 years
- International Airline Occupational Health Nurse Association
- Board of Occupational Health Nurses (BOHN)

COMMUNITY SERVICE

Manchester Association for the Hearing Impaired (2000–Present)

Healthcare

Counsellor

Angel needed emphasis placed on educational goals, as well as demonstrating career advancement. This was effectively done in the Core Skills section and the Education section showing her direction towards her doctorate.

Angel Roswell

1 Anystreet, Anytown AX0 0AA • E-mail: angel200620@email.com • 020 8123 4567

Professional Profile

Highly motivated, versatile and resourceful **professional** with **BSc** in **Psychology** and currently in a **Master's** programme specializing in **Marriage & Family Counselling**. Over five years' experience with children aged 2–6 in disciplined, learning atmosphere combined with performing human resource duties, training and counselling for teachers, co-workers and parents. Strong support experience in office atmosphere with expertise in research and writing. Eager to excel, learn quickly, personable, and appreciated among peers.

Core Skills:
- Highly effective writing skills.
- Strong research and reporting abilities.
- Experienced in budgeting, financial planning, fundraising and donation solicitation.
- Naturally intuitive to children's needs with strong insight to unspoken needs.
- Strengths in listening, evaluation and counselling.
- Effective database management and marketing.
- Development of programmes/projects with effective implementation.
- Strong presentation skills, both written and verbal.
- Proven negotiation abilities.
- Proficient in assuring compliance with city, county, local and national government agencies.
- Able to accept responsibility and delegate where needed.
- Well-developed organizational skills.
- Personable and work well with all types of personalities.
- Loyal, driven, honest and committed to a job well done.

Professional Experience

Associate Director • Educational Service • Southport • 2006–2011
Head Preschool Teacher (promoted)
Head Jr Preschool Teacher (promoted)
Assistant Jr Preschool Teacher (promoted)
Rapid upward progression in job responsibility from initial assistant, performing work as needed, to assuming Associate Director responsibilities involving the entire school, ie curriculum, teaching, training, counselling, supervising, providing assessments, budget planning, negotiations, parent involvement, marketing and fundraising.

Receptionist/Office Assistant • In Basket Business Services, Southport • 2005–2006
Receptionist for 10 companies along with answering multi-phone lines. Data entry, including invoicing, posting payables and receivables, and verification of statements. Variety of office duties.

Marketing Coordinator • Automated Machine Tool, Southport • 2004–2005
Telemarketing for strong sales leads. Relief receptionist. Maintained database, literature files and price books. Letter composition.

Certifications

Certified • City of Guilds (3049) level 3 NVQ

Education

Ongoing studies to qualify for **Doctorate Degree in Child Psychology** – *emphasis in* **Play Therapy**
Master's Degree – Marriage & Family Counselling • Southport University • *Degree expected 2015*
BSc • **Psychology** • Southport University • 2009

Guidance counsellor

SHARON WISE

1 Any Street, Anytown AA1 1AA
55555 555555 ~ sharon_wise@email.com

SCHOOL GUIDANCE COUNSELLOR

PERFORMANCE SUMMARY

Dedicated primary and secondary school guidance counsellor, skilled at providing positive direction for students' academic, social and emotional well-being. Work effectively with children with ADHD and with multicultural and diverse populations.

CORE COUNSELLING SKILLS:

Guidance Curriculum: Classroom Guidance Lessons; Career Awareness; Conflict Resolution/Social Skills; Developmental Awareness

Individual Planning: Student Assessments; Student Placement & Scheduling; New Student Transition; Academic & Career Advisement

Responsive Services: Mental Health; Family & Teacher Consulting; Crisis Intervention & Grief Management; Psycho-Educational Support Groups

Systems Support: Programme Evaluation; Programme Development & Coordination; Needs Assessment; Committee Participation

EDUCATION / CERTIFICATION

MA, *Counselling,* UNIVERSITY OF SOUTHAMPTON
MA, *Teaching,* MARYGROVE COLLEGE
BA, *Teaching – Social Studies/French,* MIDLANDS UNIVERSITY

Certified – City & Guilds Counselling Skills
Certified – *Social Studies & French*
Certified – Higher Professional Diploma in Counselling – expected completion August 2015

PROFESSIONAL EXPERIENCE

HARTLAND COMMUNITY SCHOOL, Hartland   2010–Present
SCHOOL COUNSELLOR

Provide individual and small-group counselling sessions and large-group counselling presentations within classroom and guidance office environments for a school with 800 students. Participate in parent/teacher meetings to discuss and develop emotional and behavioural strategies for students with physical, mental and emotional challenges.

- Developed 45-minute Bully-Proofing classes and presented them to students.
- Wrote a monthly article for the school newsletter on a topic of relevance.
- Facilitated students participating in the Gifted & Talented programme.
- Held orientation for new students and their parents, providing them with a timetable of classes and showing them around the building.
- Created 30-minute Career Awareness/Exploration sessions so students would become exposed to various career options. Organized a Career Day, arranging for 40 speakers in various fields to talk with the students about their profession.

Continued

Counselling and social services

SHARON WISE   sharon_wise@email.com   Page Two

- Facilitated support groups dealing with social and coping skills, and conducted needs assessment and programme evaluation with staff and students.

- Designed a survey for students and teachers to evaluate the guidance programme.

- Hung a bully-proofing display, with children earning hearts for 'acts of kindness'.

- Participated as a team member for the School Improvement Team (SCIT).

- Performed coordinator duties, planning and organizing initial mailings, assigning students to teachers, adhering to budgets, and scheduling classes.

HEADWAY COMMUNITY SCHOOL, Plymouth   2008–2010
GUEST TEACHER

Substituted in the middle school and high school, teaching most subjects. Immediately tried to develop a rapport with students and engage in discussion of relevant topics. Facilitated the discussion to steer towards daily lesson plan. Discussion and debate kept students centred, entertained and open to learning.

- Given long-term teaching assignment for students with disabilities. Taught maths, science and social studies in years 6–8 for a full term. There were 5–10 students in each of four classes, ages 11–13; many students had ADHD. Wrote lesson plans, marked assignments and consulted with parents.

DEANSWAY COMMUNITY SCHOOL, Plymouth   2001–2008
FRENCH & SOCIAL STUDIES TEACHER

Taught five classes each day, with each class having 30–35 students; engaging their curiosity and research abilities in structured classroom activities. Provided lectures, notes, study guides and projects for courses in History, Government, Economics, World Geography, Global Issues and French.

- Devised an effective structure for parent communication.

- Gathered resources as supplemental materials to be used in conjunction with assigned texts to give students a richer experience.

- Assigned different subjects each year, showed flexibility in providing first-rate learning experience for each subject.

- Developed a system to track work and assignments while moving to different rooms for each class period.

- Provided students with practical experience, such as making menus and calendars in French.

- Member of School Improvement team and on the committee to improve student self-esteem.

PROFESSIONAL MEMBERSHIPS

- British Association for Counselling

RECENT CONFERENCE PARTICIPATION

Launching Career Awareness – Education Service Agency
Legal Issues for School Counsellors – Counsellors Association
Counselling Groups in Crisis – Association of Specialists in Group Work
A.D.H.D in the New Millennium – Schools' Association
Bully-Proofing Your School – Schools' Association
The Human Spirit & Technology – Counselling Association
Understanding Attachment Disorders – Medical Educational Service
Grief Counselling Skills – University of Plymouth

Mental health counsellor (entry-level)

Having acquired her Bachelor's degree, as well as in-depth voluntary experience, Jessica is seeking a full-time entry-level position within the mental health career field.

Counselling and social services

Jessica Devlin
1 Any Street, Anytown AX0 0AA
020 8123 4567 • 55555 555555 Mobile • jessdev@home.com

OBJECTIVE: Entry-level Mental Health Counselling position, such as Residential Counsellor, Mental Health Counsellor, Mental Health Associate, Clinical Case Manager, or Partial Care Counsellor.

EDUCATION
BSc Psychology/Professional Education   May 2014
London University

Relevant Courses:

Introductory Psychology	Mental Illness	Developmental Psychology
Introductory Sociology	Psychodrama I	Educational Psychology
Physiological Psychology	Loss and Grieving	Sociology of the Family
Essential Helping Relations	Social Psychology	Field Experience I & II
Transcultural Health	Theory of Personality	Abnormal Psychology
Intro. Criminal Justice		

MENTAL HEALTH VOLUNTEER

- **Greenway Citizen's Advice**   2012–2013

Project coordinator for two Outreach Advice Projects, including implementation of Advice Helpline Website

- **Victim Support Greenway**

Counselling victims of crime with special training in Criminal Injuries Compensation Board applications, domestic violence, racial crime and child abuse cases.

EMPLOYMENT
Substitute Teacher, North Somerset   2014–present

- Teach all subjects as substitute teacher for primary and secondary schools, following lesson plans detailed by classroom teachers, as well as maintaining positive class atmosphere and discipline.

Continued

Counselling and social services

Jessica Devlin   **Page 2 of 2**

Hostess/Cocktail Waitress, Rusty Scupper, Bristol   2013–present

- Coordinate seating, efficiently and promptly, for popular city restaurant with seating for 500 indoors and outdoors. Seat 200 customers per eight-hour shift, while serving 1,000 bar customers per five-hour shift.

- Efficiently seat and serve group parties and banquets, such as four 2013 Christmas parties (75 customers each) in one day. Received recognition for top-notch customer service and positive attitude under stress.

- Entrusted with a £450 bankroll at beginning of each shift. Maintain 99+% 'count out' (cash reconciliation) accuracy for monies collected and disbursed daily.

- Chosen by management to promote upcoming shows and events via on-site and off-site marketing pieces and public relations appearances.

Administrative Assistant, XYZ Ltd, Taunton   Summer 2011

- Maintained orderly and productive environment in busy office with six staff. Effectively answered and transferred incoming phone calls on eight lines, and scheduled 50–60 appointments daily.

- Word-processed, edited and revised large volume of letters and documents weekly (20–25 documents, each 75–80 pages in length). Consistently completed assignments with short turnaround time (within 24 hours). Received live dictation, composed and sent correspondence and memos.

COMPUTER SKILLS
Windows 98, MS Office 2000 – Word, Excel, Access, PowerPoint, MS Outlook, PhotoShop, Internet Explorer

Clinical psychologist/social services professional

Veda A Merritt

1 Any Street
Anytown AX0 0AA

Home: 020 8123 4567
Mobile: 55555 5555
vamerritt@email.com

CLINICAL PSYCHOLOGY & SOCIAL SERVICES • COMMUNITY OUTREACH

PROFILE
Versatile, dedicated Social Services professional with solid clinical and administrative acumen. Committed team player and resourceful leader with proven ability to motivate and generate results through hands-on management and a sound knowledge base. Proactive community services advocate, continually seeking out new resources to aid patients.

EXPERTISE
- Counselling and therapy for individuals, couples and groups
- Identifying and matching resources to fit client/patient needs
- Teaching and facilitating workshops to train peers, subordinates and clients
- Managing cases, including writing and reviewing case notes, and auditing case files
- Networking to develop and sustain services, then propagating community awareness
- Relationship building with patients of all ages, socioeconomic and cultural backgrounds
- Formulating, launching and managing programmes; developing new methods and procedures
- Directing personnel operations, including payroll, grievance procedures, benefits administration and workers' compensation; enforcing EEO/Affirmative Action mandates

COMPUTER
Proficient in Mac &IB Platforms _ Lotus Notes _ QuickBooks _ MS Office Professional

EDUCATION
Master's Degree in Clinical Psychology – 2010
Kildare University
Master's in Business Administration – 2006
Metropolitan University
Bachelor of Arts in Management – 2001
University of the South

EXPERIENCE
Programme Manager   **2009–Present**
Comprehensive Family Services – Ipswich
- Provide counselling and therapy for individuals, couples, families and general groups.
- Team with social workers and other service providers to secure food, shelter, etc.
- Conduct Parenting Training classes. Supervise monitored on-site visits.

Continued

Counselling and social services

EXPERIENCE
Veda A Merritt, Continued

- Perform intake to assess mental history; refer to appropriate mental health agency. *To effectively deliver these services, I strive to gain clients' trust, assuage their fears, and get past the resentment and embarrassment that can ensue in these situations.*

- Facilitate multidisciplinary case planning conferences. Manage staff.

- Conduct quarterly Community Networking meetings. *Built substantial network of service providers, which fortified our ability to provide resources and secure donations for clients' welfare.*

Programme Manager   2005–2009
Helping Hands, Ipswich

Managed four programmes: *Family Preservation; Juvenile Mentoring; Healthy Start; Supervised Visits* Provided in-home counselling and therapy/Assessed clients and patients/Conducted Parenting Training classes/Hired, trained and supervised staff.

Benefits Specialist   2003–2005
Partners in Health – Norfolk

- Managed company benefits of over £2 million annually.

- Managed five programmes. Tuition Reimbursement/Employee Transportation/Service Contracts/ Workers' Early Return to Work/Retirement Plans.

Benefits Specialist/Workers' Compensation Case Manager   1998–2003
Downey Borough Council

- Increased employee benefits programme from standard plan to flexible benefits plan.

- Launched early Return-to-Work programme for employees on sick leave.

- Expedited profit realization by implementing special training for new recruits.

- Maintained up-to-date EEO/Affirmative Action Programme for managers.

AFFILIATIONS
Supervised Visitation Network; Marriage & Family Therapists

PRESENTATIONS GIVEN
In-Services/Training: Child Abuse; Mentoring; Case Management; How to Write Case Notes; Suicide: When, Why & How to Report; Working with Children's Social Workers

RECOGNITION

Awarded By:	In Appreciation For:
Home Connection...	Service and dedication to families
Children's Planning Council...	Extraordinary service and dedication to children
Dept of Children & Family Services...	Family preservation training
Diabetes Association...	Diabetes Walk-a-Thon Leadership (Team Captain)

Willing to relocate • Available weekends

Social worker

Tanya S Richards

1 Any Street
Anytown AX0 0AA
020 8123 4567
SOCIAL WORKER – MENTAL HEALTH

STRENGTHS
- Funded college education by working full-time throughout full-time enrolment.
- Interact well with diverse populations.
- Take responsibility and work well without supervision.
- Eager to relocate.

CAREER EXPERIENCE

January 2010–Present

Community Psychosocial Services, Ruston
Qualified Mental Health Professional
- Provide mental health services to individuals with mental illness diagnosis.
- Complete psychosocial evaluations to determine appropriateness.
- Work with the psychiatrist assisting in completion of the psychiatric assessment.
- Provide individual, family and group therapy as well as psychosocial skills training.
- Prepare care plans, charting and other reports necessary to provide ongoing tracking of client progress.

January 2008–December 2009

Jobcentre Plus, Rygate
Intake Officer
- Scheduled clients for pre-employment programmes.
- Interviewed applicants and recorded information to determine job skills and training, income information and programme eligibility.
- Reviewed all required documents from clients.
- Issued monthly stipend reimbursements to participants.
- Maintained records to provide a continuing history of pertinent action on each case.

January 2003–December 2007

City Hospital, West Layton
Resident Living Trainee
- Supervised mentally ill clients.
- Monitored progress on daily and monthly programme.
- Attended individual development training meetings to coordinate new programmes to help clients function independently.

EDUCATION
Metropolitan University
BA Social Welfare, 2007.

Counselling and social services

Substance abuse counsellor

Roy is a recovering substance abuser who has found his true calling in helping others overcome addiction.

Counselling and social services

ROY NASH

1 Any Street, Anytown AX0 0AA
020 8123 4567

FOCUS
To acquire field experience necessary to become an alcohol and drug rehabilitation counsellor.

CORE QUALIFICATIONS
- Former alcohol and drug abuser now in recovery, having completed a rigorous rehabilitation programme without any recidivism for over three years.
- Avid supporter of others experiencing the nightmare of addiction; keenly sensitive to their feelings and needs to enable joining with clients in early stages of interaction.
- Confident facilitator; relate comfortably with diverse cultural and socioeconomic populations in didactic sessions with groups of from 12 to over 40.
- Observant of clients' behaviours, with documentation of improvements or lack thereof, to assist authorities in planning appropriate actions upon their release from the 28-day programme.

EDUCATION
St Jude's College, Ruxton
- Graduate of the Recovery Assistance Programme Training (RAPT), 2010
- Completed 270 educational hours towards CADC certification. Curriculum included: Addiction and Its Effects; The Recovery Process; Family Counselling; Individual Counselling; Group Counselling.
- Passed written exam given by the International Certification Reciprocating Consortium (ICRC), 2010

PROFESSIONAL EXPERIENCE
Counsellor-in-Training at Straight and Narrow, a psychosocial 12-step rehabilitative agency in Newport (2010 to present).
- Conduct 90-minute didactic sessions to groups which include mentally ill chemical abusers (MICA), focusing on their recovery.
- Assist with the new client intake process, assessing and prioritizing service requirements.
- Orient prospective clients to the rehabilitative setting and the programmes available to them.
- Facilitate the adjustment of introductory groups on a daily basis, providing them with support and encouragement to stay with the programme.
- Schedule clients for art therapy and daily recreation, and coordinate their other activities.
- Ease clients' transition into didactic sessions by introducing deep breathing and relaxation techniques as a part of daily meditation preliminaries.

FORMER EMPLOYMENT
Bartender, Happy Days Lounge, Newport (1999–2009)
Server, Bartolucci's Ristorante, Newport (1997–1999)

VOLUNTEER ACTIVITIES
- Initiated support group for parents of drug addicted/alcohol dependent children and adolescents, working closely with the police department and the D.A.R.E. programme.

Early years/nursery teacher

A new mother moving back into the workforce as a nursery teacher, intending to work towards her Early Years Teacher Status (EYTS).

Education

PENNY R HAYES
020 7123 4567 • phayes@email.com
1 Any Street, Anytown, OX0 0AA

EARLY YEARS/NURSERY TEACHER
qualified by more than 10 years' experience working with children. Possess:

Solid *organizational skills* for planning and follow through and maintaining control of the classroom.

A *genuine love of children* and a desire to see each child succeed.

Superior *written and verbal communication skills*, with an ability to meet diverse personalities at their level.

Flexibility in dealing with the unpredictability of children in classroom situations.

Intention: to gain EYTS – ITET course application through graduate experience route.

'She tutors children who are in academic need and also works as an advocate for them with their teacher. I don't believe there is any task too big or too small for Penny to undertake as long as it will benefit students.'

Head
Local Primary School

RELATED EXPERIENCE
Reading Tutor
School Volunteer
Assistant Cub Scout Leader
Sunday School Teacher
Substitute Teacher

SELECTED RELEVANT HIGHLIGHTS

Reading Tutor: Selected by teachers and parents as a tutor for two Year One students failing in reading. Planned the agenda, selected age-appropriate reading and supplemental materials, liaised with teachers and parents, and supported and encouraged both students in their successful reading efforts.

Co-ordinator: Maintain a database of parent volunteers and ensure the appropriate items and volunteers necessary for special events and class parties. Act as the class representative for PTA functions.

Assistant Cub Scout Leader: Stepped in to assist the Leader, preventing the dissolution of a 12-boy troop. Facilitate meetings and manage all the paperwork and records for the troop and each scout individually.

Sunday School teacher: Use the 'Exploring Faith' early elementary curriculum to teach up to 100 children. Plan weekly lessons, arts and crafts projects, story time, and games with an emphasis on good classroom behaviour.

School Volunteer: contributed 800+ volunteer hours over the past four years including reading to children, chaperoning field trips, assisting aides and teachers, tutoring, helping PTA with hospitality, leading fundraising events, and maintaining the Book Resource Room.

EDUCATION & TRAINING

BSc Psychology – 2000
South of England University

Leadership Training – 2010
Scouts Association

Building Better Readers – 2009
Southeast Regional Vision of Education and the County Education Foundation

Volunteer Orientation – 2008 and 2009
Local Primary School

Teacher (entry-level)

Education

ALEKSANDER GRINKOB

1 Any Street, Anytown, AX0 0AA   020 8123 4567 • alek_g@email.com

GOAL   Social Studies teaching position at secondary education level, 11–16

CERTIFICATIONS   Provisional Certification in Social Studies, 2014

EDUCATION   SOUTH EAST UNIVERSITY
                     Currently pursuing Master of Arts in Teaching Social Studies, Anticipated May 2015

                     **Bachelor of Science, Business and Economics, concentration in History
                     Graduated May 2012**

Appointments   **Teaching Assistant**, North East College
                     • Selected to teach Advanced Labour theory and Microeconomics curricula.
                     • Collaborated on the development/implementation of challenging undergraduate lectures.

Internships   **Financial Analyst**, Strategic Systems, XYZ Bank, York   2010

Activities Co-founder/Captain. Farmingville Volleyball Team   2008–2012
Planned and coordinated off-site tournaments, handled group transportation and lodging arrangements, and resourcefully managed an annual budget of £10,000.

STUDENT   Brittonswoods School, Brittonwoods
TEACHING   Combined knowledge and experience in the following positions:
                     Brittonwoods High School, year 12
                     Brittonwoods Junior School, year 7

Year 12
• Team teach and observe the instruction of Advanced Placement students, as well as class discussions on current events presented by community leaders Steve Israel and scheduled guest, Rick Lazio, centred on terrorism and related issues.
• Foster a stimulating learning environment that integrates cooperative learning, role-playing, critical debates, graphic organizers, primary sources and lesson review.
• Promote higher-level thinking skills through development of reinforcement-based mastery learning techniques modelled for students' individual learning styles.

Year 7
• Held full responsibility for all aspects of instruction and classroom management activities for five daily Social Studies classes over a one-month period.
• Taught comprehensive Social Studies units on Anthropology, Archaeology, Economics, and Political Science, providing students with an understanding of past civilizations' traditions, religions, agriculture, technology, military, government and social structures.
• Formulated, administered and graded lesson-specific tests.
• Participated in weekly Parent–Teacher conferences.

                     WESTFIELD SCHOOL, Westfield
                     Per-diem Substitute Teacher, Years 7–12
• Effectively taught regular and special education while demonstrating an ability to manage classroom responsibilities and easily establish rapport with students.

WORK HISTORY   **Customer Relations Manager**, *Food & Country Magazine*, London   2009–2013

Teacher (experienced)

ROBERT A DOWNEY
1 Any Street, Anytown AX0 0HA • 020 8123 4567 • rad24@email.com

OBJECTIVE	Position teaching English at the secondary education level, 11–16
EDUCATION	SAINT JOHN'S UNIVERSITY **PGCE, 2013** **Bachelor of Arts in English, 2011** SELDEN COMMUNITY COLLEGE **Diploma, Applied Science, 2007**
CERTIFICATIONS	CPR/First Aid for Adults and Children
TEACHING EXPERIENCE	CALVERTON MIDDLE SCHOOL, Brentwood

2014–present **Replacement Computer Lab Teacher, Sixth Form**
- Facilitate the interactive learning process in a virtual classroom setting, using the School Vista programme to teach lessons and basic internet navigation/keyboarding skills
- Implemented an English/Social Studies interdisciplinary unit incorporating the use of the internet, spreadsheets, web diagrams and creative writing exercises to research, organize and depict their understanding of King Arthur and the Middle Ages

2013–2014 **Permanent Substitute Teacher, Years 6–8**
- Managed classroom responsibilities and maintained continuity of the learning process
- Incorporated cooperative education and role-playing activities to establish a relationship between course material and students' life experiences
- Devised a mock English Language Arts (ELA) test based on previous testing methodologies and content-specific rubrics; co-selected multiple choice questions for short stories; administered and proctored ELA standardized/mock tests
- Encouraged critical thinking skills through the use of challenging debate

2013 **Replacement English Teacher, Year 7**
- Worked collaboratively with English, Science, Maths and History teachers to implement an interdisciplinary unit on heritage, incorporating the use of essay writing, laboratory experiments, graphing and historical research on family roots
- Taught students to formulate DBQs, enabling students to develop an understanding of diversity, individualism and creativity through short story multicultural literature:
  - 'Aida', authored by Leontyne Price (Egyptian and Ethiopian)
  - 'The First Flute', authored by Dorothy Sharp Carter (Central American)
  - 'L.A.F.F.', authored by Lense Nemioka (Asian)
- In participation with the cooperating Social Studies teacher, implemented an interdisciplinary poetry unit to develop students' creative/critical thinking skills, and an appreciation for the causes/effects of war through the use of personification, simile and metaphors illustrated in war-related poetry
- Assisted in the planning and coordination of the 2003 Year Book, providing consultation on layout, and supervised the collection of student photographs, poetry and song lyrics
- Interfaced with Guidance Counsellors, Teachers and Parents at BPST and Parent/Teacher meetings to discuss and review curriculum development and student progress

2013	WESTFIELD SCHOOL, Westfield
2013	**Substitute Teacher, Student Teacher**
DIRECTOR	SAINT JOHN'S SUMMER SCHOOL, 2008–Present
SKILLS	Windows 95; MS Word/Excel 97; Word Perfect 6.0; School Vista; Claris Works; Internet

Teacher (specialist)

Education

CHARLENE WILSON

1 Any Street, Anytown AX0 0AA
020 8123 4567
cwilson@email.com

**Choose a job you love, and you will never
have to work another day in your life**
—Confucius

ART TEACHER

PROFILE

Detail-orientated, high-energy, with the ability to motivate students to work at optimum levels while maintaining a comfortable, creative environment, and keeping a clear perspective of goals to be accomplished. Extensive experience in helping students broaden perspectives for personal expression through visual artistry.

CORE SKILLS

Technical Skills	Self-Management Skills	Transferable Skills
Ceramics/Handbuilding	Resourcefulness	Perception & Enthusiasm
Collage	Creativity & Flexibility	Personal Expression
Paintings/Oils	Productive Competence	Artistic Impact

PROFESSIONAL EXPERIENCE

2013–2015   LIBERTY-BENTON PRIMARY SCHOOL, *Art Teacher*   Findlay

Instructed years 4 and 5 in Art Studio and Art History; created weekly art lessons with a variety of subject matters and mediums in both two-dimensional and three-dimensional projects. Instructed a small group of students in a gifted art programme; selected artwork throughout the year and facilitated the annual student art show.

2012–2013   NORTHTOWN CITY SCHOOL, *Art Teacher*   Northtown

Full-time substitute for year 12 in the Northtown City School; part-time art teacher for years 1–5 at Woodward Primary.

COMMUNITY INVOLVEMENT

SUMMER 2012   ARTS FESTIVAL, *Table Leader*   Findlay

Collaborated in meetings throughout the year to organize an art activity table.
Recruited community volunteers to assist children with art projects.

AUTUMN 2013   ARTS PARTNERSHIP   Findlay

Bank One Student Art Exhibit
Entered five students' artwork: four students received honourable mentions and one student received third place.

SUMMER 2012   RIGHT TO READ, *Committee Member*   Findlay

Helped organize a week of activities to promote the importance of reading.
Designed theme T-shirts worn throughout the Right-to-Read Week.

2010   MOTHER HUBBARD'S LEARNING CUPBOARD   Findlay

Commissioned by local store to design logo 'character' to be imprinted on bags, keyrings, bookmarks and signs.

EDUCATION

SOUTH WEST UNIVERSITY
Bachelor of Science in Education, 2010
International Scholarship Recipient to SACI School of Art in Florence, Italy, 2009

Educational programme manager

Teresa H Long

1 Anystreet, Anytown, AX0 0AA

020 8123 4567
E-mail: THLong@zero.net

Education

PROGRAMME MANAGER

Programme Management/Administration/Leadership Development

PERFORMANCE PROFILE

Fifteen years in education, training, administration and programme management in highly visible and uniquely challenging environment of Special Education. Demonstrated record of success, customized learning programmes for students at all grades and performance levels. Built positive working relationships with support staff, administrators, parents and students. These skills and experience provide the foundation for my service to West Central Joint Services as **Programme Coordinator**.

Selected Accomplishments:

- Sought by Special Education Director to serve on team to create standards, protocols and framework for assessing ED teachers and programmes
- Administrated programme needs for students and coordinated the interactions of support professionals, including but not limited to: Programme Directors, Building Administrators, School Psychologists, Physical Therapists, Occupational Therapists, Speech/Language Pathologists, Autism Consultants, Orthopaedic, Visual, Hearing and other health-impaired service coordinators
- Effective facilitator of case conferences that foster a productive partnership between parents and school personnel, and ensure that the individual needs of each student are met
- Excellent oral and written communication skills with the ability to speak on a broad range of topics; reflecting depth and understanding of the resources and programmes available to the special needs community
- Designed preschool programme with overall responsibility for recruiting, training, curriculum development and the establishment of 'hands on' learning centres
- Created 'behaviour system' for County ED Classrooms, which was used as a 'foot-print' for other programmes and buildings throughout the area
- Possess a solid working knowledge of Local Education Authority requirements that enable students to participate in programmes and services for special needs
- Experienced with the implementation and evaluation of a wide range of assistive technology, programmes have included but are not limited to: Boardmaker, PECS, Writing With Symbols, Kurzweil and Alpha Smart
- Customized curriculum for LD, ED and MiMH students and coordinated performance standards against individual Education Plans
- Thoroughly communicate the change plans and service modifications following IEP Conferences, to ensure timely implementation of new and effective educational strategies
- Established thorough working knowledge and practical understanding of various academic assessment tools
- Functioned as department and building mentor to supervise new teachers and student teachers, helping them to increase competence and adapt quickly to school policies and procedures

Continued

Education

Teresa H Long   020 8123 4567   Page 2 of 2

- Participated in two building-wide 'Climate Audits', as a staff member providing input and feedback to the review committee, and as an audit team member interviewing staff to develop a written review of results for school administration
- Recipient of the Shining Star Award, and two consecutive awards for Excellence in Education of Students with Autism

Academic Credentials:

Currently in pursuit of a **Master of Science** degree in **Education Administration**, as part of the **EPPSP (Experiential Programme for Preparing School Principles)** at Butler University.

Awarded a **Bachelor of Science** degree in Special Education from University of London. Certified in Mildly Mentally Handicapped, Seriously Emotionally Handicapped, and Learning Disabled.

Professional Development:

Formal academic training and personal experience has been enhanced with additional training from:

- The **Lindamood-Bell Institute**. Course of study included Lindamood Phoneme Sequencing Programme Visualizing & Verbalizing for Language Comprehension & Thinking, Seeing Stars – Symbol Imagery for Phonemic Awareness, Sight Words & Spelling, On Cloud Nine Maths – Visualizing and Verbalizing for Maths and Drawing with Language. Certified LAC Test Administrator; Lindamood Auditory Conceptualization Test.
- **ADOS** – Autism Diagnostic Observation Schedule, Butler University (2011)
- **Differentiating Curriculum** – Birmingham University – University of Kent
- **Multi-Cultural Education, Cooperative Learning, Applied Behaviour Analysis, and Effective Goal Writing** – Birmingham College

Career History:

Primary/Intermediate ED Teacher
Hamilton Primary School 2007–present

Private Tutor and Assessor
Lindamood-Bell Process 2006–present

Executive Director/Teacher
The Child Connection Preschool 2003–2007

Middle School Special ED Teacher
Pike Middle School 2001–2003

Learning Disabled Teacher
ABC School 1998–1999

Learning Disabled Teacher
XYZ School 1998

Secondary Teacher of Severely Emotionally Handicapped (Alternative School)
XYZ School 1995–1997

Direct Care Staff/Programme Coordinator
Northern Hills Group Homes 1994–1995

Paralegal

Jody Gilroy
1 Any Street, Anytown AX0 0AA
jgil@email.com

PARALEGAL

Skilled office professional with exceptional interpersonal and communication skills. Highly organized and detail-orientated; efficiently manages time and projects with close attention to deadlines. Effective in stressful situations and able to work successfully with diverse populations. Persuasive and tenacious.

CORE SKILLS

- Drafting legal documents, affidavits, and preparing orders
- Conducting independent interviews and investigations without supervision
- Serving as liaison between solicitors, investigators, court clerks
- Researching case law using the library and internet
- Proofreading for accuracy and consistency
- Opening and maintaining case files
- Proficient in Microsoft Office and scheduling applications

FORMAL TRAINING AND COURSEWORK IN CIVIL AND CRIMINAL LAW

Civil Litigation – Drafting of pleadings, preparation of motions, discovery and pretrial data certificates and trial notebooks

Ethics – Client confidences, conflicts of interest, unauthorized practice of law

Contracts – Offers, acceptance, consideration, illegal contracts, third-party contracts, contractual capacity, remedies, Uniform Commercial Code, discharge of obligations, provision

Research – Statutes, digest, case law, citators, encyclopedias, dictionaries, online databases

Torts – Negligence, intentional torts, strict liability, personal injury litigation, settlements

Criminal Law – Statutory and common law, criminal theory and interpretation of statutes

Public Law – Business and economic regulation and ethical considerations

EDUCATION

Higher Certificate in Paralegal Studies – National Association of Licensed Paralegals

PROFESSIONAL DEVELOPMENT

- Leadership Training
- Administrative Plan, Policies, Procedures and Programmes
- Interviewing and Interrogation (Reid Technique)
- Conflict Management

WORK HISTORY

Paralegal, XYZ Legal Services 2008–2010
Communications Officer, XYZ Ltd 2007–2008
Paralegal Trainee, ABC Co. 2005–2006
Retail Manager, DEF Ltd 2001–2005
Management Trainee, DEF Ltd 1998–2001

Legal, law enforcement and security

Police officer/security operations

Originally from the United States, Andrew has moved jobs a few times, so some short positions after his active-duty military time have been grouped together here.

Legal, law enforcement and security

ANDREW LEXINGTON

1 Any Street
Anytown AX0 0AA

020 8123 4567 (H)
Lexington@email.com

Career Focus

Law Enforcement, Security, or Force Protection Operations

Personal and Professional Value

International Police Officer, Liaison Coordinator, and Police Instructor, with six years' experience in law enforcement and military medical operations.

CORE SKILLS

- Excellent Interpersonal Skills
- Superior Oral and Written Communications
- Intelligence Analyst
- Brief High Level Delegations
- Instructor and Trainer
- Tactical Operations Analyst
- Counterterrorism Activities
- Service to Kosovo and Operation Desert Storm

- Troubleshooter and Problem Solver
- Self-motivated
- Surveillance
- Tradecraft
- Marksman
- Liaison and Intelligence Sources
- Solve Crimes
- Surgical Technical

PROFESSIONAL EXPERIENCE

International Police Officer, Contracted through Brown & Root, Bosnia   2007 to Present

- Managed regular police duties from responding to murder and other crimes to handling neighbourhood disturbances. Work with interpreters and train local national police officers in managing crime scenes including surveillance, tradecraft, report writing, investigations, interviewing witnesses and suspects.
- Conduct frequent liaison with local nationals and law enforcement agencies. Conduct hands-on training for new personnel.
- Promoted to a Primary Field Training Officer and conducted classroom training, teaching local nationals how to develop and establish a working police department. Moved on as a SWAT trainer, responsible for working with the top officers in the field. Played an instrumental role in the development and foundation building of the Regional SWAT Team. Trained the special SWAT Team in lawful breaching of buildings, tactical entry methods, antiterrorism training, firearms instruction, team building, riot control, hostage extraction, vehicle extractions, explosives, etc.
- Utilized excellent mediation and interpersonal communication skills to bring the two groups together, solve problems, discuss issues and form the multi-ethnic unit. Conducted constant liaison with local police and military forces to determine threat levels to ensure Force Protection.
- Further promoted to Liaison Officer. Gather intelligence information from various source operations and prepare and deliver briefings to high-level decision makers. Act as a bridge between NATO and the United Nations to determine when to use police forces to diffuse public or military uprisings or other threats.
- Monitor intelligence data gathering and collection activities in the tactical operations centre. Gathered information culminating in the prosecution of seven bombings under terrorist activity.

Continued

ANDREW LEXINGTON   **Page 2 of 2**

Police Officer, Manchester   **2003 to 2007**

- Patrolman working within inner city neighbourhoods. Responded to calls for service. Directed traffic at the scene of fires, investigated burglaries, or provided first aid as required to accident victims.
- Assisted other officers to secure crime or accident scenes, collect or protect evidence.
- Built relationships with local population mobilizing neighbourhoods to help fight crime.
- Investigated suspected crimes including murder, burglaries, domestic violence/disturbances, gang problems, suspicious activities, and unpaid parking tickets.
- Communicated effectively both orally speaking with people and responding to emergencies or diffusing problems at crime scenes/accidents, and in writing reports of investigation. Interviewed witnesses and suspects at the scene.

One-Year Assignments:

Sales Representative, General Insurance Company   2002 to 2003

- Certified and Licenced Insurance Sales Representative for health, fire and life insurance.

Court Liaison Officer, XYZ Associates, Manchester   2001 to 2002

- Acted as a liaison between the law firm and the court system. Filed legal paperwork with all courts.

Operating Room Technician, Infirmary Surgical Unit, Leeds   2000 to 2001

- Assisted doctors during surgery in the operating room as a sterile member of the surgical team.

EDUCATION

- Bachelor of Arts, Interdisciplinary Studies, University of the North, 2007
  Emphasis on Psychology, Sociology and Criminal Justice

PROFESSIONAL DEVELOPMENT

- International Police Programmes – Police Assessment, Selection and Training Programme (Conflict, Analysis, Beretta M-9 pistol training, defensive tactics, baton and OC aerosol irritant and Officer Safety Defensive Mindset and Surveillance Detection)
- Problem Solving, Leeds Police
- Criminal Justice Seminar
- Emergency Vehicle Operator's Course
- Computerized Criminal Justice Training
- Police Academy
- Operating Room Specialist and Certified Surgical Technical Course

Received several awards for professionalism and exemplary performance in the military and police.
Supervised and organized the donation of over 7,000 hours of volunteer service to children's organizations.
Received a National Award for Service

Legal, law enforcement and security

Security services sales

Jane Swift
123 Any Street
Anytown AT1 0BB
Tel: 020 8123 4567
Jane@anyaddress.co.uk

SALES

Professional Profile
Sales • Account Management • New Business Development Professional

Sales and Account Management Development professional with expert qualifications in identifying and capturing market opportunities to accelerate expansion, increase revenues and improve profit contributions in highly competitive industries. Outstanding record of achievement in complex account and contract negotiations.

Core Skills:

- Account development/management
- Customer service/satisfaction
- Bilingual English/Spanish
- Customer needs assessment
- PC proficient

- Consultative/solutions sales
- New market development
- Account retention
- Presentation and negotiations skills

Professional Experience
Key Account Executive, 2010–Present
A&L Security Services, Largest privately held security company in the UK with annual sales of over £400 million.
　　Recruited to start up and oversee the market development of contract security services in northern England. Conduct in-depth client need assessments and develop technology-based security strategies to ensure maximum efficiency.

- Achieved consistent annual sales production in excess of £2.5 million
- Built territory from nothing capturing 55% of the market share in region
- Expanded annual billable hours from 300 to more than 5,000, fostering a rapid growth in staffing from 30 to more than 300 employees in Raleigh branch
- Successfully negotiated and secured sales ranging from £300K to £1.2 million
- Earned several national and local awards for top sales performance, including the prestigious 'Salesperson of the Year' award

Account Executive/Loan Officer, 2006–2010
Equity Finance Ltd, UK's oldest finance company, a division of a FTSE 100 company.
　　Generated and sold consolidation loans through telemarketing.

- Consistently exceeded monthly sales targets
- Received national recognition as one of the Top 10 salespeople in the country, and Number 1 salesperson in Raleigh branch.

Education
Bachelor of Arts, Business Administration/Finance, 2.1, 2005
University of Birmingham

Loss prevention management

Jerry Zeliff

Home 020 8123 4567   Mobile 5555 55555   E-mail jerry_111@email.com

• Loss Prevention Management • Industrial Security • Fraud Investigation

PROFESSIONAL PROFILE

- Expertise in investigation, analysis and evaluation of internal and external theft cases gained through fast-track promotions over eight years in retail security positions.
- Skilled trainer and motivator of loss prevention associates for a major retail organization.
- Experienced in collaborating with police and court authorities, as well as regional and corporate level investigators in matters leading to prosecution.
- Strength in timely and accurate tracking/preparation of investigative paperwork, which includes audits of shipping invoices, sales and inventory reports, and POS transactions involving underrings, cheque, credit card or refund fraud.

CORE OPERATIONAL COMPETENCIES

Equipment: Installation, testing and use of covert cameras, VCRs, two-way radios, alarm and fire systems, closed circuit TV, and Sensormatic devices.

Methods: Undercover investigation, observation towers, two-way mirrors, cash register monitoring, recognition of suspect shopper behaviour.

Related Matters: Trained in CPR and first response techniques. Basic PC literacy for database search, inventory reporting and word processing.

CAREER PROGRESSION

ABC DEPARTMENT STORES, 2007 to Present
Shortage Control Auditor, Company headquarters (since 2012)
- Implemented shortage awareness programme through audits of all stores and distribution centres to assure compliance to company's policies and procedures. Followed up on the matters of non-compliance.
- Through the audit process, identified areas where additional training was needed and instituted such.
- Resolved shortage-related issues as they arose.
- Assisted in the development and monitoring of a high-tech security programme, designed to reduce shortages in selected stores with high occurrences.
- Participated in financial audits.
- Wrote and edited company policies and procedures, particularly in the area of inventory.
- Increased electronic communications with stores via computer and POS system.

... Continued

Jerry Zeliff   **Page 2**

ABC DEPARTMENT STORES (Continued)

Loss Prevention Manager, multistore operations (2011–2012)

- Held charge position for all internal and external investigations at store level for two locations.
- Selected to fill position left vacant for three months. In less than five months, cleared up a paperwork backlog, reinforced procedures, then hired and trained new security staff of three for each store.
- Instituted safety and security awareness programme throughout sales floors, fitting rooms and checkouts.
- Implemented £1 million budget for the security functions.

Loss Prevention Manager, Bristol (2010–2011)

- Applied and expanded security techniques for one of the largest stores in the chain, located in a busy shopping precinct.
- Communicated with other precinct store security managers in efforts to apprehend shoplifters.
- Won 'Manager of the Quarter' award, out of over 25 other managers employed in this store.
- Promoted to manage neglected multistore security situation.

Loss Prevention Manager, new store opening, Bath (2009)

- Assigned to management team to oversee the installation and testing of all security systems at new locations.
- Screened, hired and trained new security personnel. Orientated all new employees for store opening. Implemented shoplifter detection incentive programme.

Loss Prevention Manager, single store, Burford (2008–2009)

- In first management assignment at store, trained staff of three in all store-detective duties.

Manager Trainee, corporate headquarters (2007–2008)

- Intensive programme covering cash office, distribution centres, receiving, service desk, internal investigations, theft detection and statistical work.

VOLUNTEER WORK

TERRITORIAL ARMY RESERVE

EDUCATION

SIA Licensed Security Guard

Security operations management

James Sharpe

Page 1 of 2

123 Any Street • Anytown AT1 0BB • Tel: 020 8123 4567

james@anyaddress.co.uk

SECURITY OPERATIONS MANAGER

Career Profile

- Over 14 years' management and leadership experience in security operations and related functions with prominent hotels, retailers and security providers.
- Currently Director of Security for a prestigious four-star hotel, earning the highest performance ranking in the company in 2008. Have directed up to 200 officers and developed/managed £500,000+ budgets. Possess an extensive knowledge of security industry standards.
- Develop and lead effective and united teams, transforming fragmented factions into a cohesive alliance of professionals producing exceptional results and adhering to strict codes of conduct. Employ a dedicated hands-on management style that has dramatically increased effectiveness and reduced turnover.
- Certified in Security Management, Hospitality Law, Hotel Security Management, Disaster Preparedness and Emergency Response, Threat Management, Workplace Violence and HSE Regulations. Member of the British Security Industry Association.

Areas of Expertise

- Security industry standards
- Budget creation and management
- Human Resources management functions
- Recruiting, training and development
- Interviewing, selection, performance evaluations
- Departmental turnarounds
- Programme and procedures development
- Motivational team leadership
- Coaching, counselling and motivation

Career Development

Director of Security Operations, Four-Star Hotel, Irvington

2007 to Present

- Manage all aspects of the security operation of this prestigious, top-rated 600,000 square foot luxury hotel with 300 rooms, a daily roster of 1,000 employees/guests, and 14 full-time security officers.
- Dramatically reversed poor performance history of key hotel departments, achieving ranking of first in the company in 2008
  - Decreased number of security-related incidents by 30%, the lowest in hotel's history.
  - Lowered workers' compensation injuries to 7 cases (of 300 workers), the smallest in the company's history.
  - Raised quality/efficiency while reducing overtime by 65%, the lowest rate in the department's history.
  - Instituted standards that did not allow a single successful safety or security litigation in five years.
  - Earned top ranking as company's best-managed department.
  - Achieved lowest employee turnover rate in the entire company.

Produced these results by creating and implementing leading-edge programmes including: innovative training, evaluation and TQM programmes that produced employee motivation, attention, interest, cooperation, and desired response; standard operating procedures for crisis management, disaster prevention and recovery, risk management, emergency response, incident investigation, and report writing; detailed investigation standards for all security and safety incidents, including policy violations and guest or employee injuries.

Continued

Legal, law enforcement and security

Legal, law enforcement and security

Chief of Security, DeLuxe Hotel, Redcliff   2006 to 2007

Directed security operations of this three-star national chain hotel with 200 guest rooms, 200 employees and 6 security officers, devising effective security policies and procedures, and budgeting and monitoring department's expenditures:

- Produced a 20% decrease in security-related incidents.
- Reduced employee turnover by 50%.

Established new standard operating procedures. Developed and implemented emergency action plans. Contributed to creation of multiple departments' security and safety requirement training programmes. Cooperated closely with the Human Resources department on HSE, workers' compensation, and other industrial safety matters to ensure compliance.

Operations Manager, Redwood Security, Redfield   2003 to 2005

Managed over 200 plain clothes and uniform contract security officers in multiple facilities, including defence contractors and film studios. Developed and promoted a proactive culture of risk management and prevention. Promoted through the ranks from Field Officer to Operations Manager, the highest rank within the division:

- Implemented new rewards and recognition programmes that raised morale and provided continuous feedback.
- Frequently volunteered extended hours to meet clients' needs and critical project deadlines. Acted as client liaison to develop partnerships and strategic loss prevention and asset protection programmes. Oversaw Human Resources operations, including officer selection, field deployment, training, scheduling, inspections, evaluations and disciplinary actions. Established professional ties with local police authorities.

Loss Prevention Manager, J S Hoblins, Derby   2000 to 2003

Oversaw security staff and operations at this market retailer:

- Protected assets and reduced legal liability by creating ongoing prioritized loss prevention initiatives.
- Developed effective loss countermeasure strategies and prevention awareness training programmes.
- Conducted comprehensive internal audits and investigations for external/internal sources of loss and employee misconduct.
- Minimized accidents and injuries by managing effective safety programmes.

Technology Skills

- Proficient in Microsoft Word, Excel, IRIMS and PPM2000.
- PC proficient in Windows.
- Extensive knowledge of computer-based, audio/visual and access control systems.

Education and Certification

BSc Political Science, University of the Midlands
Certifications:

- Security Management (Supervisor)
- Hospitality Law
- Hotel Security Management
- Disaster Preparedness and Emergency Response
- Threat Management and Workplace Violence
- HSE Regulations and Workplace Violence
- City & Guilds: Professional Guard parts 1 & 2

Network administrator/programmer

Computer and IT

Richard Hall, MCSE, CCNA

1 Any Street, Anytown AX0 0AA • 020 8123 4567 (h) • 05555 55555 (m)

NETWORK ADMINISTRATOR/PROGRAMMER

PERFORMANCE SUMMARY

Certified Network Systems Specialist with extensive technical experience in network administration and programming. Skilled in all areas of computer technologies including: installation, configuration, maintenance, troubleshooting, design and conversion. Successful in implementing £300,000+ cost reduction programme and improving operational efficiencies. Excellent organizational, team-building and communication skills.

CORE SKILLS

- MCSE+1
- Certified Linus Administrator
- Network Administrator
- LAN/WAN
- Network Firewalls
- Router Configuration
- Workstations

- CCNA
- C Programmer
- Windows NT/2003
- Software and Hardware Configuration
- System Integration
- Internet
- MS-SQL

PROFESSIONAL EXPERIENCE

Network Administrator/Programmer
CW Associates, York, January 2008–Present
- Researched and implemented £300,000+ cost-saving technology programmes and operating systems; oversaw and supervised network conversions from FileMaker Pro, Lasso and Webstart to MS-SQL, Php and Apache; customized and monitored company search engines; configured, installed and maintained Company VPN, Cisco Pix Firewalls and Routers; updated company electronic mail system from QuickMail to CommuniGatePro.

Network Administrator
Networking Worldwide, York, February 2007–October 2008
- Designed, installed and configured computers and peripherals; maintained and repaired hardware, software and operating systems; troubleshot and resolved application and electronic mail system issues; managed four domain servers.

EDUCATION & TRAINING

North West University
MSc in Computer Science, 2010
BSc in Computer Science, 2009

Microsoft Systems Certified Engineer, 2008
Cisco Certified Network Associate, 2008

Network administrator

DAVID J WAGNER, MCP

1 Any Street, Anytown AA1 1AA

55555 555555 Home • 5555555 5555 Mobile • djwagner@anyserver.co.uk

Networks / Systems

Hardware Configuration:
Windows, UNIX, Cisco
Software Configuration
Systems Integration
Systems Configuration
Router Configuration
Intrusion Detection Systems
Frame Relay Networking
Network Planning
Network Firewalls
Peer-to-peer Networks
Ethernet Networks
Telephony & Fiber Optics
Internet Information Server
Switches & Hubs
ISDN/T1 Lines

Media & Peripherals

Voice & Data
TCP/IP

Project Management

Technology Consulting
Technology Management
Networking Infrastructures
Systems Implementation
Virtual Team Leadership
Relationship Management
Advanced Communications
Telecommunications
Security Analysis
Security Development
Applications Development
Evaluation & Testing
Troubleshooting
Resource Utilization
Inventory Management
Technology Training
End-User Training
Knowledge Transfer
Executive Presentations
Strategic Planning
Project Team Development
Team Building
Client Relations
Quality Assurance
Problem Solving

TEAM LEADER • PROJECT MANAGER • DEPARTMENT MANAGER

Network Administration • Systems Security Technology

- **Microsoft Certified Professional. A+ Certification.** Accomplished technology consultant and project manager adept in desktop and network security / systems architecture planning, design, installation, configuration, maintenance and smooth project delivery.
- Accustomed to supporting multi-user networks, as well as leading high-performance technology and telecommunications solutions. Successfully employ technology to improve operations efficiency, reduce costs, and meet reliability and security goals and deadlines.
- Proven track record in team leadership and training, supplying a balanced mix of analytical, management, coaching and technical skills.

PROFESSIONAL EXPERIENCE

Senior Computer Scientist   2008–present

AA Systems Group (Army technology consulting firm), Stockton

Technical Lead – Army Computer Systems Office (2009–present)

Focus: Rollout of Army Partnership Tool Suite (APTS) system, implementing new functionality into live networks and systems.

- Lead Consultant and liaison (chosen by government project manager) in seven-member cross-functional team deploying integrated networks, systems and technologies. Introduced real-time, peer-to-peer collaboration via new application, bringing far-flung team together and eliminating disconnects.
- Key player in development, testing and implementation process, including custom tool development, to fit client needs. Integrate configuration and supply installation support for pioneering technology collaboration.

Lead Network Engineer

Information Systems Engineering Office (2008–2009)

Focus: £24 million Communications Update & Planning System (CUPS). Evaluated, selected and integrated advanced communications and networking products for the communications collaboration team.

- Key role (network engineer/administrator/technician) leading six-member team. Honed end-to-end project management and presentation skills.
- Pioneered first-ever use of security hardware/software, including intrusion detection systems (IDS), Cisco routers, and network management apps.
- Designed robust, mobile communications (and upgrades) to facilitate efficient network convergence and bandwidth utilization. Developed network management tools for real-time monitoring and troubleshooting.
- Field-tested flying local area network (FLAN), utilizing wireless Ethernet technology, which interconnected en route aircraft to ground-based units.
- Proposed equipment purchasing savings of £2.5–£6 million through services analysis, reducing duplication of physical space and equipment.
- Introduced new traffic routing method (tech) using a defence satellite channel for communications, enabling netmetting in worldwide locations.

Continued

DAVID J WAGNER, MCP *Page 2*

55555 555555 Home • djwagner@anyserver.co.uk

Computer and IT

HARDWARE:
Sun Microsystems
IBM PCs & compatibles
SCSI & IDE Hard Drives
Cisco Routers & Switches
3COM Switches & Hubs
Ascend Pipeline Series
Netgear Hubs
RAID Arrays (Sun)
Ethernet NICs
Printers, Scanners
CD-ROMs, Modems
CD-R & CD-RW Drives
Sound Cards, TV Cards
Tape Drives

Software (UNIX):
Solaris, Linux
HP UNIX, SCO UNIX
Cisco Works Essentials
BIND 4 & 9 (DNS)
X-Windows, Open Windows
SSH, Lynx, Pine, ELM
sh, csh, bash
ftp servers & clients
Eagle Raptor Firewall
Apache, Sendmail, IRC

Software (PC):
Windows, DOS
Novell Netware
MS Office, MS Outlook
WordPerfect, FrontPage
IRC, IE, Netscape
FTP Servers & Clients
Norton, Cisco
HyperTerminal, Kermit
HP Openview
Cisco Works Essentials
Carbon Copy
Seagate Backup Exec.
SCO Xvision

Software (Cisco IOS):
Internetworking OS
Network Address Trans.
Access Lists
Context Based Access
Intrusion Detection
Remote Syslog Logging
Routing Protocols

Signal Officer (TA) 2005–present
113th Signal Battalion, Stockton

- Lead, develop and motivate 40 soldiers. Oversee inventory management of £4.8 million in vehicles, weaponry, security and communications equipment.

- Mission – establish mobile subscriber equipment network (mobile phone network for combat soldiers in the field).

Computer Scientist 2006–2008
Computer Development Services, Jersey

- Lead technical consultant – Computer Services Security Branch (Army) for set-up, testing and evaluation of networks/systems security technologies. Established configuration, installation procedures and network topologies for all support tasks. Tech reports used as management measurement tool.

- Designed secure test-bed network/domain on UNIX, Windows, and Cisco IOS providing e-mail, DNS, firewalls, routing, file serving and accounting.

- Selected to serve as test manager for dry run and official testing, personally resolving testing challenges and intrusion issues.

Systems Administrator 2005–2006
Technical Solutions & Services Ltd, Jersey

- Installation, configuration and troubleshooting software (UNIX, Linux, Windows, Solaris) on HP workstations, Toshiba laptops, and servers (Compaq, Diversified, HP, Sun). Prepared backups on multiple platforms and provided technical support to data warehousing centre.

- Oversaw corporate telecomm system, LAN physical extension, and technical purchasing (POs, quoting, authorizations and receiving).

Technology Consultant 2004–2005
Campbell & Cohen (legal firm), Trenton

- Systems and network troubleshooting (Windows & Novell Netware) at multiple locations. Peer-to-peer training. Proposed LAN and equipment recommendations to stay at the cutting edge, which were implemented.

Systems Instructor / Client Support 2003–2004
Healthcare Information Group, Oakfield

EDUCATION & CERTIFICATIONS

MS, Telecommunications Management, Midlands University – in progress
BSc, Accounting, Easton College – 2003

Microsoft Certified Professional – Windows NT, Network Essentials
A+ Certification – Computer and Network Repair
Cisco Switching 2.0 & Routing 2.0 – towards CCNP in progress
Building Scalable Cisco Networks (BSCN) course – in-house training

PROFESSIONAL ASSOCIATION

Institute of Electrical & Electronics Engineers (IEEE)

Computer support technician

Computer and IT

Joshua Michael Peterson

1 Any Street • Anytown AA1 1AA • tel: 555-555-5555 • petersonjm22@anyserver.co.uk

ENTRY LEVEL COMPUTER SUPPORT TECHNICIAN/SOFTWARE CUSTOMER SERVICE

PROFILE
- **Recent computer centre graduate with proven technical abilities.**
- Demonstrated track record of achieving goals in a team environment.
- Highly motivated and dependable. Proven skills in problem solving, customer relationship management and organization.

EDUCATION

The Computer Learning Centre, Northampton   2010–2011

Computer Coursework completed in:
- Networking Essentials
- A+ Certification
- Intermediate Word 2008
- Beginning Word 2008
- Beginning Access 2008
- TCP/IP Protocol
- Beginning Windows NT
- Administering Windows NT
- Windows NT Core Technologies
- Windows NT Support by Enterprise
- Beginning Business on the Internet
- Beginning FrontPage 2008

Northampton University   2008–2009
General first-year courses in BSc programme.

EMPLOYMENT

A Cut Above, Northampton   2007–2011
Receptionist / Cashier
- Successfully handled front desk and three incoming telephone lines for busy, upmarket hair salon. Greeted and logged in steady stream of customers, coordinating appointments with hairdresser availability.
- Developed cooperative, team-orientated working relationships with owners and co-workers in this 12-seat salon.
- Managed customer problems and complaints with tact and attention to prompt customer service. Received team and customer service awards.
- Experience gained in opening and closing procedures, cash register receipts, counter sales, light bookkeeping and telephone follow-up.

Sport for All programme   Summers 2004–2007
Trainer / Coach
- Assisted Women's Football Coach in 200-participant sports camp. Asked to return as trainer for three seasons. Worked with individuals, as well as teams, to improve their attitude and resulting performance.

ACTIVITIES

Football Semi-Pro Team   2004–2008
- Team consistently ranked in top 10 semi-pro teams in the country.

High School Football Team   2003–2006
- Captain of team that won Regional Title in 2005
- Recognized as one of the top two midfielders in the county in 2006

Data centre engineer

Jane Smith

1 Any Street
Anytown, AX0 0AA

01234 567890
jsmith@email.com

Data Centre Engineer

Performance Summary

Five years' experience in data centre management and technical support. Storage engineer at a dedicated high-security site with 800 enterprise servers for secure messaging services. Server technology and hardware replacement and upgrades: Hard Drive, CPU, RAM, etc.

Technology Skills

Hitachi Data Systems (HDS)	Event Monitoring Service (EMS)	System Security
Preventive Maintenance	Electromagnetic Interference (EMI)	Disaster Recovery, Backups
C-class Blade Installation	Hardware Upgrades	Application Support
Troubleshooting	Cabling and Testing	SN8000 B-series Brocade SAN
Rack layout, IO Card Layout	Diagnose and Repair Systems	Cooling System/Air Distribution

Hardware: Hitachi Data Systems (HDS, P9500), HP 9000 Servers and Workstations, Itanium and Intel-based Blade Servers, C-class Blade Enclosure, SN8000 B-series Brocade SAN Switches (DCX).
Operating Systems: Windows, HP UX, Brocade Fabric OS.
Applications: Remote Web Console (Hitachi Data Systems), Virtual Connect Support Utility, Brocade Fabric Manager, ICE (support ticket documentation tool), SanXpert, Support Tools Manager (STM).

Professional Experience

ABC Systems, Salford   2010–Current

Data Centre Engineer
Conducted reactive field repairs and support for enterprise-level HP servers and storage. Troubleshoot and resolve problems quickly to ensure uninterrupted operating capability.

- Provide 24/7 data centre engineering support for global financial services industry.
- Improved processes and performance in a deadline-driven environment.
- Proven ability to effectively coordinate with external vendors and internal staff; works well with others in a team environment.
- Implemented customer problem structure/flow, increasing responsiveness and decreasing resolution time.
- Responsible for improving technical protocols with real-time data collection.

Education & Professional Development

London University   2010
BSc in Business Management

Uxbridge Community College   2008
AAS in Computer Science
HIPAA Privacy and Security Awareness   2014
3PAR InServ Storage Server Hardware Introduction   2014
HP StorageWorks VLS and D2D Solutions   2013

Impeccable references available

Computer and IT

IT project manager

John Swift

1 Any Street
Anytown AX0 0AA

01234 567890
jswift@email.com

IT Project Management

Performance Summary

Fifteen years' experience in IT Project Management, from requirements identification through creation and implementation of project teams in multi-vendor environments. Extensive project management experience in IT services, financial services and H/C. Skilled in creating and presenting reports to senior management. Demonstrated experience in integrating strategies, innovation, technology and team building to achieve successful and profitable ventures.

——Professional Skills——

Project/Portfolio Management	Project Scope Management	Requirements Analysis	Project/Portfolio Governance
Stakeholder Management	Matrix Team Leadership	Partnership Management	Cross-Functional Teams
Project Status Reporting	Financial Management	Conflict Management	Capacity Planning
Team Development	Coaching and Mentoring	Lean Six Sigma	SDLC/Agile Methodology
Systems Conversion	Vendor Management	Product Launch	Systems Integrations

Professional Experience

ABC Ltd, Manchester   2009 to present
IT Project Management Consultant
Delivered high-level project management and technology needs analysis. Served as Senior Project Manager.
Projects and Accomplishments:

- Directed the implementation of £23 million Document Management systems for law enforcement agency. Included user interface, image capture, storage, batch, and bar code processing throughout multiple regions.

- Led cross-functional teams of business and IT professionals to implement defined benefit solutions at *FTSE 100* client. Mentored Junior PMs to assume more visible roles and navigate internal and client matrix structures. Managed client engagements and project budget to within 5% of plan.

- Managed the implementation of £20 million Inter-Plan Teleprocessing System Conversion of VSAM & IMS to DB2, with enabling infrastructure for front-end and web services, partnering with over 100 businesses and technology experts utilizing SDLC and Agile methodologies.

DEF Systems, Canterbury   1997 to 2009
A financial service division of a premier e-commerce organization.

Technical Project Manager
Hired to lead development of new software releases to bring the company into new technology. Charged with planning, management and delivery of £2 million to £5 million project initiatives with teams of up to 30 staff members. Led customer conferences and brainstorming sessions to gather requirements. Ensured adherence with quality assurance standards by directing test plan creation. Validated unit and system test results and assisted in creating systems, user, and marketing documentation.

Education and Complementary Experience

Certified Project Management Professional (PMP), Project Management Institute   2003
BSc, Electrical Engineering, Birmingham   1997
BSc, Information Systems, UEA   1996

Software designer

Computer and IT

Regina Pierce

1 Any Street
Anytown AA1 1AA
Phone: 55555 555555
Email: reginapierce@anyserver.co.uk

★ Software Design Engineer ★
DELIVERING SOFTWARE TO REDUCE COSTS AND INCREASE EFFICIENCIES

Detail-orientated, highly motivated SYSTEMS SOFTWARE CONSULTANT with 8+ years' successful experience in designing, developing and implementing software solutions to support strategic business objectives. Keen **problem-solving skills** evidenced by the implementation of innovative technologies across dissimilar architectures and multiple platforms to provide quality product functionality. **Effective communicator** who easily interfaces with end-users, technical teams and professionals on all levels.

Technology Expertise Includes:

- Astute strategic understanding of mainframe, client/server and Internet environments.
- Experience in Object-Oriented design and development.
- Empirical knowledge of all system development life cycle phases and a structured approach to project management. Accurately develop end-user documentation.
- Proven ability to acquire knowledge rapidly and to apply new technologies for process improvement.
- Functional knowledge of the finance, billing and operations areas of **Customer Information Systems.**

KEY PROJECT MANAGEMENT & LEADERSHIP

XYZ – * LEAD TECHNICAL ANALYST * Customer Information System for South Eastern Utility Company

Challenge: To identify and resolve critical errors of newly developed software in the Primary Test region before migrating online and batch programs to Regression Testing region.

Action: Extensively used problem-solving skills while interacting with eight-member team, Software Engineers, Data Conversion, project manager and end-users to understand client requirements. Executed and analysed test suites resulting in quality assessments that verified product requirements and high quality code.

Result: Delivered high-quality software that exceeded client expectations and was specifically requested to stay on as Technical Analyst of the Regression Test Team, supporting both test teams through first-site implementation.

XYZ – * CUSTOM DEVELOPMENT LEAD / SUPERVISOR *Customization of Client / Server Customer Information System

Challenge: To resolve technical issues of the Open Client architecture that were slowing progress on the development of a £1.8 million CIS system at a utility company. To develop a detailed design of Powerbuilder software modifications in the Operations area.

Action: (1) Supervised two developers in identifying the cause of the Open Client issues and in the completion of software modifications to resolve those issues.
(2) Developed detailed design of Powerbuilder software modifications to increase functionality and efficiency.

Result: My team successfully identified and resolved the Open Client issues ahead of schedule, streamlining the rest of the project back to schedule.

Continued

Computer and IT

Regina Pierce   Phone: 55555 555555
Page 2 of 2

COMPUTER TECHNOLOGIES

Languages: SQL, SQL*Plus, PL/SQL, Transact SQL, C, Java, HTML, COBOL, Pascal, Scheme ▪ **Databases:** Oracle
8.x, DB2, Sybase, MS Access ▪ **Environments:** Microsoft Windows 95/98/NT/2003, DOS, UNIX, VMS, CICS
▪ **CASE Tools:** ADW 1.6, ADW 2.7 ▪ **Development Tools:** JDeveloper v.2.0, Oracle Designer v.6.0,
Oracle Developer 2003 v.2.0, Oracle Forms v.5.0, Oracle Reports v.2.5, Dreamweaver 3.0
▪ **Methodologies:** Oracle's Applications Implementation Methodology (AIM) & Custom Development
Methodology (CDM); XYZ's Application Implementation Methodology (SMM).

PROFESSIONAL EXPERIENCE

Corporate Affiliations: Oracle, Healthnet, Bell South, Eaton Corporation, Kellogg Company, Kelly Services
Corporation, Price Waterhouse, ABC Power Co, XYZ Gas Co, Atmos Energy, Consumers Gas,
Consolidated Natural Gas

ORACLE CORPORATION, **Senior Consultant / Technical Analyst**   2005–Present
Installed and configured Oracle Financial Applications at five large UK companies to enhance the accuracy, availability
and timeliness of financial data for strategic planning and reporting. Identified, designed, developed and documented
customizations and interfaces to Oracle applications. Delivered excellent results to each client. Consistently commended
for ability to work independently or as a team member to complete assignments on time and under budget.

- Designed and developed online Help for a customized installation of Oracle's iBill – iPay system, a £1.2
  million Oracle initiative. Extensive use of Dreamweaver 3.0 to develop 16 HTML Web pages.
- Developed work plans for a £2.5 million implementation of the Oracle CPG/Oracle Financials solution using
  Project Workbench and Microsoft Project.
- Developed Configuration Management Standards for a £1.5 million global implementation of Oracle Applications
  at a large international temporary services agency. Developed initial template of the project's global work plan.

ABC plc, **Consultant / Programmer Analyst**   2001–2005
Demonstrated outstanding technical skills in design, development and implementation of a large Customer Information
System package at five UK companies.

- Conducted analysis of Finance System on the CIS project of a large utility company. Prepared and presented
  Joint Application Design sessions, creating modification control reports, and proposing and estimating
  solutions for complex system enhancements in the following areas of finance: Credit and Collections,
  Accounts Receivable and Payment Processing.
- Programmer/Analyst. Modified existing batch and online (CICS) programs and constructed new programs to
  support general ledger journaling and credit collection processes in the implementation of a COBOL/DB2
  Customer Information System at a northeastern electric and gas company.

EDUCATION & TRAINING

London University
BSc(Hons) Computer Information Systems

ORACLE PRODUCT TRAINING:

Oracle CRM eCommerce 3i (iStore)
Java Programming with JDeveloper v.2.0
Developer/2003 Release 2: Build Forms I and Report Builder v.3.0
Oracle Receivables Release II
Oracle Financials 10.7 SC Bootcamp: General Ledger, Purchasing, Payables, Receivables, &
Application Implementation Methodology (AIM) 2.0
Ernst & Young MCS Information Technology Individual Study (MITIS 1) & Study 2 (MITIS 2)

Software development

James Sharpe   Page 1 of 2
123 Any Street
Anytown AT1 0AA
Tel: 020 8123 4567
james@anyaddress.co.uk

SOFTWARE DEVELOPMENT

Professional Summary
IS professional recognized for broad-based skills encompassing web hardware and software solutions. Adapts readily to changing technologies. Areas of expertise encompass: project management, team leadership, staff supervision, coding, design, testing, user training/support, troubleshooting, customer relations.

Technical Skills
Software: MS Office Suites, Quattro Pro, DacEasy, Act!, Premier, Avid Cinema, Authorware, Director, PhotoShop, CorelDraw, VoicePad, Naturally Speaking Impromptu, PowerPlay, Visio
Hardware: SCSI, RAID Systems, IDE, NIC's, video/audio network hubs, switches and routers
Web/Internet: Netscape Commerce Server, MS IIS, HTML, CGI, ISAPI
Databases & Technologies: Dbase, Paradox, MS Access, MS SQL Server, Progress, DDE, OLE, OLE2, ActiveX, Automations Servers (in and out of process), Active Forms, DCOM, Memory Mapped Files, Compound Files, MS Transaction Server (version 1.0), NT Services, Named Pipes, Thunking, Multiheaded applications and libraries (Win32), WinSock, mail services, HTTP, FTP, NNTP, TCP, UDP, SMTP, POP3
Operating Systems/Services: MS DOS, MS Windows 3.11, 95, 98, NT Server/Workstation, UNIX, MS Exchange, MS SQL Server, WINS, RAS, DHCP, IIS
Programming Languages: Delphi, Pascal, Progress, C/C++, VB, Fortran, PowerBuilder, Perl, Assembly

Career Highlights
- Recruited to manage several major projects at Technical Services (TS):
  - Reconfigured entire IS department. Developed specifications for new servers for file sharing, Web and database. Redesigned network 100 Base T; installed T1; and enabled WINS, DHCP, Exchange Server, MS SQL Server and IIS.
  - Revamped networks, servers and internet connections to resolve the weekly, sometimes daily, crashing of network.
  - Project manager for medical/internet project that was designed to provide continuing education courses online.
  - Supervised two professionals in IS and web development.
  - Wrote several interfaces for authorware, I.E. 4.0 and Exchange, and created intranet as dynamic pages from MSQL database.
- Founded Holbrook Software, with sole responsibility for account development, project planning, staffing and customer relations. Developed software solutions for several public agencies and private firms:
  - Created an employee scheduling software, married filing status software with yearly upgrades and conversion programme.
  - Developed a criminal history database, investigation and complaint software packages for South Gloucester and Somerset Police.
  - Developed a UCR (uniform criminal reporting) software package. Program enables small cities, villages and towns to participate in computerized national UCR.
  - Created software to accommodate membership database, account histories, invoices, membership functions, bank deposits, reports and rosters for the J&B Association.

Continued

Computer and IT

James Sharpe 020 8123 4567
page 2 of 2

- Designed Vortex Computer Systems website, applying knowledge of HTML/CGI, security and interactive pages, among other functions.
  - Developed user-defined help feature for online help
  - Provided HTML CGI and Winhelp training
  - Created interfaces to third-party products
  - Gained extensive expertise with large relational databases

Professional Experience
Holbrook Software
2007–Present
Software Developer/Proprietor

Electronic Systems
2004–2006
Director of IS, Programming and Web Development

CIM
2002–2003
Software Developer

Vortex Computer Systems
2000–2001
Interface Developer/Web Programmer/Webmaster; Online Help Programmer

Verso & Co
1995–2000
Regional Computer Coordinator

TechuStat
1994–1995
Customer Service Representative

Professional Development
Coursework in Advanced Programming, Pascal and Fortran

Technical support specialist

Gloria Bartlett

1 Any Street, Any Town AA1 1AA

55555 555555 Home ▪ 555555 8888 Mobile ▪ gloriabar@anyserver.co.uk

APPLICATION SUPPORT ADMINISTRATOR/TECHNICAL SUPPORT SPECIALIST/DESKTOP SUPPORT

Technologically sophisticated, bilingual (Spanish/English) IT Support & Training Specialist with hands-on experience in project life-cycle management for technical and intranet applications, website development and maintenance, and workgroup support. Proven desktop and network troubleshooting skills. Expertise in:

- Help Desk & Hardware Support
- First-Level PC Support
- Project Management
- System Upgrades/Conversions
- LAN/WAN Architecture
- Escalation Resolution
- Peer-to-Peer User Groups
- Web Content Upgrades
- Customer Service

TECHNOLOGY SUMMARY

Networking – LAN / WAN, Windows 2000 / NT 4.0 Server, TCP/IP, SQL Server

Operating Systems – Windows 95 / 98 / 2000 / XP, Windows 2003 / NT 4.0 Server, DOS 6.0

Applications – MS Office Suite 97/2000/2002 (Word, Access, Excel, PowerPoint), MS FrontPage 2003, Macromedia Dreamweaver 3.0, Adobe Acrobat 5 and PDF, Flash 4.0, Novell GroupWise 5.5, Adobe Pagemill 3, Lotus Suite 96, Corel Suite 96, Corel 9, Adobe PhotoShop, Kodak digital software, Symantec pcAnywhere 32, Internet Explorer, Netscape Communicator and WinZip

Programming – HTML code, CGI, Java, JavaScript, C Programming, RPG 400, SQL, Visual Basic 5.0, Visual InterDev 6.0, AS/400, ASP code

PROFESSIONAL EXPERIENCE

XYZ Ltd, Oxford   2003–present

Senior Technician, MIS – Technical Support Activity (2009–present)

Promoted to provide help desk support for 2003+ end-users (including remote users) in nine locations throughout the UK, as well as project management team leadership for special technical assignments. First-point-of-contact (Tier 1 Help Desk Technician) for support incidents, as well as end-user training.

- **Help Desk.** Ensure effective 'one-stop' technical support for mainframe, WAN, LAN and remote system. Install and update software, and set up, configure and troubleshoot Reach Centre equipment. Track and de-escalate technology and workflow problems, and assist Desktop Support Group and other IT groups.

- **Website Development.** Project-managed website redesign to text-only version, enabling fast and easy access for all users, including vision-impaired. Supervised staff of eight.

- **Intranet Development.** Key player in creation, launch and maintenance of intranet site, providing management with easily retrievable, up-to-date information for operations decisions. Initiated, created and maintain Access users group intranet to facilitate information sharing and learning.

- **Project Management.** Led WIX CD-ROM project for two years, delivering interactive CD-ROMs with 1,000+ documents for simplified preparation.

- **ASP Development.** Played pivotal role in beta-test programming and development of causal sales application (upgraded Alpha 4 database into back-end of Access 2000 and SQL Server, front-end into Internet Explorer via ASP programming).

- **End-User Training.** Expanded Reach Centre offerings by designing, developing and delivering advanced programs and manuals for MS Office, GroupWise, Novell Network, and Internet, making information easily understood and usable. Manage all Access courses, training and supervising five adjunct team instructors.

Continued

Computer and IT

Computer and IT

Gloria Bartlett
55555 555555 Home ▪ 555555 8888 Mobile ▪ gloriabar@anyserver.co.uk   Page 2

XYZ Ltd – continued
Technical Assistant, MIS – Technical Support Activity   (2007–2009)
First-level technical support for software installation, as well as setup and configuration of new equipment (PCs, laptops, printers, scanners, projectors, digital & video).

- **IT Software Training.** Designed curriculum and materials, and delivered technical training, for introductory programs in Microsoft Office Suite (Word, Excel, Access), as well as Windows 95, keeping staff motivated and focused while improving job satisfaction and productivity.

- **Website Support.** Functioned as Web Editor for Division of Taxation's Internet/intranet website, proofing and updating website information on a daily basis.

- **Database Maintenance.** Upgraded and maintained link-shared employee Access database with Chief of Staff's office, ensuring data integrity for training. Created database reports for management evaluation.

- **Technical Development Project.** Pioneered development and implementation of storage, archive and retrieval system for electronic presentations used throughout Division of Taxation.

Principal Clerk – Technical Education   (2005–2007)
Promoted to provide installation, configuration and troubleshooting support for new equipment and software in REACH Centre, as well as evaluation and modification of skills assessment.

- **Training Centre Database.** Initiated and implemented data gathering system in Access to compile, store and retrieve statistics on computer training classes. Researched and wrote monthly reports used to evaluate training trends and staff training needs.

- **Saver Rebate Program.** Key team participant in initial, large-scale data compilation for Saver Rebate Program, including retrieval, distribution, quality control and storage of data.

Senior Clerk Typist, Clerk Typist – Corporate Business Tax   (2003–2005)
Assisted auditors by researching taxpayer information on mainframe, ordered work files for Supervising Auditor using HLLAPI information system, and prepared report statistics using Excel spreadsheets.

XYZ Accounting (temporary contract)   (2002–2003)
Data Entry Specialist / Legal Secretary
Front office support for accounts: records management, legal document preparation, purchasing, and equipment maintenance. Used IS software for research and to process complaints.

ABC BANK, Stevenage   (1998–2001)
Customer Service Representative / Supervisor Teller
Instructed employees in use of computerized banking systems and procedures. Verified and audited financial reports and balance sheets. Cash management responsibility exceeded £100,000.

EDUCATION

Instructor Certification, **HRDI – 2008**
Courses: Curriculum Design, Performance Consulting, Training Presentations, Design Surveys and Questions, Determining Training Needs, and Active Techniques for Teaching.

Certificate in Computer Programming, The Computer Institute, Guildford – 2007
Courses: HTML, CGI, Java Programming, JavaScript Programming, RPG 400, C Programming, SQL, Visual Basic 5.0, AS/400 Subfiles & Common Language Queries, MS Office, Windows NT 4.0.

Ongoing Professional and Technical Development in-house and at vendor locations (2003–present)

Technology strategist

Computer and IT

BRENDA R HINESVILE

Droid: (214) 721-5687	1 Any Street	http://brendahinesville.com
iPhone: (214) 723 7856	Anytown AA1 1AA	brenda@brendahinesville.com

TECHNOLOGY STRATEGIST / SENIOR SOFTWARE ARCHITECT
SOLID LEADERSHIP – SOFTWARE ARCHITECTURE – MOBILE
APPLICATION DEVELOPMENT – INTERNET MARKETING

PERFORMANCE PROFILE

Proven Leadership – Rare blend of theoretical and practical understanding of open source applications and server environments. Leadership and hands-on experience in regulated financial services and mobile software industries.

Senior-Level Software Professional – Strong leader. 12+ years of experience developing and managing open source software. Successful in building solid technology platforms and leading technology organizations. Career includes senior-level positions, contributing to corporate, board and division-level strategic planning, policy formation and decision making.

CORE COMPETENCIES

Software Development

- Advanced Objective-C on iPhone OS
- Advanced C/C++ on OS X, BSD, Linux
- UNIX Systems Programming
- Application Architecture & Design
- Network & Security Protocols
- Mobile Hardware/Software Limitations

Management Leadership

- Personnel Recruiting/ Management
- Regulatory Accountability/ Compliance
- Translation/Communication of Technology Needs & Issues
- Process & Policy Creation & Implementation
- P&L Accountability

System Administration

- Server & Network Administration
- Extensive Work in UNIX Shells
- Expert in Terminal Environments
- Thorough Knowledge of OS Internals
- FFIEC Technology Regulations
- Web and Server Security
- Network Protocol Analysis

PERFORMANCE PROFILE

Developed iPhone App for commercial transportation industry   **2014 to 2015**

- Ranked 2 on App Store top free business apps, June 2014.
- Featured on App Store – New and Noteworthy, June 2014.
- Featured in numerous freight publications and Morning News.
- Online Gallery, HD Screencasts, technical overview available on Project URL.

Contributed Documentation to Plone – Open Source CMS   **2014 to 2015**

- How to configure a Plone 3 production server with Squid and Apache 2 + SSL on a FreeBSD 7 server with PF, the packet filter. Comprehensive instructions for secure installation.

Continued

Computer and IT

Brenda Hinesville   iPhone: (214) 723 7856   brenda@brendahinesville.com

Developed Open Source Enterprise Software for XYZ Bank   2008 to 2013

- Deployed loan pricing and eligibility software across nation-wide network on hardened Linux servers.
- Designed extensive schema in PostgreSQL, C++ DFA for parsers, and TCL for dynamic content.
- Achieved near 100% system uptime and significantly increased bank profit margins.
- 500+ mortgage programmes, 50K+ underwriting/pricing rules, £1 million daily changing mortgage interest rates.

Migrated Bank Infrastructure to Open Source Platforms   2008 to 2010

- Deployed, managed Open Source mail / web servers on hardened Linux at SAS 70 Type II data centre.
- Drastically reduced costs, near 100% uptime, and significantly mitigated security/ regulatory risks.
- Developed CRM on Open Source CMS and deployed across nationwide branch network.
- Deployed Open Source mail / web clients on corporate workstations – trained IT department on Linux server administration and workstation software management.

Led startup of IT department for XYZ Bank   2008 to 2010

- Established bank's online presence.
- Integrated custom CRM with Google Adwords to track lead conversion quality and ratios.
- Provided technical, financial and managerial oversight of bank's technology infrastructure.
- Ensured compliance with banking Regulations.

PROFESSIONAL EXPERIENCE

LEAD SOFTWARE ARCHITECT / DEVELOPER   2014 to Present
APPLICANDY, LLC – MOBILE APPLICATION DEVELOPMENT, LONDON

Designed and developed iPhone application, iLogMiles, for commercial transportation industry. Led project, including all development, and provided training on software standards, Apple guidelines and Internet marketing. Closely followed agile design principles. Designed and managed website and web application framework.

- App released for the 'iTransport on the road' – Today's Haulage Magazine, April 2010.
- 'New iPhone App Provides Daily Log Book' – Heavy Duty Magazine, April 2010.
- 'Amid industry discussion…, smartphone logging apps proliferate' – Overdrive Magazine, April 2010.
- 'Two iPhone/iPad app developers hit milestones with iLogMiles…' – Morning News, April 2010.
- 'Software developers keep turning out the apps' – Morning News, March 2010.

SOFTWARE CONSULTANT   2013 to 2014
MORTGAGE & INVESTMENT LTD, LEEDS

Consulting services for banks and financial institutions – Enterprise software architecture, capital markets consulting – Mark to Market, Fall-Out analysis, and Hedged Pipeline analysis reports. Deployed Plone on hardened FreeBSD server at SAS 70 Type II data centre.

Continued

Brenda Hinesville   iPhone: (214) 723 7856   brenda@brendahinesville.com

HEAD OF INFORMATION TECHNOLOGY / MANAGING DIRECTOR   2008 to 2013
XYZ BANK, LONDON

Led and managed technology department and created tech strategy for bank. Architected and managed technology infrastructure, including migration strategies for accounting and loan origination systems. Trained personnel on network protocols, system admin, server security and data modelling. Performed technology assessments of prospective acquisitions. Managed project lifecycles for several software interfaces. Performed database migrations, server installations, server upgrades, performance tuning & security assessments. Managed vendor contracts.

SOFTWARE DEVELOPER   2006 to 2007
MORTGAGE PORTFOLIO SERVICES, SWINDON

Designed, developed & deployed mortgage lock platform using CGI and C++.

C++ and UNIX TUTOR   2005 to 2006
COMMUNITY COLLEGE, EXETER

Tutored 200+ students in C++ and UNIX courses.

OPEN SOURCE DEVELOPER, EXETER   2001 to 2007

UNIX systems programming on Solaris, Open/FreeBSD, RH/Slackware Linux.
Developed thread-safe, streams library in C++. The library is an extension of the C++ iostreams hierarchy. Customized streams provide support for sockets, shared memory, pipes and text files. Project URL – http://mls.sourceforge.net

EDUCATION

BSc – Computer Science, University of London   2007
- Graduate-level coursework in Computer Science
- Emphasis on operating system architecture and database design
Member of iEEE Computer Society

Notable Conferences: Apple World Wide Developer Conference; Apple iPhone Tech Talk – San Jose, 2014. Administering Linux in Production Environments – USENIX; Online Analytics – Omniture Inc.; Search Engine Strategies – Chicago, 2011.

Computer and IT

Web developer/programmer

Kelly L Hillman   1 Any Street, Anytown AX0 0HA • 020 8123 4567

Web Developer/Programmer or Database Programmer

Performance Summary

Performance Profile/Performance Summary

- 14 years of innovation in Web Development and Programming for high-profile technical companies and government organizations. Skilled problem-solver with fast learning curve for cutting-edge technologies.

- Polished communication, presentation, training and client-relations skills. Able to relate effectively to people at all levels and convey complex technical information in an understandable manner.

- Experienced in all aspects of architecture and accessibility techniques. Hands-on knowledge of Section 508 and W3C Standards.

Technical Skills

Programming/Scripting Languages: HTML, XHTML, DHTML, CSS Stylesheets, ColdFusion, Fusebox, Perl, JavaScript, CGI Scripting, XSSI, Java, Java Servlets, JSP, JDBC, Swing

Database Applications: SQL, SQL/PL, Oracle, Access, Database Design and Architecture

Software Applications/Programs: Dreamweaver, Flash, Fireworks, Adobe Photo Shop

Operating Systems/Platforms: UNIX and Windows

Professional Experience
Web Developer/IT Specialist, EXCEL SYSTEMS/EPA (Formerly LOCKHEED-MARTIN) – RESEARCH Swindon (2010 to Present): Manage the maintenance, development and enhancement of a Coldfusion application that interfaces with an Oracle database. Create, update and maintain 11,000 web pages/templates while ensuring compliance with section 508 and EPA web guidelines. Perform Java Script and PDF conversions; create high-quality graphics; produce content; integrate dynamic popup menus; update employee web-based information.

Managed the complete conversion of 20,000 EPA web pages to meet section 508 website guidelines in both appearance and compatibility.
Instrumental in successfully meeting all critical and stringent deadlines.
Recognized by management for advanced skill level and efficiency.

Continued

Kelly L Hillman   **Page 2 of 2**

Web Development/Maintenance – Newbury (2009 to 2010): Oversaw all aspects of client website development. Performed a wide range of design and coding projects using HTML, DHTML, XHTML, JavaScript and Flash. Updated and maintained content and graphics for both new and previously existing sites.

Spearheaded and managed all business, technical and client relations functions.
Developed and launched numerous high-impact websites in addition to successfully redesigning existing sites to create additional market exposure.

Junior Systems Programmer/Analyst, MCTC – Swindon (2007 to 2009): Hired to develop and code web-based applications and user interfaces in transmitting/integrating data with Oracle databases for a comprehensive government occupational network database. Served as a member of a technical team in developing multiple web, database, data search and retrieval applications.

Recruited for a part-time position, promoted to full-time.
Pioneered the research and development of guidelines for people with disabilities.

Marketing/Technical Support Assistant, XYZ CORPORATION – Swindon (2005 to 2006)

Educational & Training – MSc Computer Information Technology, UNIVERSITY OF ESSEX

BA in Sociology (2005), UNIVERSITY OF ESSEX
Information Systems Programming (2007), DURHAM TECHNICAL COMMUNITY COLLEGE – Durham, HTML_Advanced HTML_Advanced Online Java Script Training_Sun's sl285 Hands-on Java Workshop_XML Certification Training_Applied Systems Analysis and Design_Object-Oriented Software

Systems engineer

PARAG GUPTA

1 Any Street • Anytown AA1 1AA • 55555 555555 • parag.gupta@technical.com

SYSTEM ENGINEER

Motivated and driven IT professional offering 9+ years of hands-on experience in designing, implementing and enhancing systems to automate business operations. Demonstrated ability to develop high-performance systems, applications, databases and interfaces.

➤ Part of TL9000 CND audit interviews which helped Technical get TL9000 certified which is significant in Telecom industry. Skilled trainer and proven ability to lead many successful projects, like TSS, EMX and TOL.

➤ Strategically manage time and expediently resolve problems for optimal productivity, improvement and profitability; able to direct multiple tasks effectively.

➤ Strong technical background with a solid history of delivering outstanding customer service.

➤ Highly effective liaison and communication skills proven by effective interaction with management, users, team members and vendors.

TECHNICAL SKILLS

Operating Systems:	Unix, Windows (2000, XP), DOS
Languages:	C, C++, Java, Pascal, Assembly Languages (Z8000, 808x, DSP)
Methodologies:	TL9000, Digital Six Sigma
Software:	MS Office, Adobe Framemaker, Matlab
RDBMS:	DOORS, Oracle 7.x
Protocols:	TCP/IP, SS7 ISUP, A1, ANSI, TL1, SNMP
Tools:	Teamplay, Clearcase, Clearquest, M-Gatekeeper, Exceed, Visio, DocExpress, Compass
Other:	CDMA Telecom Standards – 3GPP2 (Including TIA/EIA-2001, TIA/EIA-41, TIA/EIA-664), ITU-T, AMPS

PROFESSIONAL EXPERIENCE

Technical, Main Network Division, Norwich • Jan 2004–Present

Principal Staff Engineer • **Products Systems Engineering** • Nov 2009–Present
- Known as 'go-to' person for CDMA call processing and billing functional areas.
- Create customer requirements documents for Technical SoftSwitch (TSS) and SMS Gateway products. All deliverables done on/ahead schedule with high quality.
- Solely accountable for authoring and allocation, customer reviews, supporting fellow system engineers, development, and test and customer documentation teams.
- Support Product Management in RFPs, customer feature prioritization, impact statements and budgetary estimates.
- Mentored junior engineers and 1 innovation disclosure (patent) submitted in 2012.
- Resolve deployed customer/internal requirements issues and contribute to Virtual Zero Defect quality goal.
- TOL process champion and part of CND focus group that contributed to reducing CRUD backlog (NPR) by 25% and cycle time (FRT) by 40%.
- Recognized as the TL9000 expert. Triage representative for switching and messaging products.
- Achieved 'CND Quality Award' for contribution to quality improvement in May 2012.

Continued

Senior Staff Engineer • XYZ Systems Engineering • May 2007–Oct 2009
- Led a team of 12 engineers for three major software releases of TSS product included around 80 features/enhancements to create T-Gate SE deliverables.
- Mentored newer engineers to get up to speed on TSS product.
- Created requirements for TSS product, 30 features/enhancements contributing to five major software releases. *Recognized as overall product expert with specific focus on call processing and billing.*
- Played integral role in successfully implementing proprietary commercial TSS billing system.
- Supported PdM organization by creating ROMs, technical support for RFPs (Vivo, Sprint, TELUS, TM, Tata, Inquam, Alaska, Reliance, Pakistan, PBTL, Mauritius, Telefonica, Brasicel and Angola).
- Proactively identified functional areas of improvement for requirements coverage, contributed to resolving several faults, improved customer documentation, and provided reference for future releases as well as other customers.
- *Received 'Above and Beyond Performance Award' – Oct 2008.*

Senior Software Engineer • EMX Development • Aug 2005–Apr 2007
- Successfully led and coordinated the cross-functional development teams, 30 engineers, to meet the scheduled design, code and test completion dates ensuring Feature T-Gates are met.
- Feature Technical Lead for Concurrent Voice/Data Services feature, the largest revenue-generating feature for KDDI customer.
- Feature Lead for Paging Channel SMS feature. Created requirements and design; led implementation phase of five engineers' team; supported product, network, and release testing; and created customer reference documentation.
- Performed the role of functional area lead for Trunk Manager and A1 interface functional areas. Provided two-day Technical Workshops for internal/customer knowledge sharing and functional area transition from Caltel.
- Provided customer site testing and FOA (First Office Application) support for major EMX releases and off-hours CNRC (Customer Networks Resolution Centre) support.
- *Received 'Bravo Award' – May 2006, Sep 2006, Jan 2007*

Software Engineer • EMX Development • Jan 2004–Jul 2005
- Developed design and code for SMS feature as a Trunk Manager functional area lead for the largest FA impacted by the feature. Supported product, network and release testing.
- Contributed to customer release documentation. Supported feature-level SMS testing at various internal labs and customer sites resulting in successful deployment at customer sites.
- Designed and coded phases for wiretap and virtual circuits feature development, initial assessment of internal and customer EMX PRs (problem reports) to route/classify issues and providing problem assessments for many of these PRs.
- Created an implementation process to serve as reference for new hires.
- Provided CNRC support during the Y2K transition.
- *Received 'Above and Beyond Performance Award' – Jan 2005, Dec 2005 and 'Certificate of Outstanding Achievement' – Jun 2004*

EDUCATION

MSc Computer Engineering • University of London • 2003
Bachelors of Engineering in Electronics • Technology and Science Institute, India • 2001

Significant Trainings Include

- Open Source Software
- WSG Requirements Process
- WiMAX
- Product Security
- Agile Management for Software Engineering
- Fagan Inspection and Moderation

Network architecture specialist

JOHN A CHRISTOPHER
1 Any Street, Anytown AX0 0AA • 020 8123 4567 • fax 020 8123 5678 • jacla@email.com

Applications
Adaptec Easy CD Creator
Adaptec Direct CD
Carbon Copy
Cc Mail
Clarify
HP Colorado Backup
MS Active Sync
MS Office Professional
MS Outlook 98 and 2003
MS Internet Explorer
NetAccess Internet
Netscape
Norton Ghost
Partition Magic
PC Anywhere
Rainbow
Reflection 1
Reflection X
Remedy-ARS
Symantec Norton Antivirus
Visio
Windows CE

Operating Systems
Microsoft Windows:
Microsoft Windows 8.1
    Workstation and Server
Microsoft Windows ME
Microsoft Windows 10
Cisco Router/Switch IOS
MS-DOS
UNIX

Network Architecture Specialist
Cisco Certified Network Associate

Results-driven, self-motivated professional with solid experience supporting hundreds of users in multiple departments in the corporate environment. Recognized for outstanding support and services, process development and project management. Able to manage multiple projects simultaneously and to move quickly among projects. Capable of leading or collaborating. Areas of expertise include:

- Network architectures and networking components
- Software and operating system deployment in corporate environments
- PC hardware installation/repair and disk imaging
- Troubleshoot complex operating system problems
- Call tracking, case management, solution integration

Accomplishments
- Reduced help desk calls by developing end-user training and knowledge database.
- Led migration for 3000+ client/server email accounts from HP Open Mail to MS Exchange.
- Developed data collection protocol for BLM Natural Resource Inventory.
- Mentored teammates on technical materials and procedures.
- Built relationships to quickly resolve business critical issues.

Certifications

Technical Certification for MS Network Support Program, 9/12
CCNA – Cisco Certified Network Associate, 8/12

Continued

John A Christopher   **Page 2 of 2**

Hardware
Intel-based Desktops
Intel-based Mobile
    Computers
HP Colorado Tape Backup
Cisco 2500 Series Router
Hewlett Packard Pro Curve
Switches
CD Writer

Protocols & Services
TCP/IP
DHCP
DNS
NetBEUI
Remote Access Service
WINS

Networking
Ethernet
Token Ring
Microsoft Networking

Work History

Technical Support Engineer, ABC Technologies (Holt Services), 4/13–Present

E-mail Migration Specialist, ABC Technologies (Holt Services), 11/12–4/13

PC Technician, RBM (The Cameo Group) 5/12–11/12

Customer Support Specialist, Centre Partners, 9/11–5/12

Recycle Technician, RBM (WasteNot Recycling) 2/11–9/11

Soil Scientist, Bureau of Land Management, 5/10–10/10

Education

ABC Institute Workshop – Goal Setting, Achievement, Motivation, 1/11

BSc, Soil Science: Environmental Mgt. – London University, 12/10

Awards and Honours

ABC Shining Star Award for Outstanding Customer Service, October 2014

Outstanding Services to Technical Services Division, January 2013

High Quality Customer Service Award, RBM Technical Support March and April 2012

Computer and IT

Software quality assurance engineer

Sam Smith

1 Any Street
Anytown, AX0 0AA

01234 567890
ssmith@email.com

Software Quality Assurance Engineer
Performance Summary

QA engineer with in-depth knowledge of complex wired and wireless technology. Superior testing skills with outstanding analysis, programming and debugging capabilities with the ability to identify critical software defects before market release. Backed by two promotions within four years and receipt of MVP award within last two years. MSc in Computer Science.

✔ Performs test plan creations, manual and automated product testing, troubleshooting failures, and tracking with defects.

✔ Strong interpersonal and communication skills with the ability to work with cross-functional departments, including software developers.

✔ Performs product validation automation by creating test scripts and investigating script failures.

✔ Experienced with layer 2 and layer 3 networking protocols.

Professional Skills

✢ Software Testing Methodologies	✢ Network Protocols	✢ White Box & Black Box Testing
✢ Test Plan Creation	✢ Problem Isolation & Recreation	✢ System Testing
✢ Test Beds	✢ Complex Test Scenarios	✢ Functional & Design Test Reviews
✢ Automation Scripting	✢ Troubleshooting Skills	
✢ Product Testing & Debugging	✢ Scalability & Performance Testing	✢ Regression Testing
		✢ Root Cause Identification

Work Experience

ABC Networks, Coventry

2009–Present

Software QA Engineer (WLAN Team)

2012–Present

Manages deployment of wireless networking protocol APs on wireless network; drives each user's connectivity issues to fullest resolution. Uses agile development processes for test and validation. Performs manual and regression testing of next generation access. Leads test efforts for developing an innovative and unique Adaptive radio management technology.

● Created up to 500% faster network connections for smartphones, tablets and laptops, resulting in vastly improved client and system performance.

● The network continuously optimizes client connections, keeping network capacity and performance consistent.

● Reduced help desk calls 30%.

Software QA Engineer (WLAN Team)

2009–2012

Performed manual and regression testing of next generation access points, controller and switches. Performed problem isolation and recreation in complex test scenario failures. Designed functional and interoperability-level verification test from system specifications and product requirements. Executed functional, interoperability and customer use test cases; tracked test case results.

● Achieved 2012 Q3 MVP Award by turning around a customer deal for high-density iPad performance competitive testing. Completed multiple rounds of testing under time constraints, resulting in a 30% improvement on streaming capabilities and lowering video stalling, outperforming XYZ, leading to multiple customer wins.

● Accomplished ARM2.0/1.0 feature regression testing and test plan write-ups, building test beds on multiple releases with features including Spectrum Load Balancing Band-Steering, Mode-Aware ARM, Airtime Fairness, and PerSSID Bandwidth Management and Scanning.

● Performed high-density (HD) testing on a testbed with 200+ heterogeneous client devices, resulting in improved AP performance with high client density.

● Identified significant hardware issues in early life cycle on two new AP platforms crucial to the company's new initiative in the hospitality market, resulting in decreased hardware schedule risks.

Continued

Sam Smith ssmith@email.com Page 2

Awards

Quarterly MVP Award Nominee, Q2 2013
Quarterly MVP Award, Q4 2012

Education

University of London 2009
MSc Computer Science

Lincoln University 2007
BSc Computer Science

Computer Network Skills

NX-OS and Cisco Nexus Switching: VLANs, Private VLANs, STP, Port-channels, Virtual Port Channels, Unidirectional Link Detection, Cisco FabricPath, Firewall, High Availability, SPAN, ERSPAN, Unified Fabric, Nexus 1000V, QoS, OTV, MPLS,
Layer 2: VLANs & Trunks, Inter-VLAN routing, Etherchannels, STP, High Availability
Layer 3: Routing basics, EIFRP, OSPF, Route filtering, BGP (Good concepts)
Extensive knowledge in 802.11 a/b/g/n/ac WLAN
Protocols: TCP/IP, UDP, ARP, DHCP, ICMP, 802.3, 802.1x, HTTP, FTP, TFTP, DNS, Syslog

Programming

TCL	C
Expect	C++
Shell Scripting	JAVA

Hardware

IXIA XM12 High Performance Chassis	Aruba Controllers
WaveTest 90/WaveTest 20	Cisco Catalyst 3560 & 3750 Switches
Aruba Corvina Switches	Lantronix Terminal Servers
Netgear Gigabit Series Switches	Access Points (APs)
Dell PowerEdge R620 Server	

Software Applications

IXIA: IxChariot, IxExplorer,	Testlink
IxLoad	SecureCRT
IxVeriwave	mRemote
3CDaemon	Winagents TFTP Server
iPerf	Backtrack
Wireshark	MIB Browser
Omnipeek Packet Analyzer	Linux Screen and VI Utilities
Bugzilla	

Operating Systems

Linux (Fedora, Centos, Ubuntu)	Apple MAC OS X
Cisco IOS	Windows Server 2000 & 2003
Aruba OS	Windows XP/7/8
Google Androids	Unix
Apple iOS	

Excellent references available on request

Computer and IT

Systems and network manager

James Sharpe   Page 1 of 2
123 Any Street
Anytown AT1 0BB
Tel: 020 8123 4567
james@anyaddress.co.uk

NETWORK OPERATIONS

Professional Profile
- 15 years of management and hands-on background working in IT infrastructure.
- Experience with world-class banks and financial institutions in New York, London, Paris.
- Hold MBA in Banking and Finance.
- Chosen for the 2000 International Who's Who in Information Technology.

Core Skills
network design • systems management • LAN administration • strategic planning • team formation and leadership • budget preparation • project planning and management • presentation • business writing • resource management • product and design research • vendor interface and negotiation • systems conversion • computer operations • systems implementation • branch start-ups and automation • disaster recovery • system migrations • data centre overhauls and moves • applications support

Executive Development
Major Bank, London
Chief Executive and Manager of Network Operations   2008 to Present
Control £1 million budget and oversee five technicians in the design, implementation and support of company's WAN and LAN infrastructure. Handle heavy resource management and coordination with internal departments, vendors and network integration companies to define scopes of work, technical designs, product selection, required resources, schedules and price negotiation. Budget resources and prepare reports. Hire, schedule and review technicians.

Projects
AT&T frame relay and Cisco router implementation, TCP/IP address conversion, Compuserve RAS implementation, Cisco switched Ethernet 100mb/1 gb Catalyst implementation, HP Open View and Cisco Works implementation, MS DHCP and proxy server implementation. Managed project teams at remote sites to implement NT servers, routers, PC hardware upgrades, and Windows 95/NT images. Co-managed 1,100-user move.

Major Investment Bank, London
Network Manager   2005 to 2008
Managed WAN daily support, hardware installation/configurations and network changes. Monitored/configured private frame relay voice and data network. Monitored ACC routes and NT servers. Performed Windows NT 3.51 server and workstation installations. Configured ACC routers, Adtran CSUs and Newbridge 3612 and 3606 multiplexors for remote site installations.

Continued

James Sharpe 020 8123 4567 page 2 of 2

Large Multinational Bank, Paris
Network Operations Supervisor 2002 to 2005
Managed all network and computer operations for the international hub site, reporting directly to the Technology Manager and supervising a team of technicians and computer operators. Supervised three direct reports, supported traders, reviewed/upgraded operations, handled troubleshooting, researched products and interfaced/negotiated with vendors.

- Completed full office start-up in Luxembourg in three months. Implemented LAN, voice, data, and video capabilities. Hired and trained computer operator to support local users. Implemented support procedures and documentation.

- Saved company over £50,000 annually: migrated video conferencing from leased lines to ISDN, cleaned up multiplex or maintenance contracts, discovered overpayment on WAN lines. Set up a new process to review all invoices and pre-approved all purchases and communications costs before forwarding to Technology Manager.

Technology Expertise
Hardware: Cisco 7206/4700/25XX, Cisco PIX firewall, Cabletron MMAC+/Smart Switch 6000's/ MMAC8, Newbridge 46020/36XX, IDNX 20/12, CYLINK link encryptors, Paradyne CSUs, ACC routers, Northern Telecom Option 11, PictureTel 4000/M8000, VAX 4000/6310/8000, HSC50, RA60/80/82/90 disk drives, MTI disks in DSSI architecture, HP 9000 K100, Sun Ultra 10, HP Laserjet 3/4/5 and QMS laser printers, Dell/Digital/AST/IBM PC hardware, Intel/3Com NIC cards. Cabling knowledge includes category 3/5, IBM Type 1, fibre optic multimode, v.35, x.21, RS232.

Software: SWIFT Alliance v3.0, IBIS, ST400, Montran (CHIPS), Reuters, Telerate, ADP Executive Quotes, IFSL Green Bar Viewer, Euroclear, Tracs, Soar, MS Project 95, VISIO, MS Word/Excel/ PowerPoint, Lotus Notes v4.6, MS Mail, Ami-Pro, Lotus 1-2-3, DOS, Chameleon v4.6, Sybase v11, COBOL, Pascal, BASIC.

Protocols/Operating Systems: Cisco IOS version 11.x, TCP/IP, IPX, frame relay, EIGRP, OSPF, RIP, PPP, ISDN, SNMP, DHCP, WINS/DNS, Netbeui, NeBIOS, DECnet, LAT, VAX/VMS v5.5-2, Pathworks v4.1/5.0, Windows NT Server 3.51 and 4.0, Netware 3.12, HP-UX v10.2, Solaris v2.6.1, OS/400 v2.3.

Education and Professional Development
MBA in Banking and Finance, London University
BSc in Interdisciplinary Studies, The Polytechnical Institute
Computer Operations Diploma, Institute for Data Systems
Additional technology courses: Network Design and Performance, Advanced Cisco Router, Configuration, Microsoft Project 95. SYBASE SQL Server Administration, SYBASE Fast Track to SQL Server, Fundamentals of the HP UNIX System, Pathworks V5 Migration Planning, RDB Database Administration, Pathworks Tuning and Troubleshooting, PC Architecture and Troubleshooting.

Computer and IT

Information manager

Dan Newcomb, PMP

1 Any Street   •   Anytown AA1 1AA

Mobile: 55555555 5555   •   aresumesolution.com

INFORMATION TECHNOLOGY MANAGEMENT

Technology manager with multifaceted experience in mainframe and client server environments with multiple relational databases; Informix, Oracle Sybase and SQL server. Exceptional team-building and management capabilities. Strong background in relational database management, performance tuning and high availability techniques. Skilled project manager with ability to obtain project requirements and implement solutions that drive bottom line. Talented in providing technology risk management. Developing wide-ranging talents in computer technology, staff leadership and SDLC to effectively manage organizational change, mitigate risk, infuse new ideas and deliver large-company capabilities.

➤ Excellent ability to analyse business needs and implement cost-effective solutions meeting business objectives.

➤ Solid record of achievement building and aligning organizations with strategic IT business objectives to achieve dramatic bottom-line results.

➤ Expertise providing project management, technology expertise and staff leadership.

➤ Demonstrated talents in database architecture, design and maintenance.

CORE COMPETENCIES

– £MM Project Management	– SQL	– Staff Leadership	– COBOL
– Process Management	– Informix	– Release & Change Management	– DMSII
– Software Development Lifecycle	– SDLC	– Disaster Recovery Management	– UNIX
– Telecom Systems		– Vendor Management	– C
– Client Relationship Management	– DRM	– Database Administration	– Oracle

PROFESSIONAL EXPERIENCE

XYZ FINANCE COMPANY, Birmingham – Present

Consumer division of bank providing consumer credit and home mortgages to customers throughout UK.

Application System Team Manager

Provides team leadership and project management for IT projects with price ranging in value from £50,000 to £1.5 million, ensuring timely completion. Directs and mentors four Application/Database Designers, providing prototype, design, development and implementation of database architecture and strategies and support of databases and applications. Oversees organizational change management functions, providing support and approval of over 100 change requests in one release cycle. Designs and implements ETL solutions for XML-based interface of Origination data. Assists audit organizations, providing engineering and architecture changes to necessary applications, databases and servers for SOX compliance. SME for origination data and ensures persistence of data across downstream systems. Provides support for backup applications.

Accomplishments:

• Increased client leads by 20% through development and implementation of lead registration system.

• Directed team in development and implementation of Disaster Recovery Planning efforts, providing quick restoration of critical applications.

• Spearheaded major 18-month application and database design project for implementation of application and database security ensuring compliance for entire organization with budget of £1.5 million.

Continued

Dan Newcomb   **page 2**

ABC MORTGAGE, AND FINANCE, Woking   2006–2008
Database Consultant

Designed and implemented the Enterprise wide Data Warehouse and reporting framework for the mortgage line of business with departmental data mart. Performed Dimensional data modeling to implement the data warehouse. Managed the Application and Physical DBA role for Enterprise wide Oracle and Informix databases ranging from 50 GB to 250 GB size. Established database backup and recovery strategies using RMAN and ONBAR utilities.

Performed expert object management technique like object partitioning. Performed capacity planning based on transaction volume and expected growth. Developed and implemented shell scripts, stored procedures, functions and triggers. Ensured all databases were functioning appropriately and resolved any issues on a timely basis.

Accomplishments:

- 10% reduction of time between receipt of inquiry to funding with the help of availability of daily sales, appraisal effectiveness reports.

XYZ TECHNOLOGIES, Woking   2005–2006

Leading provider of technology solutions for Telecom Industries around the globe.

Senior Database Consultant

Developed and maintained telecom clearinghouse software for telecom services providers to manage 1 million customer requests per day. Directed team of developers in support and maintenance for Exchange Link project running on an Oracle 8-I database with capacity of over 200 GB. Performed application and database tuning with object and index redesign resulting in 66% improvement in application performance. 24/7 support of application in an ASP model. Handled configuration management, change management, business analysis, and project management.

Accomplishments:

- Increased customer satisfaction through improved application support, increasing revenue from £1 million to £10 million.

ABC TECHNOLOGIES, Somerset   2003–2005

Leading provider of software for telecom service providers.

SAP Production Support Database Administrator

Served as Oracle database administrator for large 600GB database, providing 24/7 support of numerous SAP R/3 systems. Learned and quickly adapted to new technology. Analysed and resolved complex issues with over 1,000 batch jobs in SAP R/3 environment. Developed and implemented shell scripts, providing escalations based on procedure and severity. Provided support for end-users on complex issues. Configured and maintained various files. Ensured application security and provided user administration.

Accomplishments:

- Key member of team that turned six-month pilot SAP project to company-wide implementation, providing coordination between vendors, clients and implementation team.

EDUCATION
BSc (Hons) Engineering
City Engineering College, Manchester

Training:

- Certified training in COBOL, DMSII, UNIX, C, and Oracle
- Certified training in 'Structured Systems Analysis and Design'

Continued

Computer and IT

Dan Newcomb page 3

TECHNICAL SKILLS

Databases:	SQL Server 2000, DMSII, Sybase, Oracle 7, 8, 9I, 10G Informix 7.3/9.X, SQL Server 7.0
Systems:	HP9000 (HP-UX 11, 10.20), SUN SPARC-Enterprise 2000 (Solaris 2.5), SUN SPARC 6500 (Sun OS 5.6), Sun Fire 880, AIX, Linux, UNISYS A series, Windows NT
Languages:	C, COBOL74, SQL, Oracle Pro*C, PRO*COBOL, PL/SQL, VB, ASP
UNIX Programming:	Shell scripting, AWK/SED Scripting
DB Tools:	Oracle (Enterprise Manager), SQL*DBA, Import, Export, SQL Loader, SQL (Report Writer), Microsoft SQL Server Data Transformation Service, Oracle RMAN
CASE Tools:	ERWIN/ERX (both IE and IDEF1X)
Methodologies:	UML, Rational Unified process, SCRUM, Agile

Advertising sales (entry-level)

Melody J Courtney
1 Any Street, Anytown AX0 0AA

55555 555555 mobile   home 020 8123 4567

Professional Summary: Enthusiastic, creative and hard-working media studies graduate with demonstrated successful sales experience. Reputation for providing excellent customer service resulting in increased sales and improved customer retention. Eager to translate solid classroom and work-placement experience in advertising sales into bottom-line revenues in the radio/television industry.

Education: BA in Media Studies, Metropolitan University, 2008.
Coursework included advertising research and strategy, design and graphics, media planning, and sales and campaigns.

Final Year Project
- *Challenge:* Create an advertising campaign for the City Hospice Group.
- *Action:* As key member of a six-person team, performed demographics survey, developed campaign strategies, created logo and slogan, authored and designed bilingual brochures, and created media kit within £250,000 budget.
- *Result:* After presenting project to 11-person panel, won first place out of 12 teams. The City Hospice Group implemented the slogan and several campaign strategies.

Work Placements
Advertising Sales Representative, AB Advertising, Truro   Sept–Dec 2007
- Sold print advertising to local businesses using cold-calling techniques.

Production Assistant, XY Films Ltd   Jan–May 2007
- Assisted with production of 2 to 3 commercials a week. Accountable for delivering all technical equipment to the site and pre-production set up of lights, monitors, microphones and cameras. Worked closely with sales department and producer, learning both the technical side of commercial production as well as sales and customer service issues.
- Handled pre-production and on-air tasks including studio set up, script delivery, operating cameras and soundboards.

Sales/Customer Service Experience
Sales/Waiting Staff, Great Brewpub, Truro
- Consistently generated additional revenues using thorough product knowledge and friendly sales technique to sell house specials and add-on items. Contender for the '£1,000 Night' sales award.

Host/Waiting Staff, Jack's Seafood, Falmouth
- Developed repeat business by providing excellent customer service in fast-paced environment.

Awards/Memberships
- Won Silver Medal, an annual award for college students, 2007
- Served as Co-Director of Adwerks, developing ads for non-profit organizations, 2006
- Member and committee chairperson of the Ad Society, a college professional organization, 2006–2008

Salesperson

Sales and marketing

SARA FERNANDEZ, MBA

1 Any Street, Anytown AA1 1AA • Mobile: 55555555 5555 • *sara123@comcast.net*

ONLINE MULTIMEDIA SALES
Advertising, Communications and Media

Performance Profile

Ambitious, high-performing sales professional with a 20-year track record of success generating revenue and securing high-profile clients for 'best in class' companies. Recipient of **numerous prestigious sales awards** for consistently **exceeding sales goals and forecasts** and creating win-win client solutions. Uses a consultative approach to assess client needs and provide 'turnkey' solutions and programmes that meet the client's strategic goals. Possesses extensive expertise in branding, managing and positioning product lines, and implementing innovative solutions that drive revenue and bring unique products to the community. Expertise in:

Core Skills

⊹ Business Development	⊹ High-Expectation Client Relations	⊹ Overcoming Objections
⊹ Relationship Management	⊹ Employee Communication Strategy	⊹ Contract Negotiations
⊹ Strategic Alliance/Partners	⊹ Staff Motivating and Mentoring	⊹ Channel Sales Strategies

Gifted sales strategist and tactician who excels in driving revenue through innovative channel development programmes. Key skills include: the ability to produce ROI with passion, tenacity and an ethical, compliance-based stance that nurtures respect and supports growth. Excels in training and mentoring teams to outperform the competition. Possesses a high level of personal and professional integrity, a passion for achieving organizational success and a desire to **always play on a winning team**.

VALUE LTD – Axbridge • 2012–Present
Senior Sales Account Executive

Promoted and sold online advertising packages for leading investment and personal finance website. Identified and targeted key accounts and built relationships with senior level, often board level, clients and advertising agencies, building for them a 'soup to nuts' online campaign and suite of services that generated results. Charged with delivering £1–3 million in advertising revenue, by analysing existing sales channel relationships and developing a new strategy focused on market leaders.

ABC LTD – Sheffield • 2003–2012
Account Manager (2011–2012) • National Ad Agency Sales Representative (2010–2011)
National Recruitment Sales Representative (2003–2010)

Recruited to develop, revitalize and nurture productive relationships with major companies and government agencies such as XYZ Healthcare, UVW Systems, RST Air, and the NHS and HPA. Packaged and sold targeted multimedia integrated talent solutions and services to maximize effectiveness and reach to key clients.

Key Accomplishments:

➢ **Multimedia Campaign Development.** Offered existing clients an opportunity to 'fish in a different pond' by developing and recommending new multimedia account strategies targeted at niche markets. Packaged and sold non-traditional campaigns from non-print sources targeted at key audiences.

➢ **Product Development.** Credited with designing and spearheading the execution of a cutting-edge xyz.com product whereby keyword searches produced product-related ads along the margins of the website, generating more than £50K in revenue per year.

➢ **Increased Advertiser Revenue.** Through a combination of face-to-face visits to 13–15 domestic markets, the creation of various telephone sales programmes, and multiple e-mail marketing campaigns, increased ABC Ltd JOBS Advertising Unit by £10 million, an increase of 25%, representing one-third of all sales for the unit.

➢ **Sales Performance.** Consistently met and exceeded quarterly and annual sales revenue goals, up to 131% above quota.

➢ **Awards & Recognition.** Recipient of ABC Award for demonstrating a commitment to customers reflected in business performance, a high-level of sales achievement and customer satisfaction. Recipient of several prestigious awards including three Sales Achievement Awards, two Sales Excellence Awards and a Publishers Award for Sales Excellence.

Continued

SARA FERNANDEZ   page 2

JKLJOBS.COM – Bristol • 1996–2003
Managing Director – (2002–2003) • **Director of Client Services** – (2001–2002)
Account Executive – (1996–2001)

Progressed rapidly through and promoted into positions with increasing responsibility during time with JKLJobs.com. Directed all aspects of sales, marketing and operations functions, and managed full P & L (£10 million in revenue). Generated significant new client business and produced employer-branded recruitment and retention advertising campaign and execution strategies.

Key Accomplishments:

➤ **Cost Containment.** Spearheaded key cost-containment initiatives, saving thousands of pounds.

➤ **New Business Development.** Partnered with the JKLJobs sales channel in the design and implementation of a 'business case building' sales contest, increasing JKLJobs revenue by £2 million.

➤ **Sales Productivity.** Noted for driving £1 million in new business development in one year.

➤ **Process Improvement.** Spearheaded from conception to implementation an employee retention initiative. Launched monthly new hire performance appraisals, which fostered a welcoming experience for new employees and drastically improved retention. Hired, trained and supervised a staff of 12 account managers and provided ongoing staff mentoring and support enabling them to increase company's client base.

➤ **Employer Branding.** Partnered with senior level Human Resources clients in the design and development of uniquely branded corporate recruitment advertising strategies. Recommended tactical approaches for campaign execution.

➤ **Marketing Solutions.** Presented competitively positioned employee communication solutions and executed delivery of solutions such as collateral development, diversity strategies, university/college relations and creative ad design to maximize employee communication programmes.

Education

Master of Business Administration
City School of Business

Diploma, Sales and Marketing
City University

Sales representative

Jenny McClean

1 Any Street • Anytown AX0 0AA • 020 8123 4568 (Office) 020 8123 4567 (Home) • jamclean@email.com

Professional Profile

- Organized, efficient and precise with strong communication and liaison skills
- Skilled in planning and execution of special projects during time-critical assignment
- Decisive and direct, yet flexible in responding to constantly changing assignments
- Able to coordinate multiple projects and meet deadlines under pressure
- Enthusiastic, creative and willing to assume increased responsibility
- Attention to details and strong follow-through

Special Skills

- Language – Fluent in Spanish
- Computer – UNIX, VMA, Lotus Notes, MS Office, Word Perfect, SPSS 8.0, ESRI
- Certified in radiation safety
- Experience with medical terminology
- Database development

Relevant Skills

Office Administration

- Collecting and recording statistical and confidential information
- Assembling and organizing bulk mailing and marketing materials
- Data entry, with exceptionally fast typing and related office administration activities
- Organization specialist, able to ensure smooth and efficient flow of functions
- Progressive experience in office management, scheduling, and support services, data analysis, and research collection

Customer Service

- Extremely sociable and able to put visitors at ease
- Excellent verbal and written communication skills
- Highly skilled at solving customer relations problems

Education

- MA in Public Administration, Metropolitan University
- BA, Sociology, University of the South

Professional Experience
DATA ANALYST 2010–Present
ABC Health Products, Havant

ADMINISTRATIVE CLERK 2008–2010
The Valley Healthcare Clinic, West Hants

GRADUATE ASSISTANT IN CONTINUING EDUCATION 2005–2008
Metropolitan University

SALES SUPERVISOR 2004
XYZ Department Store, Plymouth

LAW CLERK 2002–2004
Patton & Page Law Firm, Plymouth

Account sales

Jalen Gilliard

1 Any Street
Anytown, AX0 0AA

01234 567890
jgilliard@email.com

Account Sales – College and Professional Sports

Performance Summary

Former professional athlete and sports management graduate with five years' experience exceeding sales quotas. Able to nurture relationships with business and sports professionals at all levels. Hands-on experience and passion for sports industry, with BSc degree in Sports and Entertainment Management. Dedicated to accepting challenges. Excels in fast-paced environments. Career history of target market development and exceeding sales goals. Strong organization and multitasking skills.

- ✔ Excels in prospecting, qualifying, developing and closing sales opportunities.
- ✔ Research and competitive analysis skills.
- ✔ Strong presentation and CRM skills.
- ✔ Strong written and verbal communication skills.
- ✔ Coachable and dedicated, with strong team-building and leadership skills.
- ✔ Technology: Microsoft Office 2007 and 2010 (Word, Excel, PowerPoint); internet savvy.

Professional Skills

Prospecting & Closing	Negotiation	Package Development
Exceeding Quotas	Cold Calling	Account Retention
Consultative Sales	Relationship Building	Networking
Package Pricing	Competitive Analysis	Lead Generation
Market Development	Industry Research	
Client Acquisition	Promotions	

Professional Experience

TicketHub, Kidderminster
Corporate Ticket Sales

2010–Present

Responsible for Sports Events ticket sales to companies, associations and advertising incentive agencies. Consistently exceeds sales quota, builds lasting corporate relationships, and manages new sales staff selection and training. Designated turnaround coach for struggling employees.

- Ranked #3 national Sports Events ticket sales 2014
- Ranked #5 national Sports Events ticket sales 2013
- Ranked #6 national Sports Events ticket sales 2012
- Ranked #8 national Sports Events ticket sales 2011

Education & Professional Development

Southern University
BSc Sports and Entertainment Management

2010

Superior References Available

Sales and marketing support

Jacqueline Alois

1 Any Street, Anytown AA1 1AA
00000 000000
jacqueline@alois.net

Database Management ◆ Marketing Communications ◆ E-mail Template Design

Performance Profile

Sales and Marketing Support Professional with more than 14 years' experience in time-sensitive, fast-paced environments. Highly developed oral and written communication skills, multitasking, attention to detail, and perseverance to completion. Keen insight into clients' perspectives, goals and target audiences. Proficient with various software programs including Word, Excel, Access and Goldmine.

Professional Competencies

- Database administration
- Market research
- Sales lead qualification
- Proactive problem solving
- Promotional copywriting

- Internal/external customer service
- Computer and procedural training
- Project coordination
- Relationship building
- New account development

Professional Employment History

ABC COMMUNICATIONS LTD, CROYDON   2007–PRESENT
Database Marketing Coordinator for trade-show design firm
- Assist the MD, Creative Director, and sales force of seven in developing targeted messages to promote company's services (trade-show display design and client training seminars). Contribute ideas in brainstorming sessions and translate concepts into persuasive written materials (brochures, web pages and e-mail templates).
- Generate leads through extensive phone contact, which has facilitated the closing of numerous sales by determining clients' interests and addressing their specific needs or concerns.
- Enter and update all pertinent information for up to 500 clients and prospects on Goldmine system; create profiles and periodically send electronically distributed promotional pieces to keep company in the forefront for future business.
- Initially train new sales consultants on data mining to their best advantage as well as empower them for success in prospecting and cold calling. Organize sales assignments to avoid duplication of efforts.
- Coordinate all pre- and post-sale details with various departments.
- Demonstrated versatility and talent in several areas.

XYZ LTD, ORPINGTON   2005–2007
Sales Representative for graphic arts supply company
- Performed duties of sales liaison, assistant purchasing agent, and customer service representative.
- Streamlined department by automating the quote process and systematizing sales literature.

Education

County College, Diploma, Marketing Communications, 2005
Shelton Institute, Applied Writing and Database Administration courses, 2006

Brand/product manager

Jackie Byrd

1 Any Street, Anytown AA1 1AA
Home Phone Mobile Phone E-mail Address

BRAND/PRODUCT MANAGEMENT, GAMING INDUSTRY

You want: Brand/Product Manager, GameKids.com
Looking for experienced Brand Manager to direct product lines, develop strategic marketing promotions, product research & positioning, and cross-departmental interfacing. Minimum three years' management/marketing experience, with game marketing experience.

I deliver:

Performance Profile

Over 15 years' experience in sales and marketing leadership positions. Demonstrate strong commitment to maintaining highest level of product quality while driving revenue growth through multiple marketing and promotional strategies. Able to identify and convey Unique Selling Proposition (USP) to customers/business partners. Skilled in all core marketing and business development disciplines, with particular strength in product marketing. Hold deep passion and interest in gaining market share for gaming company.

Gaming Highlights

- Lifelong participant in the field of gaming, worked for gaming pioneer Chaosium.
- Worked for renowned game designers Sandy Petersen and Greg Stafford.
- All editing, mapping, layouts and writing for SuperWorld and Companion of SuperWorld.
- Supplemental modules for Cthulha.
- Gaming store owner, sold business that remains profitable two decades later.

Professional Skills

Product Research & Analysis	Strategic Promotional	Editing, Mapping, Layouts,
Competitive Positioning	Campaigns	Writing
Presentations, Negotiations	Collateral Material	Vendor Relations
& Closing	Development	Recruitment, Selection
Product Line Management	Strategic Game Marketing	Performance Review
Team Building & Leadership	Point-of-Sale Displays	Advertising Performance
Customer Relationship	Prospecting & Lead	Metrics
Building	Generation	Profile Assessments
		Presentation Skills

Professional Experience

Marketing Manager (2005–Present)

ABC BUSINESS DEVELOPMENT, Cambridge

In charge of developing company marketing plan, managing vendor relationships, hiring/training sales staff, evaluating team performance, and completing sales in hands-on account executive role. Contract with companies to develop market presence for telecommunications products and services, working with broad range of clients that includes retailers, software development firms and property developers.

- Redeveloped website and all marketing materials for key client XYZ Homes. Tracked results of advertising placements, created sales/marketing plan and secured exposure in *The Business Journal*.

Continued

Sales and marketing

Jackie Byrd Page 2

- *Results: Increased sales and established pre-selling pattern affecting every community.*
- Improved management of product line (profile assessments) by writing brochure for customization to five industries, including healthcare and non-profit organizations.

Account Executive (2005–2006)

DEF COMMUNICATIONS, Cambridge

Oversaw all aspects of sales in both employment positions, with focus on medium-sized companies. Scope of responsibility included making cold calls, conducting fact-finding research, delivering presentations, securing new accounts and creating referral partner network.

- Introduced sales and marketing strategies that contributed to product improvement and revenue growth in heavily competitive market.

Account Executive (2001–2005)

GHI Ltd, Norwich

Directed sales and marketing initiatives for business clients. Managed all phases of sales cycle, progressing to consultative selling approach as company increased lines to accommodate customers.

- Played key role in driving company from start-up to New Dealer of the Year in 1998. Assisted in developing company from one to multiple carriers.

Broker (1999–2001)

JKL, Norwich

Represented supplemental insurance programmes to companies and their employees.

- Created 'package' approach to sell multiple insurance lines simultaneously, resulting in 228% revenue increase and average sales growth from £360 to £820 annual premium.
- Earned formal recognition as Number One Producer for largest supplemental insurance company worldwide; received commendations for opening most new groups in UK in 1995.

Senior Partner (1990–1998)

RESOURCE MANAGEMENT CENTRE, Norwich

Initially hired as Sales Manager and earned subsequent promotions to GM and Senior Partner, respectively. Delivered consulting and training seminars in all areas of business management, including finance and accounting, business growth, personnel law and management, taxes and reporting, and personal development.

- Spearheaded company's expansion into computer market to offer high-end accounting systems, wide area networks, centralized processing solutions, and ISDN to customers.

Professional Training Courses:

Nextel Basic, Advanced, and Consultative Selling Training – Certified PSI Disk Cashing Controllers – Certified PC Multi-User Operating System – Certified Novell Netware – License in Insurance for Health, Life and Disability – Telecommunications Training Courses: PBX Trunks, Digital Switched Service, Digital Data Service, ISDN, Frame Relay Service, Self-Healing Network Service, DS1 (includes SHARP/SHARP+), DS3, Analog Private Line

Computer Skills: Skilled in Excel, Word, PowerPoint; experienced with sales programs Onyx, Gold Mine, & ACT
Community Involvement: Work with at-risk youths in running games on late Friday and Saturday nights, providing fun, appealing alternative to prohibited activities.

Certified Facilitator; run demos of CreepyFreaks (under company's authorization) and promote Pirates of the Spanish Main, both products of the GameKid Corporation

Sales manager/office manager

Catherine M Sipowicz

1 Any Street, Anytown AX0 0AA • 020 8123 4567 • jcsipowicz@email.com

SALES MANAGER – OFFICE MANAGER

Performance Summary

Professional Sales Manager and Office Manager with over 10 years' experience in all phases of business cycle. Consistently exceeds objectives and increases bottom-line profits for employers. Quick learner and an excellent communicator with ability to perform well in a multitasking environment.

Extensive experience in the sales process from order entry through to customer service. Thrive in manufacturing and production arenas; detail-orientated individual, friendly and personable, self-starter with willingness to work well as member of a team.

Creative and skilled analyst with strong problem-solving skills offering outstanding systems expertise (conversions, upgrades and training), excellent computer and internet skills.

Professional Skills:

- Office Management
- Project Management
- Customer Service
- Customer Sales Profiles
- Inventory Control

- Credit and Collections
- Problem Identification/Solutions
- Sales Management Support
- Commission Reporting
- Sales

PROFESSIONAL EXPERIENCE

XYZ Ltd – *Jersey (2003 to Present)*
Sales Account Manager (2011–Present)

Responsible for maintaining £7 million of current business and coordinating all functions between the outside sales staff and the internal departments of the company.

- Directed and coordinated activities concerned with the sales organization including screening and evaluating new customers, performing credit authorizations, verifying client's sales history, and compiling monthly sales comparisons.
- Appointed as Sales Account Manager to handle a major supermarket chain buying £3 million of floral products, resulting in a 23% sales increase in the first year.
- Provided sales forecasts for holidays and special events which greatly increased the efficiency and accuracy of production schedules and purchasing requirements.
- Designed an innovative programme to evaluate effectiveness of new marketing campaigns. Hired and supervised a merchandiser to track the programme on a weekly basis.
- Developed an automated monthly sales comparison analysis with the IT department reducing the report generation time from eight hours to one hour.

Continued

Sales and marketing

CATHERINE M SIPOWICZ Page 2 of 2

Office Manager (2006–2011)

Managed a multitude of tasks contributing to the daily operations of XYZ Ltd. Responsible for hiring, training, motivation and supervision of the telemarketing staff.

- Developed and implemented various systems for optimizing production resources and increasing efficiency. Designed Excel spreadsheets and standardized forms for use by all departments.
- Enhanced interdepartmental communications resulting in reduced production and billing errors.

Administrative Assistant (2003–2006)

Coordinated communications between sales and production. Performed credit checks, collections, and resolved price discrepancies. Responsible for inventory, price lists and customer lists.

- Project Manager for developing, implementing and maintaining an inventory control system that used coding to correlate new orders with production scheduling.

EDUCATION

BA in Political Science, City University, 2003

Sales manager

MAX STERN

1 Any Street • Anytown AA1 1AA • Mobile: 5555555 5555 • *maxstern234@anyserver.co.uk*

NATIONAL SALES MANAGER / ACCOUNT MANAGER
Internet....High-Tech....Software Industries

Performance Summary

Award-winning and dedicated sales manager with over a decade of success generating revenue and securing high-profile clients for leading companies, such as ABC Technologies and XYZ Communications, with excellent levels of retention. Recipient of numerous prestigious sales awards for consistently exceeding sales goals and forecasts, and creating win–win client solutions. Use a consultative approach to assess client needs and provide solutions that meet the client's goals.

Professional Skills

✣ New Business Development	✣ High-Expectation Client Relations	✣ Relationship Management
✣ Key Account Management	✣ Consultation and Solution Sales	✣ Contract Negotiations
✣ Strategic Alliance/Partners	✣ Sales Training & Team Leadership	✣ Vertical Channel Sales

Proficient in all sales cycle phases from lead generation and presentation to negotiation, closing and follow-up. Excel in training and mentoring teams to outperform the competition. Possess a high level of discipline, professional integrity, a passion for achieving organizational success and a desire to always play on a winning team.

PROFESSIONAL EXPERIENCE

DEF TECHNOLOGIES – Sterling   10/2010–Present
DEF Technologies provides trusted, neutral and essential addressing, interoperability, infrastructure and other clearinghouse services for communication service providers and enterprises worldwide.

National Sales Manager   3/2011–Present
Promoted from Account Executive to National Sales Manager in six months due to the consistent attainment of breakthrough sales results. Oversee national sales programmes and supervise 15 sales representatives. Recruit, interview, hire and train staff and evaluate performance for regional placements. Conduct quarterly sales meetings, develop goals and coordinate all local, regional and national training efforts.

- **Sales Performance**. Achieved **100% of sales quota despite a 60% reduction in staff.**
- **Awards & Recognition. Received 2005 Star Award, DEF's most prestigious distinction,** which rewards superior performance and strong commitment to operational excellence. Nominees undergo a rigorous nomination and selection process, and awards are granted to the **'top-talent' (less than 5%)** of the company.
- **People Leadership.** Empowered staff and built a focused and loyal national sales team that consistently generated higher-than-budget sales.
- **New Business Development.** Key player in cultivating relationships with national clients including ABC Systems, DEF Ltd, and GHI Media. Personally conducted assessment interviews with prospective clients to identify needs and formulate appropriate solutions.

Account Executive   10/2010–3/2011

- **Vertical Sales Campaign Management.** Through rigorous cold-calling and prospecting, launched company into the online advertising vertical, setting the stage for colleagues to follow. As a result, an impressive 65% of all online advertising currently comes through DEF, and recurring monthly revenue exceeds £150,000.

XYZJOBS.COM – Guildford
XYZJobs has revolutionized the way people manage their careers and the way companies hire talent, and puts job seekers in control of their careers, making it easier for employers and staffing firms to find qualified candidates.

Continued

Sales and marketing

MAX STERN • page 2

Southeast Account Executive 6/2009–9/2010

Aggressively sold XYZ business solutions including database, web job hosting, and job posting packages within the Central and Southeast regions. Applied a solutions selling methodology to the sales cycle, promptly completing proposals and sales activities, closing sales opportunities quickly and efficiently, and completing necessary paperwork steps to successfully set projects in motion.

- Revenue Generation. Consistently exceeded monthly revenue target of £15,000. Cold-called and closed new business with major retail clients including Sainsbury's and Asda.

JKL SOLUTIONS – Hendon

JKL is a trusted source for the complete Oracle suite of data-centric solutions, including database, Oracle Fusion Middleware, and packaged applications.

Account Executive 1/2009–6/2009

Managed Sales for Oracle's 9iAS and Collaboration Suite, and developed new territory in district, including several key accounts such as MNO and Mediastore. Managed a staff of 25 sales representatives.

- **Marketing.** Generated £1 million in new business development by creating local and national marketing programmes to generate buzz around Symantec products.
- **Campaign Management.** Prospected for new business through various marketing campaigns, including telemarketing, direct mail, targeted seminars, and partnerships with leading software firms.
- **New Business Development.** First to sell the hosted Collaboration Suite product to the Armed Forces Retirement Home, and secured the RSA relationship at JKL.
- **Trade Show Participation.** Networked extensively throughout the business community at industry trade shows, obtaining over 7,000 leads on average per event.
- **Awards and Recognition.** Generated the highest volume of accounts company-wide and was recognized with the JKL's prestigious 'Sales Leader Award'.
- **Partner Development.** Liaised with JKL staff and Oracle team to successfully manage the Symantec relationship.

ABC TECHNOLOGIES – Swindon

ABC Technologies is a leading media and entertainment company, whose businesses include interactive services, cable systems, filmed entertainment, television networks, and publishing.

National Account Sales Manager 3/2003–10/2008

Sold print and online advertising across all ABC properties (159 websites and publications) including DEF Times, Computer Journal, XYZ News and Media News. Interfaced directly with board-level executives, negotiated high-level contracts and coordinated implementation. Managed accounts in three major verticals (retail, travel and tourism, and online gaming) and orchestrated post-sale professional services and resources. Recognized market needs and provided clients with new solutions, ultimately expanding their customer base.

- **Revenue Generation.** Booked £2.3 million in new revenue from a previously dormant category, exceeding £1.8 million revenue quota within eight months.
- **New Business Development.** Created £1.5 million in new business opportunities through presentations, cold-calling and successful final negotiations.
- **Training Course Development.** Designed and implemented a live prospecting training class focused on topics such as using unique online tools (ad relevance and niche online sites, etc) and capturing contact information from prospects and leads.
- **Customer Relations and Retention.** Forged strong partnerships with both clients and ad agencies, and increased advertisers' retention rates by encouraging collaboration between both groups.
- **Sales Presentations.** Completed intensive national sales and presentation training, and ranked 1 (out of 30) and 7 in the country in both 2005 and 2006, based on number of deals closed.

EDUCATION & TRAINING

Advanced Leadership Programme
DEF Technologies • Sterling • 2013
MBA
City University • London

Senior sales and marketing manager

JAMES SHARPE
123 Any Street • Anytown AT1 0BB
Tel: 020 8123 4567
james@anyaddress.co.uk
Page 1 of 2
SALES AND MARKETING

PERFORMANCE PROFILE

Top-producing sales and marketing professional with nine years of management experience in world-class organizations. Consistently successful developing new markets, penetrating new territories, identifying and capturing new business, and managing large-scale events for blue-chip companies worldwide. Goal-driven manager committed to developing outcomes mutually benefiting company and client. Excellent qualifications in building corporate relationships with industry leaders.

CORE COMPETENCIES

- New Account Development
- Key Account Management
- Client Needs Assessment
- Contract Negotiations
- Competitive/Strategic Planning

- Large Scale Meeting/Event Planning
- Catering Planning/Management
- Co-Marketing Partnerships
- Relationship Management
- Customer Service/Satisfaction

PROFESSIONAL EXPERIENCE

E&R LEISURE, Hilverside   2009 to Present
Senior Sales Manager
Joined company to lead market entry/penetration initiatives throughout the Northeast region of the UK for this privately held exclusive leisure complex with 800 suites, a 60,000 square foot conference centre, and a full range of guest amenities. Managed business growth among blue-chip corporate accounts and national association accounts.

- Developed and maintained relationships with corporate meeting planners of major accounts including FCS, TS&H, Chanteclere, Niki Portman, S&G, Kentland, Glentrich and others to develop custom-tailored business meeting packages.
- Worked closely with corporate planners throughout all phases of strategic and tactical planning, coordination, and execution of major events to ensure superior service and guest relations.
- Captured national association accounts including National Cancer Society, Heart Association, The Law Society and Chartered Institute of Psychologists.
- Sold and orchestrated multiyear bookings to numerous associations and corporate accounts.

Achievements
- Built territory and increased revenues from £1 million to over £7 million within first year.
- Achieved 157% of annual booking goals (2,500 room nights per month).

ALDEBURGH HOUSE, Aldeburg   2006 to 2009
Catering Sales Manager
Challenged to develop new markets and products for visiting multicultural groups.
- Identified target market, initiated contact with prospects, developed proposals, and forged major account relationships.
- Worked closely with corporate planners at DeLa Mere, FTA, Foresham, Newsline and others to create unique and extravagant parties and events ranging up to £2 million per event.
- Sold, planned and coordinated catered group events for corporate accounts and private parties ranging from 2 to 19,000 guests.
- Developed comprehensive strategic and tactical plans for every phase of event including logistics, transportation, food and beverage, entertainment and gifts to create a memorable occasion.

Continued

Sales and marketing

James Sharpe 020 8123 4567   page 2 of 2

- Oversaw scheduled events and served as troubleshooter and liaison between staff, event managers and corporate clients to resolve issues and ensure guest satisfaction and loyalty.

- Compiled planning, tracking and forecasting reports using proprietary computer system.

Achievements

- Achieved 130% of Catering Sales and Service Team Goals, 2009.

- Consistently exceeded individual annual sales goals.

INTERNATIONAL HOTEL, Southgate   1998 to 2006
Fast-track promotions through a series of increasingly responsible positions based on business growth and improved sales revenue for this high-volume airport property.
Sales Manager-North (2005 to 2006)
Sales Manager-South (2002 to 2005)
Associate Director of Catering (1998 to 2002)
Catering Manager (1998)

- Created innovative guest packages for corporate accounts locally and nationally for this first-rate property with 300 rooms, a 12,000 square foot conference centre and several guest services facilities.

- Developed corporate and professional relationships throughout the industry and coordinated with other properties to accommodate extremely large groups.

- Identified target accounts and consistently developed new business driving increased revenues.

- Promoted property through trade show and convention participation, including public-speaking engagements for large groups.

- Planned and coordinated exclusive large-scale intimate client events for the affluent.

Achievement

- Achieved 131% of sales goals throughout the Northern region, 2006.

CHINESE COURT RESTAURANT, Midvale   1996 to 1998
Catering/Sales Manager
Successfully sold Chinese-themed parties to international wholesale and corporate convention groups.

EDUCATION
Diploma in Marketing – Institute of Marketing
Diploma in Multinational Business Operations – Institute of Marketing
Diploma, Certificat de Langue Française, Institut Catholique De Paris, 1996 (Study Abroad Programme)

PROFESSIONAL DEVELOPMENT
Sales Training:
International Hotel, BEST programmes (Building Effective Sales Techniques), Top Achiever Sales, Travel Management Companies, Best Practices

Designation
Certified Meeting Professional (CMP)

Affiliations
Meeting Planners International, Member
Society of Association Executives, Member

International sales/marketing manager

MEGHAN M ENGLAND

1 Any Street • Anytown AA1 1AA • 55555 555555 • email@email.com

INTERNATIONAL SALES/MARKETING MANAGER
Strategic Planning/Staff Supervision & Training/Business Development

PERFORMANCE PROFILE
Innovative marketing professional with key domestic and international experience penetrating new markets, expanding existing accounts and boosting profits. Fluent English and Spanish. Results-orientated and visionary leader with proven success in new market identification, regional advertising, branding and competitor analysis. Skilled in staff supervision and training, client relations and strategic planning. Polished communication, presentation, negotiation and problem-solving skills. Thrive in intensely competitive, dynamic environment.

CORE COMPETENCIES
- Strategic Business Planning
- Budget Management
- Business Development/Planning
- Staff Training & Development
- Marketing Programme Design

- Market Identification
- Team Building & Leadership
- Account Relationship Management
- International Client Relations
- Key Networking Skills

PROFESSIONAL EXPERIENCE

AMERICA/CHILE/LATIN AMERICA
Fast-track progression through the following key international marketing management positions:

South American Marketing Manager, XYZ LATIN AMERICA – London (2008 to Present)
Direct and manage 360-degree company marketing programmes throughout Argentina, Bolivia, Brazil, Chile, Colombia, Mexico, Paraguay, Peru, Puerto Rico, Venezuela, Uruguay and the Caribbean Islands for the third largest software company worldwide. Oversee all aspects of Latin American regional marketing operations with broad responsibility for strategic planning and the indirect supervision of a staff of four marketing managers and various partner PR/advertising agencies.

Initiate, develop and nurture new leads to generate additional sales revenues; collaborate with sales representatives to turn over leads and establish key relationships. Accomplish marketing goals by launching comprehensive marketing, advertising and branding plans. Manage PR marketing functions through press releases, executive interviews, press conferences, professional networking and by creating an educational focus to allow greater company exposure. Ensure top-level customer satisfaction; collaborate with various outside agencies to administer and analyse customer surveys.

Develop and manage a £3 million marketing budget encompassing strategic industries such as banks, the public sector and utility companies, as well as strategic solutions involving customer relationship management, enterprise resource planning, supply chain management and small to mid-sized businesses. Design and implement regional advertising/branding strategies and analyse progress through brand-tracking studies and competitive reports. Pioneer and manage key relationships with high-profile industry analyst firms. Interact with an outside global advertising agency to arrange internationally syndicated relationship marketing campaigns. Serve as a company representative, liaison and central point-of-contact for providing vital information, managing market research and resolving issues at all levels.

Key Accomplishments:
- Spearheaded and manage a highly effective electronic quarterly newsletter, resulting in increased communications among Latin American employees.

Continued

MEGHAN M ENGLAND   **Page 2**

- Directed an extensive eight-month regional team project in successfully training and educating all Latin American marketing personnel on the newly implemented CRM system in the areas of budgeting/planning, campaign planning, preparation, execution/analysis, lead management and reporting.

- Developed and initiated the first regional budget with the global marketing team.

- Pioneered the centralization of advertising, resulting in greater discounts and significant savings.

- Accomplished greater recognition for the company including the first, and many additional publications of the company president in regional magazine articles.

Marketing Manager, XYZ CHILE – Santiago de Chile (2006 to 2008)

Spearheaded, built and launched the first marketing department for the company's Chilean subsidiary, with full responsibility for hiring, training, scheduling, supervising, mentoring and evaluating marketing coordinator and marketing analyst staff members. Managed an £800,000 Enterprise Resource Planning marketing budget. Interacted directly with the sales team to implement marketing strategies and meet goals. Managed extensive market research and analysis functions by collaborating with a local agency to conduct focus group interviews in evaluating both company and competitor solutions. Involved in all aspects of production, public relations, sales, relationship building and customer service.

Key Accomplishments:

- Created and implemented a lead-generation programme, resulting in an increased amount of qualified leads for Account Executives and improved revenues due to shorter sales cycle.

- Built solid PR operations by developing and managing high-impact press strategies; concurrently continued to initiate key media relationships, conduct press conferences and executive interviews.

South American Coordinator, XYZ LATIN AMERICA – London (2003 to 2006)

Managed the international roll-out and training for the company's Sales and Marketing Information System. Travelled extensively to various international locations to oversee all implementation and training functions. Concentrated on providing a full range of support to Finance and Marketing Directors.

Spanish Teacher, ABC CHEMICALS LTD – Luton (2003)
Taught Spanish to top-level executives.

Education & Credentials

BA in International Studies
CITY UNIVERSITY (2002)

Language Studies
Seville/Segovia, Spain (2002)

Comprehensive Spanish Language Studies
Adelaide, Australia (2001)

Additional Professional Training in Business and Communications

Private Pilot Licence with instrument and commercial ratings

– Excellent Professional References Available on Request –

Sales executive

MARY ANN BURROWS
1 Any Street
Anytown AA1 1AA
55555 555555

Outside Sales/Account Manager/Customer Service

PERFORMANCE PROFILE

Energetic and goal-focused sales professional with solid qualifications in large account management and customer relationship building/maintenance. Proven ability to develop new business and increase sales within established accounts and mature territories. Self-confident and poised in interactions across all business hierarchies; a persuasive communicator and assertive negotiator with strong deal-closing abilities. Excellent time-management skills; computer-literate.

CORE SALES SKILLS

- Sales Growth / Account Development
- Commercial Account Management
- Prospecting & Business Development

- Customer Liaison & Service
- Consultative Sales / Needs Assessment
- Territory Management & Growth

PROFESSIONAL EXPERIENCE

XYZ Ltd, Wolverhampton   2008–Present
SALES EXECUTIVE (2010–Present)
Promoted and challenged to revitalize a large territory plagued by poor performance. Manage, service and build existing accounts; develop new business, establishing both regional and national accounts. Serve as key liaison for all customers and work as the only sales representative in the company. Produce monthly reports for major national accounts.

Selected Results

- Reversed a history of stagnant sales; delivered consistent growth and built territory sales 22%, to £4.75 million annually, in less than two years.
- Surpassed quota by a minimum of 20% for 14 consecutive months.
- Personally deliver 95% of all sales generated for the company's main site.
- Prospected aggressively and presented products to key decision makers during cold calls; opened more than 60 new commercial accounts.
- Improved account service and applied consultative sales techniques; grew sales in every established account a minimum of 15%.

MANAGER, Hartlepool Store (2008–2010)

MANAGER TRAINEE, Wolverhampton Store (2008)
Initially recruited as a management trainee and rapidly advanced to management of a retail location generating £1 million annually. Supervised and trained 12 employees. Budgeted and produced advertising, oversaw bookkeeping, and set/managed sales projections and growth objectives.

EDUCATION AND CREDENTIALS
BA BUSINESS MANAGEMENT, 2008
Wilmington College, Newcastle

Additional Training
Building Sales Relationships, 2011
Problem Solving Skills, 2011

Professional & Community Associations
Member, Chamber of Commerce, 2009–Present
Member, Country Club and Women's Golf Association, 2009–Present
Youth Sports Coach and FIFA Certified Referee, 2012–Present

Senior account executive

BOB M SMITH
bms@email.com

1 Any Street • Anytown AA1 1AA
Home: 55555 555555 • Mobile: 5555555 5555

Software and Technology Sales
✣ ✣ ✣

PERFORMANCE REVEW

Strong background in sales, sales management, new business development and account management in collaborative environments. Skilled in Enterprise Software Sales, Enterprise Content Management (ECM), Business Process Management (BPM) and Business Process Outsourcing (BPO). Increased sales by developing strong relationships with clients, staff, partners and management from initial contact through implementation. Demonstrated talents in building brand awareness through various marketing techniques.

- Exceptional ability to research, analyse and translate information to diverse audiences.
- Skilled in developing and implementing marketing techniques that drive revenue and increase sales.
- Excellent communicator with a consultative sales style, strong negotiation skills and a keen client needs assessment aptitude.
- Strong background in selling to board-level executives of large organizations.

CORE PROFICIENCIES

- Business Process Analysis
- Sales & Marketing
- Document Management
- Contract Negotiations
- Relationship Development
- Technical Sales
- Order Management
- Strategic Accounts
- Business Development

PERFORMANCE HIGHLIGHTS

- Created a niche market at ABC Solutions, providing a repeatable business process management (BPM) solution for national financial services and mortgage industries, using FileNet technologies. Project resulted in significant increase in profit margin by 35%.
- Awarded FileNet's 'Innovative Solution of the Year' at XYZ LTD for development of a repeatable Business Process Management Solution in financial services industry (2012).
- Met and exceeded quota by 103% and added four new named accounts in 2011 at XYZ Limited.
- Recognized as top Southern Region performer at ABC Ltd (1996–2001).

PROFESSIONAL EXPERIENCE

XYZ LTD – London
Senior Sales Executive / Business Development Director   **2010–Present**
Performs direct software sales for organization which specializes in 100% Open Standards-based Enterprise Document Generation. Focuses on financial services and government programmes, including lending and unemployment insurance. Negotiates contracts with new vendors and partners. Cultivates relationships from initial contact through to implementation with partners, clients, staff and management.

- Hired as first direct sales staff member for start-up operations in UK, gaining four new named accounts in first year.
- Organized 'Lunch & Learn' programme for FileNet System Consultants and integration partners to provide product education.
- Established strategic partnerships with UNISYS, BearingPoint and IBM Global Services, as well as several other system integrators.

Continued

BOB M SMITH

TECHNICAL SOLUTIONS LTD – York

DIRECTOR OF SALES & MARKETING   2006–2010

Charged with providing sales and marketing for systems integration and professional services organization. Increased brand awareness through development of comprehensive marketing materials. Analysed business needs and implemented solutions that drove business growth. Created new pricing model and product structure. Provided sales and deployment of ECM and BPM solutions nationwide. Managed relationships with FileNet, Captiva and Kofax. Implemented Business Process Analysis methodology that analysed and documented customer's current processes, and how the technology could streamline these processes. Customers included: ABC Bank, DEF Trust, GHT, JKL Ltd.

- Awarded FileNet's 'Innovative Solution of the Year' for development of Business Process Management Solution in financial services industry (2007).

- Exceeded quota by over 100% in two out of four years.

- Earned membership in FileNet's ValueNet Partner Club (2007–2009).

- Developed and implemented new change management marketing programme assisting companies with installation of complex technology.

JKL SYSTEMS LTD – York

REGIONAL SALES DIRECTOR   2002–2006

Directed and managed sales staff throughout the UK. Oversaw and managed budget of £6.2 million. Created and implemented new value-based sales process for rapid prototyping technology. Developed and installed Rapid Manufacturing Application within the Aerospace industry. Provided global sales support for ABC Motor Company, DEF Engineering and GHI Autos. Trained sales and engineering staff members. Oversaw all regional operations, including deals and resources on a national basis. Established and managed relationships with Business Process Outsourcers (BPO).

- Reduced operating costs for field operations by combining facilities.

- Facilitated professional sales training boot camps.

- Discovered highly complex application, resulting in creation of InVisiLine braces.

- Transformed 3D Solutions sales force from product focus to solutions-orientated focus, through process analysis, training and ROI models.

- Grew annual sales 15% by focusing sales teams on solution sales.

ABC Ltd – York

DISTRICT MANAGER/SENIOR ACCOUNT EXECUTIVE   1995–2002

Promoted from Senior Account Executive in 2000. Provided direction and management to 14 staff members, charged with providing large enterprise document management and BPM solutions. Gained new channel partners with application providers and consulting vendors. Charged with selling £MM solutions to board-level executives at large organizations, including ABC Aircraft Engines, Medical Mutual, DEF Tyre and Rubber, GHI Products, JKL Holdings, MNO Health Systems, PQR Bank and STU Bank.

- Increased indirect sales channels by 100%.

- Awarded 'Top Performer' for exceeding quota by 125%, 1996–2001.

- Received 'Eastern Region Top Producer', 1998.

EDUCATION

BA Business Administration • City University

Internet sales

JANE SWIFT

01234 567890   1 Any Street, Anytown, AX0 0AA   jswift@email.com

Internet Sales

Performance Summary

Top-producing Internet Sales Professional with history of delivering business solutions that align client objectives with available technical resources. Strong technical background and in-depth product knowledge help identify customer needs, allay concerns, and become trusted customer resource and advisor. Proven ability to resolve complex problems, open new markets and close multimillion-pound sales.

- Solid understanding of key account management, with a highly accessible service orientation and rigorous follow-up.
- High energy, action oriented, and ready for challenges; seizes and acts upon opportunities that others often overlook.
- Expert in building and maintaining relationships with key corporate decision makers and establishing large-volume, high-profit accounts with excellent retention/renewal rates.
- Strong business and analytical acumen, adept at using data to uncover opportunities.

Professional Competencies

✔ Consultative Sales	✔ Account Development & Retention	✔ Problem Resolution
✔ Active Listening	✔ Presentation	✔ Negotiation
✔ Closing	✔ Project Management	✔ Financial Analysis/ROI
✔ Customer Service	✔ Collaboration	✔ Entrepreneurial
✔ Prioritizing	✔ Independent Action for Opportunities	✔ Brainstorming Ideas

Performance Highlights

- Retained £250K annual account and renewed for additional two years (client had been planning to change providers) by leveraging resources and applications.
- Captured £240K in new sales and monthly revenue increase of £20K in usage fees by pinpointing lead management opportunity for outside field sales.
- Grew annual sales from £240K to £720K among group of related companies by securing introductions and building/nurturing division manager relationships.
- Secured more than £500K in revenue and opened new market by establishing presence in reseller market.
- Increased adoption rate of online bill pay by 44%, generating additional £3 million in sales in first six months of promotion.

Professional Experience

XYZ, Watford   2012–Present

Wireless Sales Executive

New account generation, plus retention and growth for large enterprise customers as well as mid-market businesses and organizations. Billed revenues in excess of £3 million.

- Captured £1.65 million in new sales and increased usage fee revenues £20K per month with data analysis.
- Retained dissatisfied client and increased annual revenue from £250K to £350K.
- Saved departing client, raised revenue from £200K to £450K and increased commitment from two to three years.

Continued

ABC, Watford   2007–201₂
Sales Associate
Sold mapping software to major companies. Accounts included Microsoft, Cisco, MetroQuest, TicketHub an
others.

- Captured over £30 million in annual revenue by successfully managing development of CompuServe and Netscape e-mail applications.
- Routinely exceeded quotas and increased sales from £650K to £1.7 million over five years.
- Delivered approximately £3 million in revenue by migrating thousands of e-mail users onto mail platform over one-year period.
- Closed reseller deal, generating more than £600K in sales.

Application Sales Project Management
Sold CompuServe and Netscape e-mail applications, generating over £90 million in annual revenue.

- Successfully developed comprehensive project plans that included internal and external dependencies, schedules, risk analysis and risk management plans.
- Proactively systemized and simplified chaotic data and vague requirements, which kept teams and projects productively focused.
- Meticulously tracked and monitored projects, communicating status to senior management, project teams and key stakeholders.
- Negotiated £10 million in annual agreements by selling unused network bandwidth.
- Increased adoption rate of online bill pay by 54%, generating additional £3 million in sales in first six months.

Professional Achievements

- Honoured with 'Excellence to Sell' award for overall sales attainment in 2010, competing with 300 other sales executives
- Sales Achievement Excellence Award, four consecutive years
- National Accounts Sales Achievement Award from Engineering Team

Education

BA, Social Science, Bristol University

Superior references available

Sales and marketing director

Kevin J Bordon

SALES AND MARKETING

1 Any Street
Anytown, Anycounty AX0 0AA
020 8123 4567
E-mail: kevBordon@email.com

Professional Profile

Sales and account management background, encompassing client relations and new business development; delivered presentations before FTSE 100 companies, manufacturers and distributors.

Planned and conducted networking, canvassing, lead generation and direct marketing campaigns, as well as trade show presentations; recruited, trained and supervised employees; developed rapport with senior management, department heads, vendors, clients and sales personnel.

Professional Skills

- National Sales Management
- Corporate Advertising
- Supervision of Employees
- Training and Motivation
- New Account/Business Development
- Contract Management

- Marketing Programmes
- Team and Relationship Building
- Performance Improvement
- Representative Liaison
- Purchasing/Inventory Control
- Vendor Relations

Professional Experience

DX TUBE CORPORATION, Clifton   **2008–Present**
Director of Sales & Marketing

DX is the producer of welded pipe and welded tubing. Introduced a large customer base from the stainless steel industry to contract and continue as DX's clients in the welded pipe and tubing area of the business.

- Hired eight sales representatives to sell DX's products in different regions in the country.
- Developed new pricing strategies including rebates, freight considerations for inventory, business, and direct business to attract new accounts for long-term relationships.
- Personally covered local sales territories including Gloucester, Wiltshire and North Devon.
- Ensured trust and service for new customers.
- Set up a sales group for sales training.
- Developed a new brochure and detailed chart for field sales presentations to enhance our company's communications.
- Created programmes for advertisements in various trade magazines and promotional vehicles that were successful in bringing in new enquiries regarding our products and ultimately new customers.
- Arranged outings for social events and served as liaison that designed new markets for growth opportunities.
- Defined markets and targeted the right customer populations for the sales force.

Continued

Kevin J Bordon | **Page 2 of 2**

Professional Experience (continued)

AB TUBE, LTD, North Branch 1993–2008

Sales Director 2001–2007
Sales Manager 1993–2001

Assumed full responsibility for all sales and marketing functions for this steel company. Played a key role in the organization's growth from £12 million to over £40 million in annual revenues, initiating and managing a series of business development strategies to increase activity from new and existing accounts.

Spearheaded programmes to target previously untapped markets, which included a campaign geared towards the beverage industry that produced £8 million in annual sales.

- Secured lucrative agreements with such industry giants as CDE Ltd and FG Oil, strengthening the company's overall competitive position.

- Built productive relationships with 10 independent representative agencies, instituting incentives, which heightened their efforts to promote the company's lines.

- Improved the performance of sales employees through effective training and motivation generating significant new business.

- Enhanced the company's image and visibility by launching aggressive advertising and marketing campaigns, which included ads in trade magazines, brochures and promotional items.

- Devised methods to facilitate more open communication between sales representatives and other departments in the company, including production, quality control and finance.

TUBE SALES, Canterbury 1987–1993

Purchasing & Inventory Control Coordinator

- Directed purchasing and inventory control activities for over £20 million of stainless steel tubing.

- Established a centralized purchasing system that generated substantial savings through more advantageous rates.

Education

City College, London
BA in Business

Affiliations

City Recreation Centre, Coach
Forest Gate Country Club Member

Additional Keywords: stainless steel industry, welded pipe, welded tubing, steel industry, management, business development, sales, manufacturing sales, vendor negotiations, advertising, marketing, manufacturing account management, sales management.

Sales and marketing

International marketing director

John Smith

1 Any Street   Anytown, AX0 0AA   01234 567890   jsmith@email.com

International Marketing
Market & Product Strategist/Business Developer/Negotiator

Performance Profile/Performance Summary
20+ year track record driving revenue growth and market share. 'C' level relationship builder. Delivers strong and sustainable revenue gains. Increases business unit performance and negotiates the deals that guarantee success.

Contracts with:

- Xerox
- EDS
- Visa
- Bank of America
- Microsoft
- Oracle
- Nortel
- Lockheed Martin
- Boeing
- Nordstrom
- Fuji
- Morgan Stanley
- Gap
- Sun
- AMD
- Apple

Core Competencies

- Strategic Planning
- Product Management
- Market/Product Strategies
- Global Practices
- Contract Negotiations
- Global Account Management
- CRM
- Sales Management
- Process Re-engineering
- Reseller Channels
- Pricing Models
- Global Account Development
- P&L Responsibility
- Packaging
- Product Re-engineering
- Budgets
- Market Strategy
- Acquisition Management
- National Accounts
- Hands-on Sales
- Business Unit Re-engineering
- A/R & Bad Debt
- Business Development
- Lost Account Recovery
- Contracts
- Program Development
- International Markets
- Recruitment & Selection

Accomplishments

- Conceived and coordinated the global account management process; grew market share from 7% to 100% and revenue from £330,000 to £6 million per month. First pre-paid international contract, allowed company to accelerate into international markets achieving £1+ billion in revenues.

- Business unit turnaround, successfully recovering 60% of lost accounts plus new business to increase revenues by £5+ million in the first 12 months.

- Revitalized dying product with International Reseller Channel, extended product life by two years.

- Designed and implemented National Accounts Programme. Increased revenue from £12 million to £27 million per month.

- Led the company's new technologies market development (VPN, Web Hosting), securing sales in excess of £15 million within six months.

Continued

John Smith   01234 567890   jsmith@email.com   **Page 2**

Professional Experience

Software Company, Guildford   2011–Present
CEO, Business Development and Alliances

- Recruited to drive the product development process and expand market reach through the implementation of an international reseller channel and strategic business alliances.
- Negotiated contracts with Fuji Xerox, Xerox, Accenture and Lockheed Martin capturing £10 million in potential revenue.
- Managed the renegotiation of two existing alliances that will net the company at least £2 million over the next 12 months.
- Established a new technology relationship with Open Text, extending the company's reach in the Life Sciences market.

International Telecom, Nottingham   2002–2009
Regional Director National Accounts

Full P&L, £20 million operational budget, 250+ personnel, mandate to build a national account programme during a 15-company acquisition period; consistently exceeded all business objectives.

- Managed the best corporate A/R and bad debt levels, achieved outstanding customer retention level of 94%, and managed corporation's lowest employee turnover rate of 10%.
- Developed and implemented a National Account Programme, expanding revenues within the first year from £180 million to £260 million.
- Averaged a 21% annual internal revenue growth and was selected to the President's Club from 2003 through 2008.

ABC Telecom, Esher   2000–2002
Executive Director – Global Accounts

Promoted to manage 139 sales and support staff (five direct reports) and to oversee 35 national accounts.

- Managed and negotiated £750 million in contracts, including BofA, Visa, Microsoft, Gap, Sun, Apple, Oracle, AMD and Nordstrom. Grew market share from less than 15% to 48% in two years.
- Averaged 122% of revenue target each year.

ABC Telecom, Birmingham   1997–2000
Branch Manager

Recruited to grow and manage the account for a major bank, successfully leading a team of 39 cross-functional members.

- Grew annual sales and revenue from £3.6 million to £80 million within two years, attaining 100% market share.
- Spearheaded largest commercial sale in ABC history, valued at £400 million, successfully converting the entire network to ABC in less than six months while maintaining 100% customer satisfaction.

Continued

Sales and marketing

Sales and marketing

| John Smith | 01234 567890 | jsmith@email.com | **Page 3** |

DE&F, Salford   1991–1997
Field District Manager

Consistently exceeded quota, averaging 112%, and made President's Club every year while in sales/sales management positions.

- As staff member for DE&F Information Systems, was responsible for revenue and issues for approximately 200 accounts, achieving 109% of the revenue quota.

DE&F Headquarters, York   1988–1991
National Account Management

Negotiated and implemented the largest local government equipment contract, valued at £20 million.

- Named to Management Development Programme (top 2% of all management personnel), recognized for superior executive and leadership potential.

Education

Bachelor of Arts, York University

Career Development: Intensive 18-week DE&F account management and product training seminar.

Public accountant

John Smith, CPA

1 Any Street
Anytown, AX0 0AA

01234 567890
jsmith@email.com

Certified Public Accountant

Performance Summary

CPA with 10 years' experience in delivering tax services for: sales and use tax, premium tax, surplus lines tax, estate tax and income tax on behalf of corporations, partnerships, limited liability companies, individuals and trusts. Reviews data to ensure accuracy and compliance with Generally Accepted Accounting Principles (GAAP) and Sarbanes-Oxley Act (SOX) policies and procedures. Income tax preparations and recommendations regarding tax reporting issues and compliance requirements.

Professional CPA Skills

Forecasting	GAAP	Tax Strategies
Financial Analysis	FASB	Income Tax Research
Account Reconciliation	Internal Controls	Sales and Use Tax
Accounts Payable (AP)	SOX Compliance	Accruals
Accounts Receivable (AR)	Risk Management	Strategic Planning & Execution

Professional Experience

First Choice, Manchester 2010–Present
Certified Public Accountant
Tax return preparation and review of trusts, estates, individuals, partnerships and corporations for various industries, including Tax and VAT audits. Expanded services for three existing clients and obtained six additional clients.

- Generated more than £28,000 net savings by resolving a sales tax audit that had remained unsettled for 10 years.
- Averted penalties and additional taxes imposed on a clergy tax paper by resolving complex tax audit.
- Researched GAAP procedures and utilized PPC Accounting and Auditing Guidance as a springboard to assist in the audit plan for an A-133 Single Audit to request government funding.

ABC, Manchester 2005–2010
Tax Specialist
Prepared monthly/quarterly state sales and use tax returns. Compiled and reviewed information for VAT and state income tax returns. Completed pre-audits on past sales and used tax returns for parent company and newly merged company to prepare for state audits.

- Streamlined and decreased monthly sales/use tax compliance processing time by 66%, from 15 working days down to 5 working days.

Certifications

Certified Public Accountant (ACPA UK) Certificate 2007

Professional Affiliation

Certified Public Accountants Association (CPAA) Current

Superior references available on request

Financial services and insurance

Compliance officer

John N Smith

1 Any Street
Anytown AX0 0AA

Home 01234 567890
Mobile 01234 567890
jsmith@email.com

Compliance Officer
'Keeping profits within the company, and compliance problems without.'

Performance Summary

Compliance Officer with five years' experience working for a leading financial institution. Minimizes risk by executing policies and processes that prevent fraud and loss of assets. Natural ability to analyse data, investigate transactions and document findings. Additional knowledge of Treasury AML guidelines, data protection, Securities Rules, ISO 27001 certification and suspicious activity reporting requirements.

Professional Skills

Anti-Money-Laundering Guidelines	Case Management	Code of Ethics	AML Investigations
Collection and Examination	Detection & Prevention	Document Review	Data protection
Fraud Investigations	Conduct Due Diligence	Risk Mitigation	Quality Control
Report Development	Monitoring	Policies & Procedures	High-Risk Jurisdiction
Identifying Terrorist Financing	Transactional Review	Customer Asset Movements	Information Security

Professional Experience

WXYZ, Birmingham   **2011 to Present**
A multinational financial services company.
Compliance Analyst
Ensures employee compliance with Employee Code of Ethics policies and procedures. Analyses and resolves inquiries on external trading accounts, investments, and general Code of Ethics policies and procedures. Served as subject matter expert for Markets and Banking employees, ensuring compliance with internal and external Code of Ethics.

- Reduced supervisory review time of employee brokerage accounts 35% by assisting in development and reconciliation of web-based New Hire Account Disclosure application.
- Completed training of 12 new staff members on policies and procedures in conducting reviews of Code of Ethics documentation three months ahead of schedule.
- Assists in implementation of employee annual certification process and implemented new processes for divisions, ensuring external activity requests are reported and current.
- Ensured that marketing and banking for Mid-Atlantic Division adheres to identical new employee outside activity documentation by leading coverage scope project.

Compliance Assistant   **2010–2011**
Provided administrative research and project management support for compliance officers.

Education & Affiliations

ICA Diploma in Governance, Risk & Compliance
Manchester Business School, University of Manchester   2009
National Association of Compliance Officers (DC Chapter)   Current

Excellent references available on request

Insurance adjuster/investigator

John Smith

1 Any Street
Anytown, AX0 0AA

jsmith@email.com
01234 567890

INSURANCE ADJUSTER/INVESTIGATOR

Performance Profile/Performance Summary

Logical and analytical approach to identifying and resolving situations with high potential for conflict. Organized and creative, with solid approach to comprehensive information gathering.

Police-trained investigator, superior questioning and analytical skills, experienced in negotiations, able to develop trust and open communication.

Calm under pressure. Committed to applying a trained and seasoned detective's skills to the insurance profession.

Core Competencies

- Investigative Techniques
- Courtroom Representation
- Risk Assessment
- Needs Assessment
- Witness Questioning
- Incident Documentation
- Report Writing
- Conflict Resolution
- Legal Compliance
- Negotiating
- Safety Principles
- One-to-One Training

Professional Training

- Police Science
- Reconnaissance
- Photography
- Crisis Evidence
- Investigation Techniques
- Surveillance
- Family Violence
- Public Relations
- Security
- Accident Investigation
- Child Abuse/Rape
- Communication Skills

Police Service

Avon & Somerset	2009–2014
Detective Fraud Squad	
Avon & Somerset	2006–2009
Detective Serious Crimes	
Greater Manchester	2000–2006
Officer Canine Unit	
Greater Manchester	1999–2000
Patrolman	

Education

MSc, Leadership and Organizational Change	2013
Bristol University	
BSc, Criminal Justice	1998
University of Manchester	
Information systems security coursework	2014
ABC Community College, Clevedon	

Superior references available upon request.

Financial services and insurance

Credit and collections

JAMES HOFFMAN
1 Any Street, Anytown AA1 1AA 55555 555555
PORTFOLIO MANAGEMENT

PROFESSIONAL PROFILE
Financial services professional with expertise in commercial collections, credit administration and financial analysis/structuring.

CORE FINANCIAL COMPETENCIES
- Extensive general business experience in the financial services industry, with credentials in both line and staff positions. Areas of expertise:

  - credit/portfolio administration
  - asset structuring/restructuring
  - commercial collections
  - loan documentation
  - regulatory compliance

  - financial analysis
  - risk assessment/underwriting
  - problem asset resolution/loan work-outs
  - operations/information integration
  - lender liability issues

- Background in diverse environments ranging from major regional financial holding companies to large and small community banks.
- Driving force in the establishment of a newly chartered commercial bank in the Bristol area.
- Customer-focused professional whose philosophy is to 'do it right the first time'.
- Viewed by clients as an individual who is worthy of their trust, and who holds their best interests paramount.
- Effective at building sound internal/external relationships to support client and organizational goals.
- Actively involved in leadership roles focused on community development.

EDUCATION
MBA   **Financial Administration**
North West University, 1992

BA   **Business-Economics**
City University, 1990

Executive Professional Development Programmes:
- Management School for Corporate Bankers
- National Commercial Lending Schools
- Certified Commercial Lender
- Computer School for Executives
- Leadership and Lending – Credit Executives Association

Continued

JAMES HOFFMAN   PAGE TWO

EXPERIENCE
ABC BANK, Preston   2008–Present
- Founder/Charter Director/Executive Director and Senior Lending/Compliance Officer.
- Member of three-person team that founded and organized a new commercial bank. Established nine-member Board of Directors.

Key Accomplishments:
- Led efforts in generating £17.2 million in start-up capital.
- Developed bank into a profitable organization with £120 million in assets, while maintaining strong loan quality.
- Personally managed 70% of the bank's borrowing client base and 60% of £72 million in total loans outstanding.

XYZ, Teddington   2005–2008
- Senior Director, Leasing – Managed lease origination process for a national leasing company. Products included private label programmes for five FTSE 100 companies. Trained, supervised and developed new team members.

Key Accomplishment:
- Introduced commercial bank quality underwriting procedures to correct prior portfolio deficiencies for leases averaging £75,000 per transaction.

DEF BANK, Ilminster   1999–2005
- Director and Senior Lending Officer – Responsible for bank's credit administration and management of commercial, consumer and residential lending. Chaired loan and Community Reinvestment committees.

Key Accomplishment:
- Developed and implemented new credit culture, achieving an all-time bank record of 1.12% ROA, from a negative .67%.

GHI BANK, Chichester   1993–1995
- Commercial Lending Officer – Special Loan Division – Established and managed new loan workout activity to support the bank's domestic commercial lending group.

Key Accomplishment:
- Directed reduction of internally classified credits and nonperforming assets by 70% each.

CIVIC AND PROFESSIONAL ACTIVITIES
- Board of Directors and Past Chair, Local Chamber of Commerce
- International Association of Bank Executives, Charter Member and Board of Directors
- Senior Board Member, National Banking Institute

Non-profit fundraising consultant

NORMAN BEACON
1 Any Street • Anytown AA1 1AA
Home 55555 555555 • Mobile 5555555 5555 • NormanBeacon@email.com

PUBLIC RELATIONS / FUNDRAISING CONSULTANT
Verifiable Record of Raising Significant Amounts of Money for Charitable and Community Causes

Performance Profile

Retired Executive, committed to providing expertise in communications to promote the public good. Combines distinguished career leading successful company growth with extensive background contributing to charitable causes.

- Proven strengths in the art of communication and negotiation with the ability to establish confidence and trust, resolve conflicts, build consensus and motivate parties with divergent opinions towards common goals.
- Excellent listening skills with focus on a 'win/win' philosophy.
- Extensive network of contacts.

PROFESSIONAL BACKGROUND
SPECIALITY CONFECTIONS, Leicester
Managing Director / Chief Operating Officer • 1987 to 2011

Launched and directed activities of confectionery manufacturing company from start-up through 20 years of successful operations.

- Built business from initial capital investment of £10,000 to annual revenues in excess of £40 million.
- Established and nurtured key contacts with retail and wholesale operations on local, regional and national level including major chain stores.
- Sourced vendors and contractors and directed manufacturing operations in UK and abroad.
- Negotiated with union and non-union personnel, consistently achieving a win/win outcome.
- Generated widespread goodwill for company through extensive, ongoing involvement with numerous community organizations.
- Named 'Local Business of the Year' by *Business Journal*.

EDUCATION
BA (Hons) Humanities, University of London

COMMUNITY ACTIVITIES – Partial List
Head of Fundraising – Friends of ABC Hospital
Chair of Steering Committee – ABC Youth Association
Member, Past-Officer – Anytown Chamber of Commerce
Member, Board of Directors – Neighbourhood Youth
Chair – ABC Community Association

ADDITIONAL INFORMATION
Foreign Languages – Fluent in Spanish
Computer Skills – PC and Mac Proficient on Microsoft Office Suite
Activities & Hobbies – London Marathon (annually since 2000), Golf, Tennis Event Planner

Accounting and administrative assistant

Jean English

1 Any Street, Anytown AX0 0AA
Home 020 8123 4567
E-mail: jenglish@email.com

Accounting & Administrative Assistant
Accounts Payable and Receivable/Payroll/Computer Systems Expert

Organized and responsible Administrative & Accounting Assistant with more than 12 years' experience across diverse industries. Educated and energetic professional, quick learner with exceptional computer skills and the unique ability to manage several tasks in a stressful environment. Excellent communicator seeking a challenging position using current skills and abilities, with the opportunity for professional growth.

- Accounts Payable/Receivable
- Payroll/Payroll Systems
- Employee Scheduling
- Purchasing/Lease Agreements

- Microsoft Windows, Excel, Word
- Daily Ledger/Bookkeeping
- Customer Service
- Database Development

PROFESSIONAL EXPERIENCE

Manager of Casino Administration/Analyst   2006–present
Casino Royale, Windsor
- Responsible for tracking, analysis and payment approval of all accounts payable for the department averaging £100,000 monthly.
- Created a computerized daily tracking system used by all managers and the casino President due to its flexibility and user friendliness.

Pit Manager   2004–2006
Casino Royale, Windsor
- Accepted the challenge to learn the scheduling system for staff of 1,000 during a crisis, allowing payroll to CV uninterrupted for the entire casino.

Floor Supervisor   2002–2004
Casino Royale, Windsor
- After just one year as a dealer, was promoted to Floor Supervisor managing up to 300 dealers on a shift.

Agency Office Manager   1995–2002
Gulliver's Travel, Windsor
- Managed all day-to-day operations including accounts receivable, accounts payable, bookkeeping, payroll, budgets, employee training and customer service.

Travel Agent   1990–1995
Gulliver's Travel, Windsor

EDUCATION AND PROFESSIONAL CREDENTIALS

Computer Programmer Analyst, three-year business programme including accounting
St. Clair College of Technology, 1991–1994

Microsoft Excel Advanced, *2006*   **Microsoft Access Advanced**, *2006*
Microsoft Excel Intermediate, *2005*   **Microsoft Access Intermediate**, *2005*
Microsoft Excel, *1999*   **Microsoft Word**, *1999*
St. Clair College of Technology

Bank branch management

SCOTT E BOWMAN

1 Any Street • Anytown AA1 1AA • 55555 555555 • bowman@email.com

Branch Management/Customer Service – Finance

PERFORMANCE PROFILE

Results-orientated **Finance and Banking** professional with demonstrated ability to develop corporate growth, stability and financial performance. Skilled analyst with strong organizational and communications abilities and proven leadership qualities. Comprehensive understanding of financial needs at all levels of business including evaluating, analysing and communicating financial data.

Recipient – Commerce Capital Markets Referral Award – July/August 2004

CORE BANKING COMPETENCIES

Finance & Banking	Project Management	Teller Operations
Marketing Financial Services	Customer Service Relations	Loan/Account Origination
Team Management	Sales Management	Problem Solving
e-Business Management	Communications	Continuing Education
Supervision/Leadership	Branch Management	Strategic Management

PROFESSIONAL EXPERIENCE

ABC BANK, Newport – 2004 to Present

Customer Service Representative (CSR)

Extensive knowledge of lending policies, practices, compliance and underwriting criteria. Experienced processing collateral loans, unsecured personal loans, asset-based loans and mortgage-based loans. Process all loan documentation, performing research activities as necessary.

Counsel clients in the selection of financial products in order to meet their financial planning and banking needs.

- Create and process client accounts providing excellent customer service.
- Sell bank products based on specific sales focus.
- Identify prospective clients and develop and implement presentations for clients.
- Originate and process consumer and mortgage loan applications.

Accomplishments

- Consistently met and exceeded sales quotas and standards by cross-selling and up-selling bank products and services.
- Increased branch loan production volume.
- Sold a variety of loans, creating loan worksheets, and making recommendations to lenders upon request.
- Ensured that loan policies and procedures were followed in accordance with audit guidelines.

AUTOGRAPHS LTD, Manchester – 2004 to Present

BUSINESS MANAGER/PRINCIPAL

Established and currently manage internet and mail order entertainment media business. Implemented strategic marketing programmes successfully retaining clients and achieving market position. Instituted pricing structure after conducting extensive marketing research using industry resources. Explored marketing and advertising opportunities adding value to new initiatives. Tracked data and improved business operations accordingly.

Accomplishments:

- Grew annual revenues to £30K.
- Authored inventory item descriptions and managed customer service relations.

EDUCATION/TRAINING

CITY UNIVERSITY

BA – History and Politics

ABC BANK COURSES

Finance, Supervision, Business Management, Consumer Lending, Customer Service, Loan Products, Privacy Compliance, Loan Underwriting, Foreign Assets Control, Bank Secrecy, etc.

COMPUTER SKILLS

Microsoft Office, Lotus Notes, dBase, Basic, HTML

Insurance claims specialist

Laura D Wenn　　　　　　　　　　　　　　　　　1 Any Street, Anytown AX0 0AA •
Insurance claims specialist　　　　　　　　　　020 8123 4567 • ldw@email.com

Professional Profile
Resourceful fast-track insurance claims specialist with an outstanding record of success in winning settlements and reducing claims payouts to acceptable and just amounts. Investigate, negotiate and settle complex claims.

Areas of Expertise

Administration

- organized and effective performance in high-pressure environments
- presentation development and delivery
- word processing and spreadsheet development (type 60 words per minute)

- claims investigation with meticulous documentation
- handled phones/switchboard
- skilled customer care
- Microsoft Office, internet and intranet proficiency

Insurance Claims

- commercial and personal lines liability
- property damage and bodily injury claims
- claimant, solicitor and litigation representation
- settlement and target value range setting
- medical and liability evaluation

- general liability, auto, homeowners and products liability
- injury exposure values
- complex arbitration and mediation negotiation

Highlights

- Handle caseload of up to 230 pending commercial and personal claims. Establish contact within 24 hours, maintain impeccable documentation and determine value of case based on liability/injury. Decide claims values up to £50,000. Negotiate/settle cases in mediation, arbitration or litigation.
- Delivered a £15,000 saving to XYZ by obtaining a defence verdict on a case that a judge suggested XYZ 'buy out' for £15,000. Communicated with solicitors, evaluated liability/facts and determined feasibility for trial. Case went to trial and XYZ paid nothing but legal costs.
- Saved ABC £40,000 on complex £100,000 second-degree burn claim by determining case's suitability for mediation, and meeting with judge and plaintiff's solicitors. Case was settled for a fair £60,000 without incurring major legal costs for ABC.
- Promoted onto ABC fast-track after only one year; became the youngest adjuster in company history. Track record of positive mediation, arbitration and litigation outcomes is equal to or better than that of more senior professionals.
- Possess outstanding administrative/organizational skills, superior presentation and negotiation abilities, a passion for excellence and a contagious enthusiasm. Work well in independent or team environments. Tenacious, with the stamina needed to function in high-pressure environments.

Employment

XYZ Insurance Ltd, Claims Assessor	2006 to Present
ABC Claims Services	
Claims Specialist	2005 to 2006
Loss Adjuster	2003 to 2005
Claims Assistant	2002 to 2003

Education and Professional Development

CICCIA　　　　　　ACII　　　　　　CII Insurance Foundation Certificate

Industry Courses:　Commercial General Liability, Claims Statements, Property Casualty Principles, Litigation Guidelines, Medical Terminology and Treatment, How to Handle Cases to Avoid Litigation, Accurate Reserving

Financial services and insurance

Internal auditor

1 Any Street	**Jane Smith**	012345 67890
Anytown, 0AX 0AA	**CPA, CIA**	jsmith@email.com

Internal Auditor

Performance Summary

CPA and CIA with 15 years' experience in accounting and financial services for global organization. Considered, decisive and effective financial strategist with proven success ensuring compliance with government and internal corporate regulations and policies. Maintains the overall integrity of accounting and financial systems. Skilled in coordinating with regional finance teams on statement preparation. Prepares financial statements for management and key stakeholders. Impeccable integrity and work ethic.

Professional Skills

Financial Analysis	Variance Analysis	GAAP	SAP & PeopleSoft
Financial Close	Sarbanes-Oxley	FCPA	Staff Leadership
SOX/Non-SOX	Communication	Relationship	Report Development
Controls	Financial Statements	Development	Documentation
Account	Issue Resolution	Internal Controls	Compliance
Reconciliations		Financial Reports	
Microsoft Office Suite			

———**Professional Experience** ———

ABC Ltd, Peterborough   2010 to Present
Provider of recycling and waste management services
Internal Auditor

Management support for internal audits for multiple business units. Performs comprehensive risk-based analysis of the control environment. Identifies findings for entry into audit reports. Leads closing meetings; discusses necessary action plans related to audit findings and coordinates with area management to resolve outstanding issues. Responsible for sending draft and final audit reports to management.

- Key contributor to integrated IT Audit, resulting in £165,000 reclassification of revenue.
- Identified £120,000 of unbilled revenue that current billing system was unable to accommodate.
- Performed testing controls on behalf of ABC's external auditors, resolving questions.

ABC, Cardiff   2009 to 2010
Offshore energy services
Internal Auditor

- Directed internal audits at offshore facilities. Ensured compliance with Foreign Corrupt Practices Act. Provided assistance in preparing annual risk assessment for use in development of internal audit plans. Spearheaded the development of audit programmes for unaudited processes.

Continued

Jane Smith   012345 67890 jsmith@email.com   **Page Two**

- Identified £75,000 in obsolete inventory by performing a review and analysis of the inventory accounts for tracking shipments to worldwide locations by contracted freight forwarder.
- Reduced liability to less than £2 million by facilitating tax audit conducted by government.
- Reversed £80,000 in accrued balance after review of balance sheet reconciliations and labour laws, determining contingent severance liability was incorrectly recorded.
- Saved the company £14,000 over three months by coordinating with an in-house travel agent to reduce cost for tickets frequently booked to company operating locations.

DEF Vision, Salford   2005 to 2009
Manufacturer of optical lenses
Internal Auditor

Responsible for internal audits of lens manufacturing facilities, including post-acquisition audits to assess local management compliance with commercial policies. Managed closing engagements for newly acquired businesses, meeting with local area management to outline steps necessary to ensure accurate assertions.

- Selected to assist in a special project to analyse structure of pricing, including coordination with corporate pricing staff to analyse pricing strategy.
- Identified non-compliance with standard accounting procedures, including failure to perform aged receivable analysis and record bad debt reserve and failure to record accruals for inventory purchases, SG&A expenditures, and expensing amounts that should have been established as pre-paids.

GHI, Kettering   2000 to 2005
Global Logistics company
Accounting Research Analyst

Provided maintenance of the accounting data for long-term aircraft leases, ensuring all leases were accrued on straight-line basis and amortizing gain on sale-lease aircraft. Reviewed expense line items for leased property and equipment expense, as well as long-term aircraft lease expense, including analysing account variations, obtaining explanations of business reasons for variation and reporting findings to management. Provided quarterly summary of accounting information for management review. Prepared monthly summary of underutilized leased property.

- Selected to research accounting matters for the Accounting Group through preparation of a quarterly summary of accounting-related information for management review. Report summarized new or proposed issues and draft proposals.

——Education and Professional Accreditations——

BSc, Finance, University of London   1999

Certified Public Accountant (CPA)   2004

Certified Internal Auditor (CIA)   2006

IAA Certificate in Internal Audit and Business Risk   2008

Human resources manager

Jane E Barron

1 Any Street
Anytown AX0 0AA
020 8123 4567

HUMAN RESOURCE MANAGER

Professional Profile

Dedicated, results-orientated manager with ability to build rapport at all levels... successful track record motivating employees to obtain maximum performance and increase bottom-line profits for the company... developed internal training programmes that resulted in increased productivity and office innovation... experienced supervisor, multitasker... enjoys working in a fast-paced challenging environment.

Core HR Skills

- Recruiting
- Training and Development
- Employee Relations Programme
- Office Management/Administration

- Counselling/Coaching
- Compensation
- Systems/Computerization

Experience

ABC SERVICES LTD, Preston   2005–Present
Human Resources Manager
Responsible for all aspects of human resources for this nationwide mailing list company. Initially recruited for start-up operations and increased Human Resources functions to include responsibilities in three other satellite locations: Bristol, York and Cambridge.

Director/Human Resources

- Direct all programmes regarding employee relations, health and welfare of the staff. Serve as a resource for new employees, counselling staff from executive levels to entry-level personnel. Travel to satellite locations to direct human resource functions.
- Serve as a coach and counsellor for personal and career transitions within the company. Attend various human resources seminars. Keep abreast of the latest legal and professional advances in the field.
- Direct all recruiting operations; create job descriptions and internal job postings. Initiate job offers. Monitor costs of classified advertising and employment agency usage.
- Create, implement and enforce the policies and procedures for formal disciplinary actions and dismissals.
- Execute exit interviews and assist hiring managers with human resource functions in their respective departments.
- Computerized human resources office systems to enhance productivity and online database administration.

Training and Development

- Work with each department in developing specific training programmes required for each position. Assist in preparing training materials to support departmental needs.
- Develop and implement training programmes for general business functions including basic writing, stress management and human relations.
- Prepare annual budgeting information regarding training programmes and present policy recommendations to the Director.

Continued

Human resources

Human resources

Jane E Barron Page 2 of 2

XYZ MARKET RESEARCH, Canterbury 2003–2004
Office Manager/Administrative Director

- As Office Manager, responsibilities included preparing departmental budgets and hiring and training of 10+ employees. Performed complete office purchasing for the facility.

- Implemented a customized computer database that monitored travel expenses for sales representatives and executives. The system tracked pertinent account data and human resource information. Prepared reports; interfaced with management regarding suggestions for budgeted versus actual expenses.

- Instituted new policies and procedures to guide the entire sales force regarding purchasing and administrative procedures.

- Coordinated a departmental move to a larger facility; worked closely with interior space planners and designers.

DEF SOLUTIONS, INC., Canterbury 1997–2003
Director of Human Resources

- Total responsibility for all activities relating to human resources including staff supervision, recruitment, training, personnel relations and goal setting.

- Analysed and procured appropriate insurance coverage for all areas of liability.

- Organized programmes, parties and other company-wide events to encourage 'team' environment and a positive work atmosphere.

Business Administrator

- Initiated professional business practices and management to organize all aspects of office operations.

- Researched and recommended purchase of computers and appropriate software to meet financial and clerical needs.

- Trained other staff members in computer applications.

- Assumed responsibility for all accounting activities, including A/R, A/P, G/L and P/R procedures.

- Analysed cash flow for top management review.

Prior Employment

GHI SERVICES, Edmonton 1995–1997
Group Leader
Adjustment Analyst

JKL MANAGEMENT, Painswick 1994–1995
Assistant Supervisor

Education and Training

CITY UNIVERSITY, 1990 Courses in finance and commerce
Completed numerous corporate seminars in Management and Human Resources encompassing legal issues, recruitment, compensation and administration. Member, Society of Human Resources Managers

Human resources

Human resources

Joseph D Morten

---

1 Any Street, Anytown AX0 0AA • 020 8123 4567 (H) • 020 8123 4568 (Fax)
jmorten@email.com

Human Resources/Corporate Training
Supervision – Business Management – Employee Relations – Coaching

Professional Summary

Energetic, reliable and adaptable with solid understanding of human resources, business operations and various corporate environments. Proven abilities in creatively identifying methods for improving staff productivity and organizational behaviour. Recognized for ability to incorporate innovative management techniques to a multicultural workforce.

Results-oriented with excellent communication and interpersonal skills. Accurately perform challenging tasks with precision and attention to detail. Excel at organizing and setting up new procedures, troubleshooting and taking adverse situations and making them positive.

Core Competencies

- Human Resources Management
- Operations Management
- Team Building/Leadership
- Organization and Project Management

- Training and Development
- Staffing Requirements
- Problem Resolution
- Employee Relations

Professional Experience

ABC Waste Removal, Preston (August 2010–Present)

Administrator

ABC Waste Removal is the nation's largest full-service waste removal/disposal company

- Maintained and monitored multiple databases for more than 120 pieces of equipment in the company inventory.
- Generated accurate reports of budgets, repair costs and personnel scheduling.
- Dramatically improved maintenance-shop productivity through close budget monitoring.
- Served as a key link between management and mechanics, using excellent interpersonal and communications skills. Acknowledged for improving the overall flow of information throughout the organization.
- Initiated, planned and managed the implementation of high-turnover inventory management systems and procedures. The new inventory system was credited with improving the operation of a very high volume parts operation.
- Assumed a leadership role in the company by completely reorganizing the physical inventory process to assure greater accuracy and system integrity.
- Managed the successful integration of two new parts operations, turning a possible negative situation into a very positive one.

Continued

Joseph D Morten Page 2 of 2

XYZ Video, Coalport (March 2007–August 2010)

Store Manager
Retail video rental and sales chain with over 600 outlets and 5,000 employees worldwide

- Managed all daily store operations including a staff of five employees. Responsible for recruitment, hiring, firing, training and scheduling of all staff members.

- Ability to train and motivate staff to maximize productivity, and control costs with hands-on management and close monitoring of store budgets.

- Attained a 25% increase in sales over a 12-month period, leading all 45 stores in the district. The store ranked 40th in overall sales volume of the 600 stores in the company.

- Maintained a consistent Top 20 ranking for sales.

- Used excellent leadership, team building and communication skills to develop subordinates and encourage cooperation and responsibility. Ensured compliance with company HR programmes.

- Developed and implemented creative and aggressive promotional techniques that resulted in the store consistently exceeding its sales goals.

Education
BA – Psychology, North West University

Human resources

Senior personnel manager

Human resources

Jane Swift
123 Any Street
Anytown AT1 0BB
Tel: 020 8123 4567
jane@anyaddress.co.uk
SENIOR PERSONNEL MANAGER

PROFESSIONAL PROFILE
Well-organized, disciplined, used to working calmly, effectively and efficiently under pressure. First-rate communicator, both orally and in writing. Outgoing personality with excellent interpersonal skills, enjoys working with a wide range of people. Self-motivated with the skill and determination to succeed.

CORE COMPETENCIES
Recruitment and Selection • Employee Development • Employee Relations • Employee Services • Motivation and Reward • Human Resources Planning

EXPERIENCE
Montgomery Bank plc

SENIOR PERSONNEL MANAGER   2008–Present

PERSONNEL MANAGER   2005–2008

Covered all aspects of Human Resources Management from recruitment to redundancy.
- Held a senior management position in an organization employing over 800 staff
- Managed, organized and developed a team of six personnel managers and 20 support staff to cover all aspects of personnel management
- Developed excellent communication and motivational skills encouraging staff to achieve their objectives
- Successfully implemented an appraisal scheme for Head Office staff and for personnel in 35 branches across the UK
- Recruited specialist staff for all departments
- Introduced new and rigorous absenteeism review procedures which led to a 25% annual reduction in absentee levels
- Developed excellent working relations with the Staff Association greatly facilitating successful negotiations on matters of pay and conditions
- Negotiated new working practices as new services introduced, resulting in a 15% increase in production with a staff reduction of 2% through natural wastage
- Resolved serious disciplinary matters not dealt with at line-manager level

SENIOR PERSONNEL ASSISTANT (EMPLOYEE SERVICES)   2002–2005
- Authorized all staff borrowing from the bank
- Authorized personal loans and overdrafts up to £50,000
- Stood in for the Personnel Manager in their absence
- Acted as a point of contact for staff on all account issues for managers and staff throughout the organization

Continued

Jane Swift

PAYROLL CLERK   1999–2002
- Updated and maintained employee records
- Achieved weekly and monthly payroll deadlines
- Provided payroll assistance to bank staff
- Handled all payroll procedures, including PAYE, SMP and SSP
- Used both manual and computerized systems

EDUCATION AND TRAINING
Diploma in Personnel Management
CIPD Professional Qualification Scheme – Core Management; Core Personnel and Development
CLAIT

MEMBERSHIP OF PROFESSIONAL BODIES
Licentiate Member of the Chartered Institute of Personnel and Development (FCIPD)
Currently studying to become Graduate Member

Human resources

Director of recruitment

Jane Smith
1 Any Street
Anytown, AX0 0AA

01234 567890   jsmith@email.com

Director of Recruitment

Process Reengineering/Project Implementation/Organizational Growth and Turnaround

Process development, service delivery and enhanced profits

Performance Profile/Performance Summary

Talented and forward-thinking senior recruitment leader with proven track record of success turning around company performance by distilling and managing processes, enhancing organizational structure and developing skilled self-managed teams.

The 'go-to' person for diverse organizational and process-related challenges. Confident and passionate individual with a mission to create 'best in class' recruiting departments through comprehensive use of marketing tools and cutting-edge sales practices.

Recruitment Competencies

Project Implementation	Strategic Planning	On-boarding/Referral Programmes
Process Re-engineering	Sales and Marketing	Role Competency Design
Training and Development	Recruitment Metrics	Workforce Planning
Turnaround	Financial Analysis	Strategic Planning
Disbursed Management	Sourcing Channels	Proposal Generation
CRM	Advertising	Tracking Systems
	Performance Metrics	Contracts
	EOC legislation	

Professional Experience

ABC Ltd, Dagenham   2006 to Present
Leader in Recruitment Process Outsourcing
Recruitment Process Manager

Sourcing strategies to support the strategic, operational and business plan for the company. Influence senior business executives on strategy, resources, hiring forecasts and capacity planning. Establish and oversee maintenance of effective candidate sourcing channels and both internal and external CV tracking systems to speed the process of identifying qualified candidates and tracking effectiveness and efficiency metrics.

- Assist with proposal generation, implementation, training and daily oversight of key account service delivery teams, overall delivery of key account results, and the management and nurturing of client relationships to deliver the highest calibre client results.
- Provide timely feedback to management and clients regarding workload and accomplishments, ensuring accuracy of data and timely, thorough completion of assignments.

Continued

| Jane Smith | 01234 567890 | jsmith@email.com | Page 2 |

XYZ Ltd, Salisbury   2004 to 2006
Design construction
Director, Recruitment

230-person corporate recruiting function. Report directly to CEO. Provided strategic direction and tactical follow-up on all levels of recruitment process redesign.

- Managed the internship programme and volunteered to represent student construction organizations establishing a future flow of qualified construction management majors.

- Improved the 'candidate experience' by instituting full life-cycle recruiting at the company.

- Spearheaded company-wide skills matrix to aid in succession planning and resource management.

- Partnered with IT to create and launch career site.

- Orchestrated a comprehensive multi-prong employee retention process overhaul.

- Established a 30-60-90 new employee review process, introduced buddy system, and re-engineered new hire on-boarding procedures, reducing communication breakdowns and ensuring employees' complete preparedness for first day of employment.

START UP AIR, Doncaster   2002 to 12/2004
A low-cost airline
Recruitment Manager

Hired to develop and implement recruiting function for a start-up airline to support 2,000 hires. Assisted with the creation and management of a £1 million advertising budget. Presented detailed and comprehensive reports and analysis on staffing metrics including attrition, programme results and recruiter performance. Implementation of Sarbanes-Oxley narrative.

- Exceeded 2004 headcount targets by 20%, employing 2,000 external and 500 internal employees.

- Board-level approval for the implementation of an applicant microsite, which significantly increased the performance of the baggage-handler screening process.

- Rebuilt recruitment and selection cycle. Conducted quarterly internal audits to ensure compliance.

- Created a robust Employee Referral Programme (ERP) that propelled referrals to 13% of total hires resulting in lower cost-per-hire for hourly airport employees.

- Implemented legally defensible behavioural interviewing with recurrent training for hiring managers, resulting in a significant reduction in EOC claims.

- Designed and implemented a Service Level Agreement (SLA), greatly impacting the time-to-offer metric by eliminating communication disconnects. Time-to-offer on corporate hires went from 65 days to 30 days.

- Influenced two major internal departments to use in-house recruitment function rather than headhunting services, resulting in a savings of approximately £300k in 2004.

Continued

Human resources

Human resources

| Jane Smith | 01234 567890 | jsmith@email.com | Page 3 |

OEF COMMUNICATIONS, Doncaster 1999 to 2003
Voice, data, converged and managed services
Staffing Manager
Responsible for 37-market telecommunications corporate, technical and sales recruiting efforts for 1,200-member organization. Engaged external agencies and internal recruiters in a massive hiring effort for top performers in sales arena, meeting the business objective of 300 hires in a timeframe of three months and dramatically impacting sales for the last quarter.

- Introduced SLA to firmly establish the recruitment strategy, reducing time-to-offer by five days. Significantly reduced time-to-offer to 27.01 and time-to-start to 40.01 after the initiative implementation completion.

- Successfully established solid customer service best practices and hired 700 sales employees.

- Reduced offer turnaround to a five-day administrative cycle from a 2–3 week cycle.

- Implemented technical pre-screen process to eliminate unqualified candidates.

GHIJ 1996 to 1999
Global staffing company
Recruiter

Used both traditional and non-traditional search resources and techniques to identify and target top talent professionals including cold-calling, advertising, networking and professional associations.

- Sourced, reviewed and screened CVs for a variety of technical and corporate positions.

- Conducted preliminary IT candidate interviews and arranged for subsequent interviews with hiring managers and clients.

- Expanded growth of business by initiating direct placement contracts and placements service.

'Recruitment is the lifeblood of success. I know the challenges, the problems, and their solutions. I deliver.'

Operations manager

HOWARD MORRIS
1 Any Street ◆ Anytown AA1 1AA ◆ 55555 555555 ◆ howard.morris@myemail.com

OPERATIONS MANAGEMENT
Information Technology • Process Improvement • Financial Services

Performance Profile
Operations Management Executive with solid background in operations, business development, information technology, staff training/development, change management, project management and turnaround situations with large and small organizations in multiple industries. Results-orientated, decisive leader, with proven success in streamlining operations, reducing costs and boosting profits. Thrive in a fast-paced, growth-orientated, highly competitive environment. MBA Finance and Marketing; BSc Mechanical Engineering.

Core Competencies

- Visionary Leadership
- Operations Management
- Process Restructuring
- Project Management

- Technology Integration
- Business Development
- Market Identification
- Strategic Business Planning

- Turnarounds
- Strategic Alliances
- Staff Development
- Communication

Professional Experience

Project Manager / Process Improvement Manager
ABC TECHNOLOGIES, Cambridge (2009 to Present)

CEO / Director of Operations & Technology
DEF CONSULTANTS, Cambridge (2006 to 2009)

Director / Client Administrative Services
GHI GROUP LTD, Guildford (2005 to 2006)

Business Manager / Agent
JKL LIFE, Bolton (2003 to 2005)

Project Manager / Systems Engineer
MNS COMPUTERS / MARKETING & SERVICES DIVISION, Bolton (1992 to 2003)

Education & Training

UNIVERSITY OF LONDON
MBA in Finance & Marketing ◆ BSc Mechanical Engineering

Business ◆ Project Management ◆ Leadership ◆ Finance ◆ Management ◆ Sales Customer
Service ◆ Technical ◆ Product Information & Education

Professional Certifications: Society of Pension Actuaries
Registered Representative, Life & Disability Licence
Certified Financial Planner

Operations manager

NATHAN W BETHEL
1 Any Street • Anytown AA1 1AA
5555555 5555 Mobile • 55555 555555 Home • nwb@email.com

BUSINESS MANAGEMENT PROFILE

• EXPERTISE IN WATER PARKS •

Operations / Project Management • Staff Training & Management • Safety Initiatives

Top-performing water park operations management professional with broad range of business, organizational and interpersonal skills. Natural leader, able to develop strong working relationships with management, staff and the general public to ensure positive, high-quality guest experiences. Expertise in increasing company revenues through customer loyalty.

Core Competencies

- Outstanding track record of strategic contributions envisioning, planning, strategizing and accomplishing a range of business-related initiatives, with significant success in developing concepts into full-fledged, high-performance realities.

- Offer a valuable blend of leadership, creative and analytical abilities that combine efficiency with imagination to produce bottom-line results. Proven success in planning, directing and coordinating staff activities to minimize costs and produce optimal outcomes.

- Calm under pressure; diplomatic and tactful with professionals and non-professionals at all levels. Recognized for ability to negotiate, manage and deliver positive results and to readily transcend cultural and language differences.

- Technically proficient in use of Microsoft Office Word, Excel, PowerPoint, Outlook, on Windows and Macintosh platforms.

Professional Experience

ABC WORLD – LIVERPOOL   2014–Present

Professional Internship
Recruited, following a productive four-month lifeguard internship, to contribute to the ongoing success of this popular water park attraction.
Performed a variety of management-level functions and team-building training for staff, and developed key organizational systems to standardize strategic functions.

Continued

Nathan W Bethel **Page 2**

Key Contributions:
- Spearheaded, developed, created and implemented the Beach and Lagoon Evacuation Operations Report, coordinating all strategic safety and evacuation information. Documents included map of park, procedures, phone lists of all lifeguard stands, and inventory supply lists.
- Promoted the ABC anniversary theme of 'A Year of a Million Dreams' by participating in the 'Magical Moments' programme to create special, unique, memorable guest experiences.
- Developed a signage system to assist patrons in finding their way through the park.
- Conducted monthly in-service staff trainings. Developed and delivered training materials on a variety of topics including CPR, team building and water rescues.
- Selected to serve as a 'Safety in Motion' (SIM) instructor, training staff in becoming aware of workplace safety issues and how to safely perform all required responsibilities.
- Achieved 100% completion of staff ABC Fundraising Drive.
- Assisted in planning and executing various events, including a get-to-know-you party for interns.

Lifeguard Internship
Served as one of 80 lifeguards at ABC's famous water park.
Received special training in Lifeguarding (XYZ Lifeguard Training), and worked throughout the water park with fellow staff to provide assistance and protection to participants. Patrolled or monitored recreational areas on foot or from lifeguard stands. Rescued distressed people using rescue techniques and equipment. Contacted emergency medical personnel in case of serious injuries. Examined injured persons and administered first aid or cardiopulmonary resuscitation as required, using training and medical supplies and equipment. Instructed guests in proper use of waterslides and other features and provided safety precaution information. Reported to the Lifeguard/Recreation Manager.

Key Contributions:
- Saved several lives in backboard and other types of rescues and resuscitations.
- Received many commendations for performance above and beyond the call of duty.

Manager, Miniature Golf
Completed internship in the Miniature Golf park to further develop management knowledge.
Oversaw a wide variety of staffing and administrative functions, supporting ABC initiatives and instructing others in company policies and procedures.

Education

BA (Hons) Business Administration
CITY COMMUNITY COLLEGE
Anticipated Graduation, May 2015

XYZ & Associates Lifeguard Training
ABC WORLD, LIVERPOOL

Operations and logistics

Inventory manager/operations executive

DAN DOLAN

1 Any Street, Anytown AX0 0AA • (H) 020 8123 4567 • 55555 555555 (M)

INVENTORY MANAGER/OPERATIONS EXECUTIVE

Operations – Sales – Business Management

Delivered strong and sustainable revenue and profit gains in highly competitive markets

PROFESSIONAL SUMMARY

Empowering manager with multiple responsibilities and the ability to direct a large staff. Focus group efforts; counsel, mentor and train employees. Experience in directing new store openings and store remodelling projects. Proven ability to perform multiple tasks at once with special attention to detail.

Consistently meet and/or exceed corporate goals and operational deadlines. Responds well in high-pressure managerial situations calling for excellent organizational skills and interpersonal communication skills.

Problem solver with strong leadership ability and an in-depth understanding of profitable business operations across many disciplines. Known for successful implementation strategies with a high commitment to excellence.

CORE SKILLS

- **Inventory Control**
- **Store Operations**
- **Customer Service**
- **New Store Startups**
- **Troubleshooting/Problem Solving**
- **Leadership/Mentoring**
- **Employee Staffing and Scheduling**
- **Shrinkage Control**
- **Productivity Improvements**
- **Payroll Forecasting**
- **Logistics**
- **Team Building and Training**

BUSINESS EXPERIENCE

ABC LTD   2006–Present

ABC LTD, Luton   2008–Present

Operations Executive
- Use a strong strategic planning management style to supervise a staff of 125.
- Responsible for the operations and flow of all merchandise from warehouse to sales floor. Annual sales of the store total £40 million.
- Direct the staffing and daily operations of six managers and their teams.
- Selected by ABC as one of four senior managers of the 'New Store Team'. Participated in start-up of the Luton store in March 2008.

Continued

Dan Dolan   Page Two

ABC LTD (Continued)

- The Luton store was in the top 10% of all ABC stores nationwide for operational excellence in 2010.
- Selected as Risk Assessment Manager for the district for last two years.
- Selected for the High Level Management team for the district.
- Completed the interview process and on the list to be the ABC's next new store manager.
- Chosen as District Trainer, mentoring five additional flow executives at other stores.

ABC LTD, Manchester   2006–2008

Sales Executive/Logistics Executive

- Hired as Logistics Executive responsible for all stock into the store.
- Promoted from Logistics Executive to Sales Executive with responsibility for sales and sales floor management.

OFFICE DEPOT   2002–2006

OFFICE DEPOT, Liverpool   2005–2006
Store Manager

- Responsible for all facets of daily business functions and operations for the entire store. Store revenues grew to exceed £5 million.
- Responsible for staff of 40, including scheduling, sales quotas, performance reviews, daily staff duty assignments and employee training.
- Implemented and maintained store policy and procedures as directed by company standards.
- Used a passionate execution style and strategic planning to develop the Liverpool store into a top performer in the region.

OFFICE DEPOT, Bridgend   2004–2005
Sales Manager

- Increased sales by 20% in first year as Sales Manager.
- Increased gross margin by 32% through an increase in extended warranty sales of 17%.
- The store was the winner in a company-wide contest for having the highest warranty sales to overall sales ratio.

OFFICE DEPOT, Preston   2002–2004
Operations Manager

- In charge of all incoming stock, staff scheduling and inventory rotation.
- During first year as Operations Manager, shrinkage decreased from 3.2% to .32%.

EDUCATION

North West University
BSc Environmental Economics – 2002

Operations and logistics

Director of operations

Jane Swift   Page 1 of 2

123 Any Street
Anytown AT1 0BB
Tel: 020 8123 4567
jane@anyaddress.co.uk

DIRECTOR OF OPERATIONS

PROFESSIONAL PROFILE

Director of Operations, Manufacturing, for US subsidiary. 20+ years' experience in the creative leadership of multisite manufacturing operations to improve productivity, quality and efficiency. Facilitated significant cost savings.

CORE COMPETENCIES

- Operations Systems
- Strategic Planning
- Cost Management
- Facilities Design
- Offshore Production

- Manufacturing Process
- Quality Control
- Supplier Partnership
- Human Resources/Labour Relations
- Compliance

PROFESSIONAL EXPERIENCE

ABC Automotive Products, Houston, Texas   *2009–Present*

A national leader in the manufacturing of automotive water pumps with annual sales of £380 million and 1,500 employees.

Director of Operations

- Managed the company's two plants in Texas and Mexico. Directly supervised two plant managers, a materials manager, advanced manufacturing systems manager, distribution manager, manager for special projects, and training and a Quality Control Division.
- Initiated and secured ISO9002 certification in two plants on the first application.
- Reorganized preventive maintenance schedules that decreased scrap rates by 50% and virtually eliminated rework rates.
- Orchestrated teamwork and communication between marketing and production to ensure customers received precise delivery dates and improved quality.
- Guided efforts with a major supplier to turn around its sub-quality standards. Avoided a change to the competition's vendors that could have been costly. Result: vendor achieved ISO9000 certification and is now rated top in field.

Continued

Jane Swift 020 8123 4567
page 2 of 2

A1 Heating plc   *1999–2009*
  A residential and industrial water heater manufacturing company.
    Director of Operations, Leeds   2005–2009
    Plant Manager, Glasgow   2001–2005
    Manufacturing Manager, Leeds   1999–2001

- Instituted a quality control system that resulted in highest product quality in industry. Responded to suspicions from customers and suppliers about quality of product by arranging for decision makers to see plant in operation.
- Reduced accident rate 20% and turnover rate (from 12% to 3% per month in four years) in Leeds by implementing unilateral training programmes (eg skills, teamwork, supervisory).
- Negotiated commitments from vendors to ensure JIT system.
- Established a 5,000 square foot distribution centre to improve service to mid-continent customers.
- Prevented theft of valuable copper shipments by working with police.
- Selected by senior management to solve problems on Glasgow site, which resulted in opening on schedule.
- Improved Leeds plant operations efficiencies as a result of executing a comprehensive study. In four years increased output significantly and profits by 200% by optimizing space, decreasing product damage during production and consolidating shipments.
- Oversaw Glasgow plant closing and transfer to modern facilities. Responsibilities included identification of most economical way to equip new plant, comprehensive study on disposal of buildings, and employee transition management. Production levels remained stable and efforts led to promotion to Director of Operations.

Hillside Water Products plc, Darlington   *1990–1999*
  Manufacturing Engineer

EDUCATION
MBA, School of Management, University of the North
BSc (Hons) 2.1, Mechanical Engineering, University of the North

ONGOING PROFESSIONAL DEVELOPMENT
- Strategic Planning Seminar, South West University Executive Programme
- Leadership at the Peak, Centre for Creative Leadership
- World Class Manufacturing & Process Capability Studies
- Human Resources Seminar, The Manufacturing Association
- The Employee Team Concept, The Centre for Productivity

Operations and logistics

Supply chain/logistics manager

Operations and logistics

John Smith MBA

1 Any Street, Anytown, 0XA, 0AA   01234 567890   jsmith@email.com

Supply Chain/Logistics Management
'21 years with world leader, from the loading dock to the negotiating table'

Performance Profile/Performance Summary

MBA with 20+ years of progressive growth with XYZ in Supply Chain/Logistics Management, streamlining operations across a wide range of industries. Proven record of delivering a synchronized supply chain to optimize ROI and manage risk. Excellent negotiation and relationship management skills with ability to inspire teams to outperform expectations.

Core Skills

Supply Chain Mapping	Cost & Process	Facility Redesign
Contingency Planning	Competitive Analysis	Risk Management
Distributive Computing	Budget Management	Labour Relations
Recruitment	Training/Development	Organizational Change
Project Management	Haz Mat Compliance	Order Consolidation
Order Process Automation	Demand Response Model	Vendor/Client Negotiations
Supply Chain Process	Financial Logistics Analysis	Inventory Planning, Control &
Costing		Distribution

Supply Chain Strategy: 500+ supply chain initiatives, negotiating agreements from £5k to £27 million. Implemented technology and processes changes to reduce redundancies and staffing hours, improving both efficiency and productivity. Industries: automotive, industrial manufacturing, consumer goods, government and defence, healthcare, high tech, retail.

Logistics: All modes of transportation; Ocean, Air Freight, LTL/TL, Mail Services and Small Package.

Project Management: Implemented complete £1.2 million redesign for 11 new XYZ customer centres. Managed vendor and lease negotiations, developed budgets, training and sales structure. All 11 centres operational, on-time and on-budget.

Project Cost, Process and Reorganization Impacts

➢ Reduced transportation expense by 15%, increased production levels by 25%, reduced inventory by 15% and staffing by 20%.

➢ Improved service levels by 30%, reduced damage by 45%, shipping process automation reduced billing function staffing hours 50%.

➢ Sales force realignment and reporting structure increased sales calls by 20%, reduced travel mileage 23%, and head count by nine; total annual cost savings of £920k.

Professional Experience

XYZ, Aberdeen   **1986–Present**
World leader in supply chain services
DIRECTOR/AREA MANAGER – SUPPLY CHAIN SALES   **2005–Present**

Leads a cross-functional sales force of 18 in consultative supply chain management services to UK businesses.

Continued

John Smith	01234 567890	jsmith@email.com	Page 2

DIRECTOR/AREA MANAGER – SUPPLY CHAIN SALES continued

Direct development of integrated supply chain management solutions across all modes of transportation, closely mirroring client business plans. Mentor team in Demand Responsive Model, a proven methodology to quickly align internal and external resources with changing market demands, situational requirements and mission critical conditions. Manage £100 milion P&L.

Accomplishments

➤ Implements over 100 multi-million-pound supply chain integrations per year with 14% annual growth on 8% plan.

➤ Develops future organizational leaders; four staff members promoted through effective mentoring and development.

➤ Choreographed a supply chain movement for a Global fast-food chain to deliver 300k cartons to 15k locations all on the same day. Used modes of Ocean, TL, air and ground services, allowing for a national release synchronized to all locations on the same release date.

➤ Designed and implemented an automated reverse logistics programme for a nationally recognized health food/supplement distributor. Automated returns process to reduce touches and costly staffing hours. Eliminated front-end phone contact using technology and web automation.

MARKETING MANAGER   2004–2005

Fast-tracked to streamline sales processes, increasing performance. Performed analysis of sales territory, historical data, operations alignment, reporting structure and sales trends to devise solutions. Managed and coached area managers in business plan development and execution of sales strategies. Delivered staff development in cost-reduction strategies and compliance requirements. Accountable for £500 million P&L.

Accomplishments

➤ Drove £500 million in local market sales. Grew 2004/2005 revenues 12% and 7% respectively.

RETAIL CHANNEL/OPERATIONS MANAGER   2002–2004

Charged with underperforming business unit turnaround. Managed development and implementation of new retail strategy across the UK. Re-branded XYZ customer centres and the XYZ stores. Performed vendor negotiations and collaborated with nine regions to support additional implementations.

Accomplishments

➤ Key revenue-generating initiatives across multiple channels: 65% growth in discretionary sales. Several strategies adopted across the national organization.

➤ Re-engineered inventory for over 1,000 locations, reduced lease expenses by 45%; inventory levels by 40% by SKU development, order process automation and consolidation.

➤ Implemented new retail sales associate structure in 1,100 locations; scored highest national service levels by mystery shoppers.

➤ Selected as corporate team member on Mail Boxes Etc. acquisition integration.

Continued

Operations and logistics

John Smith	01234 567890	jsmith@email.com	Page 3

PROJECT MANAGER   2001–2002

Selected to support several underperforming business areas. Managed key segments of district business initiatives and compliance measures for 1,000 drop-off locations. Staff of 16; negotiated vendor and lease agreements.

Accomplishments

➢ Rolled out and managed ongoing Hazmat compliance programme for all locations.
➢ Generated £6 million in sales through cross-functional lead programme and increased participation from 20% to 100%.
➢ Attained union workforce sponsorship of support growth programme through careful negotiations and persuasion.

SENIOR ACCOUNT MANAGER   1999–2001
£2.8 million in growth on £1.1 million plan
ACCOUNT MANAGER   1997–1998
£1.3 million sales on £500K plan.
SERVICE PROVIDER   1994–1996
378 hours under plan first year with zero accidents or injuries.
SUPERVISOR OF PACKAGE OPERATIONS   1994
Managed 65 full-time service providers. Performed post-routine analysis, operating strategy development, compliance, payroll, service failure recovery and new technology implementation. Met 100% DOT and Hazmat compliance. Reduced post-delivery staffing time by 50% and missed pick-ups by 65%.
SUPERVISOR OF HUB OPERATIONS   1988–1994
100 union employees and staff processing 75,000 pieces per day involving 40+ outbound bays. Designed new management reporting format, reducing admin. time by 20% and improving load quality by 30%.
OPERATIONS DOCK WORKER AND TRAINING LEAD   1986–1987

Education

MBA
Edinburgh University

BA, Business, Supply Chain Management
South Bridge College

Additional Specialized Courses:

- Supply Chain Mapping, 20 hours
- Financial Logistics Analysis (FLOGAT), 10 hours
- Hazardous Materials, 20 hours
- Labour Relations, 30 hours
- Managers Leadership School, 100 hours
- Supervisors Leadership School, 100 hours

International trade compliance consultant

John Smith

1 Any Street
Anytown, AX0 0AA

01234 567890
jsmith@email.com

INTERNATIONAL TRADE COMPLIANCE
TACTICAL MANUFACTURING OPERATIONS • INTERNATIONAL LOGISTICS • AUDITING • GLOBAL
TRADE • TRANSPORTATION MANAGEMENT

Performance Summary

Diversified management and leadership background featuring significant global trade compliance accomplishments. Talent for analysing business data and identifying opportunities to improve operational efficiencies and reduce expenses within domestic and international marketplaces.

Ability to guide and empower cross-functional groups to resolve complex import and export issues and accomplish objectives. Creative problem solver who controls cost and minimizes risks while simultaneously driving desired results for bottom-line profitability.

Core Competencies

- Strategic Business Planning
- Contract Negotiations
- Business Re-engineering

- Regulatory, Compliance & Auditing
- Import and Export Operations
- Research and Data Management

- Transportation & Logistics
- Project Management
- Reporting & Administration

PROFESSIONAL EXPERIENCE

INTERNATIONAL TRADE INC., Baltimore, MD   2000 to Present

Senior Consultant, Policy & Compliance

Focal-point leader and advisor for Trade Compliance Programme across 120+ countries. Maintain knowledge of current import/export regulations, evaluate proposed regulatory changes, and write business impact and recommendation reports. Create manuals, guidelines, standard operating policies, internal control programmes and other tools needed for import/export compliance. Develop and conduct customs/export training programmes for employees, customers and third-party logistics providers.

Key Achievements:

- Discovered £1.5 billion in errors and other significant compliance deficiencies during international audit.
- Recognized as subject matter expert for development of numerous software applications. Automated and streamlined operations by at least 50% while simultaneously increasing global trade regulatory compliance.
- Conceived, developed and implemented countless ideas for increasing Global Trade Compliance among numerous business units around the world, including immediate funding and IT resources. Successful in improving productivity and increasing due diligence for regulatory requirements.

AMERICAN FREIGHT CORPORATION, Lancaster, PA   1995 to 2000

Senior Transportation Analyst

Produced Request for Quotations for domestic and international transportation, freight forwarders and other logistics services. Analysed bid packages and participated in negotiations with carriers and logistics service contracts. Identified corrective actions for domestic and international shipments. Supervised and trained three staff members in export compliance, packaging, freight damage claims, and freight payment with full accountability for budget of over £4 million.
Key Achievements:

- Restructured and streamlined international transportation and logistics processes/procedures resulting in net savings of £8.3 million through initiatives with transportation and logistics impact assessments, import port-of-entry points and port-of-export points.

Continued

Operations and logistics

Operations and logistics

John Smith   01234 567890   jsmith@email.com   Page 2

Senior Transportation Analyst *continued*

- Slashed 5% on freight payments (£7 million) through efforts in auditing transportation/accounts payable.
- Played key role in leveraging global transportation, customs brokerage and freight forwarding services.

ABC MANUFACTURING COMPANY, South Ridge, RI   1990 to 1995

Corporate Transportation Manager

Full P&L accountability for receiving, raw material inventory, and shipping departments. Managed, prepared and submitted applications to government agencies for approval of import and export licenses. Hired, trained and supervised staff of 22 in raw material inventory, receiving, shipping, importing, exporting, regulatory compliance and freight payment. Negotiated and managed contracts for domestic, international transportation, customs brokers, freight forwarders and other logistics services.

Key Achievements:

- Saved £500,000 in immediate refunds and reduced all future duties by more than £2 million annually through initiating reclassification of company's imported products with Customs Office.

- Instrumental in streamlining operations, optimizing transportation and international activities along with implementing legal measures to comply with import and export regulations.

- Successfully classified products according to harmonized tariff schedule numbers, assigned Export Control Classification Numbers, and assured compliance to country-of-origin marking requirements, NAFTA regulations, and Valuation Rules for imported and exported merchandise.

EDUCATION

Master of Business Administration – Univérsity of Southern England
Bachelor of Science, Finance – London University

CERTIFICATIONS

Certified United States Export Compliance Officer (CUSECO) International Import-Export Institute Certified in Transportation & Logistics (CTL) American Society of Transportation & Logistics Licensed United States Customs Broker Department of Homeland Security/Customs & Border Protection

PROFESSIONAL AFFILIATIONS

Chairperson, American Society of Transportation & Logistics (AST&L)
Member, Institute of Internal Auditors (IIA)
Member, International Compliance Professionals Association (ICPA)

Management consultant

James Sharpe
123 Any Street ● Anytown AT1 0BB
Phone: 020 8123 4567 ● james@anyaddress.co.uk
PROJECT MANAGER – INTERNATIONAL OPERATIONS

Professional Profile

Senior executive with successful track record in international operations and project management. Recognized for exceptional problem solving and motivational skills as well as the ability to **negotiate, deal and close successfully across cultural barriers**. Extensive experience in management consulting in diverse industries, ranging from unit construction and mining/drilling operations to industrial equipment procurement, sales and distribution. **Bilingual with extensive international experience**, including Africa, the Middle East, South Asia and Western Europe.

Core Competencies

- International Conflict Resolution
- Operation and Project Management
- Global Emergency Planning

- Worldwide Corporate Security
- New Business Development
- International Public Relations

- Risk Assessment
- International Law
- Recruitment/Training

Career Highlights

- Successfully providing diplomatic, risk management and crisis resolution services to a broad range of blue-chip companies, Ambassadors, Heads of State, cabinet ministers and senior government officials, UK and foreign.
- Successfully negotiated, on behalf of OCL Oil, with an East African government to resolve a cross-cultural crisis and avoid closure of a £1 billion distribution facility.
- Developed and implemented logistics and training programmes involving several thousand UK and foreign personnel and a £40 million annual budget. Effectively achieved all objectives with budget savings of 12%.
- Directed Smith & Jones Trucks Ltd, and Haulage International in the successful negotiation of more than £15 million of capital equipment sales to a West African government.
- Conducted numerous feasibility studies and risk assessments, both political and economic forecasts, for a variety of projects including gold, platinum and diamond mining, nuclear energy development, port, railroad and packaging facilities.

Employment History

International Affairs Consultant 2005–Present
Professional Services Provided to: Whitway International, Vella Properties International, OCL Oil, OACH Petroleum, Haulage International, Smith & Jones Trucks Ltd, Flight Airlines, Technology Co Ltd, MSC International Ltd, National Telecommunications Co Ltd, OX Technologies

National Security Agency 1998–2005
Near East and Africa Referent ... Chief of Station ... Chief of Operations ...
Chief of Branch, Counterterrorism ... Deputy/Chief of Station.

Education

Doctorate, *International Law*, University of London
Master of Arts, *History*, University of the South
Bachelor of Arts, *History*, New College, Oxbridge

Purchasing manager

Management

MARC M KELLEY

1 Any Street
Anytown AX0 0AA

020 8123 4567
Email@email.com

PURCHASING MANAGER

PERFORMANCE PROFILE

Consistent success in controlling costs and improving net profitability while continuing to support critical operations. Background includes procurement responsibility of up to £5 million annually. Excellent communicator with a good attitude and sense of humour. Tenacious negotiation with keen vendor management skills. Strong research and analysis, organization and decision-making abilities. PC proficient with Word, Excel and MainSaver.

PROFESSIONAL EXPERIENCE

Purchasing/Maintenance Assistant, ABC Ltd, Hambourne, 2007–present
Progressed from Purchasing Assistant to Maintenance Assistant. Selected by upper management to train as Assistant Plant Operator.

- Conducted and oversaw all procurement operations – requisitions, purchase orders, price negotiation, receiving, delivery verification. Commodities consisted of chemicals, hardware, consumables, office supplies and maintenance equipment.

- Prepared weekly and monthly reports of pounds committed and delivery status. Ensured inventory was current and needs were met. Performed preventive maintenance and assisted mechanic with machinery repairs.

Subcontract Administrator, Huge Aircraft Company, Bristol, 1997–2006

- Administered yearly government subcontract purchases of £1+ million. Solicited bids, negotiated prices, awarded jobs. Interfaced with representatives of many different organizations. Coordinated with Engineering, Programme, Quality, Price, and Cost Analysis staff through completion.

Received High Achiever Award for saving over £100,000 annually.

Purchasing Manager, XYZ Ltd, Manchester, 1994–1996

- Procured electronic components of purchases in excess of £5 million annually, including price negotiation and delivery. Ensured compliance with applicable Government Procurement Regulations.

Buyer, Huge Aircraft Company, Bristol, 1990–1994

- Placed purchase orders for computer and test equipment, electronic hardware, optics and other commodities.

Received Superior Performance Award for outstanding attitude and work performance.

EDUCATION/ADDITIONAL TRAINING

BA, General Business Administration, University of London
CPR/First Aid Certification – Licensed Forklift Driver
Continuing Education includes Teaming Techniques, Negotiation Skills and other relevant courses.

Purchasing manager

HERMAN KEYNES

1 Any Street
Anytown AA1 1AA

55555 555555
Hkeynes@email.com

PURCHASING

Buyer/Planner Skilled in Sourcing, Negotiations and Inventory Management

➤ Expertise in purchasing, inventory planning/control, warehouse operations and customer service.
➤ Skilled in sourcing and selecting suppliers, with a track record of consistently negotiating highest quality merchandise at favourable prices and terms.
➤ Accurate in monitoring inventory levels to minimize lead times, ensure accuracy and contribute to efficient, cost-effective operations.
➤ Analytical, with excellent decision-making strengths, team-building and leadership qualities.
➤ Highly computer literate with experience on mainframes and PCs. Systems/applications include AS-400, CAPRMS, BPCS, COPS, UPS Online, Simbill, Microsoft Word, Excel and Outlook; internet, e-mail.

CORE SKILLS

MRP ◆ JIT ◆ TQM ◆ ISO 9001 ◆ KanBan Inventory ◆ Vendor Sourcing, Selection, & Negotiations
Raw Material & Inventory Planning/Control ◆ Spreadsheets & Report Design/Preparation

PROFESSIONAL EXPERIENCE

MAJOR HEALTH PRODUCTS, Thaxted * 2003 to Present
£54 million international manufacturer and distributor of medical devices. Division of major company with 350 employees.

Buyer/Planner (2005–Present)

Oversaw material planning, inventory management, vendor sourcing/selection, and negotiation of pricing and delivery terms for components required for custom surgical kits, injection moulded products, and foam positioning products. Worked closely with cross-functional teams including marketing, R&D and product development. Processed material rejections and replacements; resolved quality and vendor problems; maintained intercompany transfers. Authorization for purchase orders up to £50,000.

● Served as key member of team in charge of transferring product line to overseas manufacturing facility, implementing closure of Essex facility, transfer of inventory to Thaxted facility, and transfer of new product line into facility – all within 10-month period.
● Reduced costs by £500,000 annually through new vendor sourcing and purchase negotiations.
● Identified and selected local vendors, reducing lead time by 50%.
● Implemented KanBan inventory management system.

Shipping Manager – XYZ Controls / ABC Industries (2003–2005)

Supervised staff of 20 including warehouse staff, fork-lift drivers, order pullers and office staff. Responsibilities were diverse and encompassed overseeing order processing and shipment at 66,000 square foot warehouse.
Maintained inventory transaction accuracy of 99%.

➤ Established procedures for online receipts of inventory to create live inventory transactions.
➤ Assisted management in closing and opening distribution facilities.

EDUCATION / WORKSHOPS / SEMINARS

TQM (including problem solving, team skills and conflict resolutions)
ISO 9001, GMP Overviews & Practices, Kaizen Blitz Training

Manager

KEN DAVENPORT

1 Any Street ◆ Anytown AA1 1AA ◆ 55555 555555 ◆ kendaven@email.com

Electronics Manufacturing Management

Performance Summary

15+ years' electronic manufacturing services management experience involving operations, finance supply chain project and materials management, including six years managing cross-functional teams and customer relationships. Skilled at evaluating complex issues, identifying key elements, creating action plans and guiding execution. MBA in Finance and General Management.

Core Competencies

- **Revenue & Profit Increases**
- **Cost Reduction & Cost Avoidance**
- **Process & Efficiency Improvement**
- **Customer Relationship Management**
- **Contract Development & Negotiation**
- **Team Building & Leadership**
- **Materials & Supply Chain Management**
- **P&L Management**
- **Metrics Management & Analysis**

Recognized by management as a key contributor and consistently promoted to positions with increasing responsibility.

PROFESSIONAL EXPERIENCE

High-Tech Circuits Ltd, South Shields   2003–Present; 1994–2002

Business Analyst, Business Unit Financial Analyst (2011–Present)

Perform extensive analysis and reporting for a business unit group of 300+ employees. Key actions and accomplishments include the following:

- Revitalized the Time Clock project, which was behind schedule. Established close interaction with offsite project manager and completed assembly, installation and testing ahead of schedule. Recognized for contribution to efficiency improvement and more effective plant operation.
- Compiled and updated quarterly customer QBR reports using Excel pivot tables and Access database information. In addition, generated and reported quarterly bonuses for employees.

Business Unit Manager (2008–2011)

Managed a challenging £25 million/year account and approximately £18 million of materials to maintain profitability. Major areas included forecasting, contract negotiations, supplier performance, financial management and HR issues. Developed and coordinated activities of cross-functional teams. Key actions and accomplishments included the following:

- Spearheaded revision and execution of full manufacturing contract within four months versus expected 6–12 months.
- Grew revenue 330% in fiscal year 2011.

Continued

Business Unit Coordinator *(2006–2008)*
Managed accounts valued at £12 million per year. Interacted with customers to ensure high satisfaction. Contributed to cost-reduction and efficiency improvements that included developing Excel macros to use purchasing and inventory data more efficiently and an Access database to track ECN changes and impact.

Master Planning Supervisor *(2003–2006; 2001–2002)*
Established rules, procedures, tools and techniques to develop plant from prototype to volume production. Managed master scheduling for multiple programmes, as well as work cell material management and metrics. Key actions and accomplishments included the following:

- Achieved smooth transfer of £30+ million programme to another facility through detailed material transactions and planning.
- Reduced excess inventory by £400,000 and increased inventory turnover by 20%.
- Promoted from Master Planner position in less than a year.

Previous positions: Master Planner; Accounting Manager

ABC Laminate Systems, Hillingdon   2002–2003

Production/Scheduling/Inventory Manager
Served as a member of Leadership Team and as High Performance Work Team coach for Shipping department. Additional actions and accomplishments included the following:

- Promoted continuous improvement and elimination of waste by initiating changes that included reducing product travel from 5,000 to 2,000 metres.
- Contributed to £500,000 inventory reduction and 98% on-time shipping record.

EDUCATION & CERTIFICATION
Master of Business Administration-Finance & General Management
City College
BA (Hons) Accounting and Finance
Northeastern University
Certified in Production & Inventory Management (CPIM)
Certified Supply Chain Professional (CSCP)

PROFESSIONAL AFFILIATION
Member, UK Production & Inventory Control Society

COMPUTER COMPETENCIES
MS Office: Word, Excel (including pivot tables and macros), PowerPoint, Access; Visio; SAP ERP

Management

International trade manager

Management

DAVID M GOLDEN

1 Any Street
Anytown AA1 1AA

55555 555555 (Home)
dmgolden@email.com

—— INTERNATIONAL TRADE COMPLIANCE PROFESSIONAL ——

TACTICAL MANUFACTURING OPERATIONS • INTERNATIONAL LOGISTICS • AUDITING • GLOBAL TRADE • TRANSPORTATION MANAGEMENT

Task-orientated, resourceful professional offering diversified management and leadership background highlighted by significant accomplishments governing global trade compliance. Innate ability to motivate and empower cross-functional groups to accomplish objectives and resolve complex import and export issues. Visionary and creative problem solver who controls cost and minimizes risks while simultaneously driving desired results for bottom-line profitability. Talent for analysing business data and identifying opportunities to improve operational efficiencies and reduce ongoing expenses within domestic and international marketplaces.

—— CORE COMPETENCIES ——

- Strategic Business Planning
- Contract Negotiations
- Business Re-engineering

- Regulatory, Compliance & Auditing
- Import and Export Operations
- Research and Data Management

- Transportation & Logistics
- Project Management
- Reporting & Administration

EDUCATION

Master of Business Administration – University of London
Bachelor of Science, Economics – City University

PROFESSIONAL EXPERIENCE

INTERNATIONAL TRADE LTD, Basildon   2005 to Present
Senior Consultant, Policy & Compliance
Focal point leader and advisor for Trade Compliance Programme within and across 120+ countries. Maintain knowledge of current import/export regulations, evaluate proposed regulatory changes, and write business impact and recommendation reports. Create manuals, guidelines, standard operating policies, internal control programmes and other tools needed for import/export compliance. Develop and conduct customs/export training programmes for employees, customers and third-party logistics providers.

Key Achievements:
- Discovered £1.5 billion in errors and other significant compliance deficiencies during international audit.
- Recognized as subject matter expert for development of numerous software applications. Automated and streamlined operations by at least 50% while simultaneously increasing global trade regulatory compliance.
- Conceived, developed and implemented countless ideas for increasing Global Trade Compliance among numerous business units around the world, including immediate funding and IT resources. Successful in improving productivity and increasing due diligence for regulatory requirements.

XYZ FREIGHT LTD, Lancaster   2000 to 2005
Senior Transportation Analyst
Produced Request for Quotations for domestic and international transportation, freight forwarders and other logistics services. Analysed bid packages and participated in negotiations with carriers and logistics service contracts. Identified corrective actions for domestic and international shipments. Supervised and trained three staff members in export compliance, packaging, freight damage claims and freight payment with full accountability for budget of over £4 million.

Emerging technologies executive

Louis Edwards

1 Any Street • Anytown AA1 1AA • 999 999 9999 • louis@email.com

Emerging Technologies Globalization Executive
Deal Maker / Market & Product Strategist / Business Developer / Negotiator

Performance Profile

Telecommunications Industry Executive with a 20+ year successful track record driving revenue growth and winning market share primarily in turnaround, start-up, and high growth situations.

Consistently delivers strong and sustainable revenue gains through combined expertise in Strategic Business Planning, Product Management, Market Strategy, Contract Negotiations, and Customer Relationship Management.

Recognized for exceptional ability to assess business unit capabilities, identify and implement appropriate business and product re-engineering measures thus assuring bottom-line growth.

Rare ability to establish the organization's vision, develop business relationships and negotiate the deals that guarantee success.

Professional Accomplishments

- Business relationship builder with track record of personally negotiating contracts with companies such as Xerox, Lockheed Martin, ABC Bank, Morgan Stanley, EDS, Visa, Oracle, Microsoft, Nortel, Boeing, Nordstrom and Gap.

- Consistently developed contracts and terms that used company capabilities and met customer needs, including first prepaid international contract which allowed the company to accelerate into the international market achieving £1+ billion in revenue. This approach became the industry standard.

- Turned around underperforming business unit lacking leadership by redesigning and motivating sales and services teams, successfully recovering 60% of the lost accounts and adding new business. Increased revenues to £5+ million annually in the first 12 months.

- Conceived and coordinated global account management process; identified customer needs and product capabilities, spearheaded product and service level agreement changes to win the first global contract. Grew market share from 7% to 100% and revenue from £330,000 to £6 million per month, setting new industry standards in global business practices.

- Revitalized product by identifying and implementing an International Reseller Channel. Re-engineered existing product through the addition of a conversion process adding packaging enhancements and aligning a service/support structure extending the product life by two years. Captured a potential revenue of £10 million annually.

- Within 45 days, conceived and implemented National Accounts Programme, establishing pricing model, sales organization structure and customer service delivery format. Successfully increased revenue from £12 million to £27 million per month. This programme became the standard for the entire company.

- Led the company's new technologies market development (VPN, Web Hosting, co-locating internet) securing sales in excess of £15 million within six months.

Employment Summary

Software Company Ltd   **2009–Present**
Director, Business Development and Alliances, London
Recruited to drive the product development process and expand market reach through the implementation of an international reseller channel and strategic business alliances.

- Negotiated contracts with Fuji Xerox, Xerox, Accenture and Lockheed Martin, capturing £10 million in potential revenue.

- Managed the renegotiation of two existing alliances that will net the company at least £2 million over the next 12 months.

- Established a new technology relationship with Open Text extending the company's reach in the Life Sciences market.

Continued

Management

Louis Edwards page 2   Ph: (999) 999-9999

International Telecom Ltd   2002–2009

Regional Director National Accounts, Newbury

Recruited to develop a major account programme and subsequently developed a national account programme. Responsibilities included full P&L, £20 million operational budget, and more than 250 personnel.

- During a 15-company acquisition period, including the ITI acquisition (the largest in Telecom history), consistently exceeded all business objectives.
- Managed the best corporate A/R and bad debt levels, achieved outstanding customer retention level of 94% and managed corporation's lowest employee turnover rate of 10%.
- Developed and implemented a National Account Programme expanding revenues within the first year from £180 million to £260 million and achieved award for outstanding revenue increase.
- Averaged a 21% annual internal revenue growth and was selected to the Gold Award Club from 2003 through to 2008 by continually identifying new business opportunities and establishing the right teams, resources and support to grow the organization and meet the customers' expectations.

ABC Telecom Ltd   2000–2002

Executive Director – Global Accounts, Cambridge

Promoted to manage the UK team of 139 sales and support staff, 5 direct reports and to oversee 35 national accounts.

- Managed and negotiated £750 million in contracts with companies including BOA, Visa, Microsoft, Gap, Sun, Apple, Oracle, AMD and Nordstrom. Grew market share from less than 15% to 48% in two years.
- Averaged 122% of revenue target every year.

ABC Telecom Ltd   1997–2000

Branch Manager, Cambridge

Recruited to grow and manage the XYZ Bank account, successfully leading a team of 39 cross-functional members.

- Grew annual sales and revenue from £3.6 million to £80 million within two years, attaining 100% market share.
- Spearheaded largest commercial sale in ABC history, valued at £400 million, successfully converting the entire XYZ Bank network to ABC in less than six months while maintaining 100% customer satisfaction.

BS&S Ltd   1991–1997

Field District Manager, Swindon

- Consistently exceeded quota, averaging 112% and achieved Gold Award Club every year while in sales/sales management positions.
- As staff member of BS&S Information Systems, was responsible for revenue and issues for all national accounts, approximately 200 accounts, achieving 109% of the revenue quota.

BS&S Ltd   1988–1991

National Account Management, BS&S Headquarters, York

- Negotiated and implemented government equipment contract, valued at £20 million.
- Promoted to Management Development Programme (top 2% of all management personnel), recognized for superior executive and leadership potential.

Education

Bachelor of Arts, York University

Career Development: Intensive 18-week account management and product training seminar

Senior technology executive

James Sharpe   Page 1 of 2
123 Any Street
Anytown AT1 0BB
Tel: 020 8123 4567
james@anyaddress.co.uk

TECHNOLOGY • INFORMATION • MANAGEMENT

PERFORMANCE SUMMARY

Accomplished Management Executive with 15+ years' experience and a verifiable record of delivering enhanced productivity, streamlined operations and improved financial performance. Natural leader with strong entrepreneurial spirit and a special talent for turning strategy into action and achievement. Highly effective team-building and motivational skills.

CORE SKILLS

- Corporate Information Technology
- Staffing & Management Development
- Quality & Productivity Improvement
- Marketing Strategy & Management

- Strategic & Business Planning
- Customer Service & Satisfaction
- Operations Management
- Team Building & Leadership

PROFESSIONAL EXPERIENCE

InterTech Group plc   2000–Present
CHIEF INFORMATION OFFICER (2000–Present)
CHAIRMAN, Martins Systems (InterTech subsidiary) (2005–Present)

Appointed to these dual senior-level positions and challenged to create and execute technology strategy for InterTech and subsidiaries of the £700 million Information Services Group. Concurrently provide executive oversight for the development and deployment of software products/services and MIS solutions for Martins Systems, affiliate offices and 3,900 independent agents.

Provide leadership for a team of 200 management and support personnel. Administer a £16 million annual budget. Scope of accountabilities is expansive and includes planning and strategy, operations management, human resource affairs, customer service, marketing, management reporting and communications.

Key Management Achievements

- Built the complete corporate technology infrastructure from the ground up. Developed technology strategies and tactical plans mapped to align with corporate goals.
- Served as a member of the corporate Leadership Council. Defined corporate vision; developed business plans, created strategies and establish tactical goals for all business units.
- Established a high-performance management staff and created a team-based work atmosphere that promotes cooperation to achieve common corporate objectives. Instituted a series of initiatives that substantially improved communications between staff and management.
- Developed and integrated programmes to maximize productive and efficient use of technology throughout the corporation. Instituted 'user champions' to serve as technical experts within each business unit, launched executive 'boot camps' to train management in aggressive computer use, and built responsive help centres for technical support.
- Spearheaded creation and implementation of a customer information and marketing team responsible for developing an award-winning marketing programme, promotions, direct-mail campaigns, and demonstrations and tours.
- Created innovative processes using product specialists for management of sales leads and distributor networks, resolution of customer escalated issues, and provision of work-flow and engineering consulting for company offices and agents.

Continued

Management

Management

James Sharpe 020 8123 4567
page 2 of 2

Key Technical Achievements

- Led implementation of client/server software suite that won the industry's 2004 and 2003 Title Tech Discovery Award for best and most innovative title industry software.

- Spearheaded development of numerous technical infrastructure projects, including the corporate internet presence, corporate intranet, Web-hosting solutions for independent agents, and electronic commerce solutions for offices, agents and service providers in the property management industry.

- Orchestrated development of an award-winning marketing programme, Power Tools for the Modern World, that won the local and district awards for best overall marketing programme.

- Guided development and implementation of a title industry software suite installed in 400 systems throughout the distributor network. Designed and deployed training programmes to ensure high-quality service levels.

- Managed creation of an Electronic Underwriting Manual that was selected as best policies and procedures implementation in the National Awards competition, 2001.

- Led design and implementation of a 1,200-user corporate WAN, a centralized help desk, a 2,000-user corporate e-mail system, and a comprehensive training centre for desktop applications.

CHIEF EXECUTIVE, InterTech (1996–2000)
Promoted to manage all operations for this subsidiary. Took over leadership for a staff of 25 and recruited/ built to 90+ personnel. Oversaw all management reporting, finances, marketing, product delivery and closing services.

Key Management Achievements

- Delivered profits throughout a severe recession.

- Maintained a consistent 15% market share despite a tripling in the local competition.

- Achieved standing in the top 15% in profitability and revenues across all company offices nationwide.

- Created and deployed a marketing programme including a series of 20 seminars; built strong industry relationships and established a reputation as the area's premier experts.

- Pioneered innovative marketing strategies to reach new markets and build a network of industry professionals.

COMMERCIAL SALES (1993–1996)
Hired to develop and manage a commercial closing division. Achieved the highest market share of commercial closings in the local market.

EDUCATION
MBA, University of the West (1993)
Bachelor of Arts, Business, University of the West (1987)

PROFESSIONAL ACTIVITIES
Frequent Lecturer, Technology Conferences, 2003–Present
Member, Systems Committee, Technical Association, 2002–Present
Member, 'Technology 2000' Planning Committee, 2002–Present

Senior technology executive

BRENDA FRANKS

| 1 Any Street | Anytown AA1 1AA | 55555 555555 | Bfran@email.com |

SENIOR TECHNOLOGY EXECUTIVE
Project Management ◆ *Multimedia Communications & Production* ◆ *MIS Management*

PERFORMANCE PROFILE
Exceptionally creative management executive uniquely qualified for a digital media technical production position by a distinctive blend of hands-on technical, project management and advertising/communications experience. Offers a background that spans broadcast, radio and print media; fully fluent and proficient in interactive and internet technologies and tools.

Proven leader with a strength for identifying talent, building and motivating creative teams that work cooperatively to achieve goals. Highly articulate with excellent interpersonal skills and a sincere passion for blending communications with technology.

CORE SKILLS

- ◆ Project Planning & Management
- ◆ Account Management & Client Relations
- ◆ Multimedia Communications & Production
- ◆ Information Systems & Networking
- ◆ Conceptual & Creative Design

- ◆ Work Plans, Budgets & Resource Planning
- ◆ Department Management
- ◆ Interactive / Internet Technologies
- ◆ Technology Needs Assessment & Solutions
- ◆ Team Building & Leadership

PROFESSIONAL EXPERIENCE
LRI Investments Ltd, Liverpool   *1994–Present*
DIRECTOR OF MIS (2005–Present)
ASSISTANT DIRECTOR OF IT/CORPORATE COMMUNICATIONS   (2000–2005)
CORPORATE COMMUNICATIONS OFFICER   (1996–2000)
ASSOCIATE   (1994–1996)

Advanced rapidly through a series of increasingly responsible positions with this UK-based, European investment group. Initially hired to manage market research projects, advanced to plan and execute corporate communications projects, and in 2000, assumed responsibility for spearheading the introduction of emerging technologies to automate the entire company.

Current scope of responsibility is expansive and focuses on strategic planning, implementation and administration of all information systems and technology. Lead technical staff members, manage budgets, select and oversee vendors, define business requirements, and produce deliverables through formal project plans. Manage systems configuration and maintenance, troubleshoot problems, plan and direct upgrades, and test operations to ensure optimum systems functionality and availability.

Technical Contributions

- Pioneered the company's computerization from the ground floor; led the installation and integration of a state-of-the-art and highly secure network involving 50+ workstations running on six LANs interconnected by V-LAN switching technology.
- Defined requirements; planned and accelerated the implementation of advanced technology solutions, deployed on a calculated time frame, to meet the short- and long-term needs of the organization.
- Orchestrated the introduction of sophisticated applications and multimedia technology to streamline workflow processes, expand presentation capabilities, and keep pace with the competition.
- Administered the life cycle of multiple projects from initial systems/network planning and technology acquisition through installation, training and operation. Saved hundreds of thousands in consulting fees by managing IS and telecommunication issues in-house.

Continued

Management

Brenda Franks 55555 5555555 page 2 of 2

Business Contributions

- Created and produced high-impact multimedia presentations to communicate the value and benefits of individual investment projects to top-level company executives. Tailored presentations to appeal to highly sophisticated, multicultural audiences.
- Assembled and directed exceptionally well-qualified project teams from diverse creative disciplines; collaborated with and guided photographers, videographers, copywriters, script writers, graphic designers and artists to produce innovative presentations and special events.
- Performed market research and analyses to determine risks and feasibility of multiple investment projects valued at up to £150 million. Developed and recommended tactical plans to transform vision into achievement.

Broadcast, Print, and Radio Advertising & Production *1988–1994*

DIRECTOR OF ADVERTISING, ABC Advertising Associates, York (1992–1994)

ADVERTISING ACCOUNT EXECUTIVE, Scope, York (1992) / Rainbow Advertising, Bristol (1991–1992) / Marcus Advertising, Bristol (1990–1991) / Brunel Radio, Bristol (1989–1990)/XYZ Advertising, Lincoln (1988–1999)

WRITER/PRODUCER, RADIO PROGRAMMING, Brunel Radio, Bristol

Early career involved a series of progressive creative and account management positions spanning all advertising mediums: multimedia, television, radio and print. Worked directly with clients to assess complex and often obscure needs; conceptualized and developed advertising campaigns to communicate the desired message in an influential manner.

Achievement Highlights

- Designed, wrote, produced and launched advertising campaigns that consistently positioned clients with a competitive distinction. Developed a reputation for ability to accurately intuit and interpret clients' desires and produce campaigns that achieved results.
- Hand-selected and led creative teams consisting of graphic designers, artists, musicians, talent, cartoonists, animators, videographers, photographers and other freelancers and third-party creative services to develop and produce multimillion-pound advertising campaigns.
- Won accolades for the creation, production and launch of a four-colour fractional-page advertisement that generated the greatest response in the history of the publication. Honoured with a featured personal profile recognizing achievements.
- Developed and applied a unique style and advertising philosophy that accounted for the nuances of human psychology and used innovative, and sometimes startling techniques to capture attention and influence the target market.

EDUCATION & TRAINING

HND Media Studies, City College, 1988

Continuing education in Marketing Research and Broadcast Production, 1992–1994

City School of Visual Arts

TECHNICAL QUALIFICATIONS

Innate technical abilities and interest in emerging technologies and digital communications. Trained and fully versed in all aspects of network design, implementation, installation and maintenance. Advanced skill in the installation, configuration, customization and troubleshooting of software applications, hardware and peripherals within the Windows environment. Proficient with most Web development, multimedia, word processing, spreadsheet, graphic/ presentation, and database tools and applications.

Senior management executive

Management

JANE B URATA

1 Any Street, Anytown AA1 1AA
Home: 55555 555555 • Mobile: 5555555 5555 • E-Mail: ju_arborist@email.com

New Business Development • Secure e-commerce Product Marketing

PERFORMANCE SUMMARY

Accomplished Senior Executive with strong affinity for technology and keen business sense for the application of emerging products to add value and expand markets.

Proven talent for identifying core business needs and translating into technical deliverables. Launched and managed cutting-edge internet programmes and services to win new customers, generate revenue and increase brand value.

Unique combination of technical and business/sales experience. Articulate and persuasive explaining the benefits of e-commerce technologies and how they add value, differentiate offerings and increase customer retention. Highly self-motivated, enthusiastic and profit-orientated.

PROFESSIONAL COMPETENCIES

• Sales & Marketing • Business Development • Strategic Initiatives
• Business Planning • Project Management • Strategic Partnerships
• Business & Technical Requirements • Revenue Generation
• Contract Negotiations • Relationship Management

TECHNICAL COMPETENCIES

• Electronic Commerce • Encryption Technology • Key Management
• Public Key Infrastructure • Firewalls • Smart Cards • Stored Value
• Digital Certificates • Internet & Network Security • Complex Financial Systems
• Authorization, Clearing, Settlement • Dual and Single Message

PROFESSIONAL EXPERIENCE

ABC Credit Card, Maidstone   *2007 to Present*
E-COMMERCE AND SMART CARD CONSULTANT

- Developed strategic e-commerce marketing plans for large and small merchants involving web purchases and retail transactions using a multifunctional, microcontroller smart card for both secure internet online commerce and point-of-sale offline commerce.
- Combined multiple software products for internet and non-internet applications: home banking, stored value, digital certificates, key management, rewards & loyalty programme, and contactless microcontroller with RF communications without direct POS contact.
- Consulted on business and technical requirements to define new e-commerce products and essential deliverables for ABC Credit Card, valued at £2.5 million, supporting and enhancing internet transactions.
- Analysed systems relating to the point-of-sale environment in the physical world and at the merchant server via the internet for real-time authorization, clearing and settlement.
- Managed projects including the management system for electronic commerce affecting core systems: authorization, clearing and settlement. Provided expertise about business and technical issues including the Credit Card Payment Service.

Continued

Management

Jane B Urata	55555 555555	Page 2 of 2

Communications Technology Ltd, Manchester   *2002 to 2007*
MANAGER OF WESTERN REGION CHANNEL PARTNER PROGRAMME

- Developed and maintained business relationships with large blue-chip customers and partners that use or resell client-server software for applications and contracts involving e-commerce and smart card technology for a variety of internet/intranet products: home banking, EDI, stored value, digital certificates, key management, perimeter defense with proxy firewalls, secure remote access.

- Negotiated an exclusive contract with one of the largest government and commercial contractors in the industry, projected to generate £2–4 million over a 24–36 month period. Contract includes secure remote access, telecommuting, secure healthcare applications.

Avanta Ltd, Heybrook Park   *1998 to 2002*
SENIOR SOFTWARE ENGINEER/SOFTWARE INSTRUCTOR

- Designed new programs and trained software engineers in object-orientated analysis and design using UML. Solutions were implemented in C++ in a UNIX environment.

- Managed a software engineering group of 53 individuals. Developed in-house programme that saved over £150,000 in training costs for state-of-the-art communications system software development.

- Received award for outstanding performance; earned a performance evaluation rating of 4.2/5.0.

- Developed and maintained C and C++ communication software in a UNIX environment.

- Created curriculum and course materials that reduced overall training costs by more than £150,000. Coordinated and presented software training programmes.

EDUCATION AND CREDENTIALS

- BSc Electrical Engineering, University of London: Emphasis, software engineering
- Top Secret Security Clearance with Polygraph

Purchasing director.

PETER M RABBIT

1 Any Street ■ Anytown AA1 1AA
(H) 55555 555555 ■ (M) 5555555 5555
ptrrbt@anyserver.co.uk

PURCHASING DIRECTOR
SENIOR PROJECT MANAGER
SENIOR OPERATIONS MANAGER

Performance Summary

Senior Operations Manager offers extensive hands-on experience and a consistent track record in large-scale domestic and international capital projects, **fostering growth** and **delivering strong and sustainable gains**. A self-starter with a proven ability to conceptualize and implement **innovative solutions**. Applies **cutting-edge technologies** to update processes/systems. **Highly effective leadership and motivation skills** support the development of cohesive teams in achievement of strategic goals. **Extensive experience** partnering with influential business leaders.

■ CORE COMPETENCIES ■

Business Planning	Financial Analysis	Quality Assurance
Business Process Re-engineering	Influencing Skills	ERP/MRP
Contracts Administration	Negotiation Skills	Supplier/Vendor Management
Cost Containment	Logistics Management	Systems Implementation
Efficiency Improvement	Project Management	Warehouse Management

Career Highlights

- **Reduced operating costs by £500,000 per year** by outsourcing an 'in-house' printing department.

- Provided comprehensive capital procurement services for **£300 million construction and start-up of two newspaper printing press facilities.**

- **Significantly increased waste recycling revenues by £545,000 per year** through successful negotiations with individual recycling firms.

- Directed **operating budget of over £180 million** during construction and operations of the **Famous World Exhibition.**

- Initiated development and implementation of **budget tracking and reporting system in support of a £90 million capital project** which accelerated successful completion **90 days ahead of schedule and £1 million under budget.**

- Security operations **reduced in-house theft, drug and alcohol abuse by 99%, while reducing costs by £100,000 per year.**

Continued

Management

Management

Peter M Rabbit, page 2.

PROFESSIONAL EXPERIENCE

NEWSPAPER COMPANY, Manager, Procurement & Security   **2005 to Present**

- Established clear processes and procedures, and centralized purchasing and inventory management via first-ever electronic system in the newspaper system, reducing costs by £500,000/year.
- Introduced new technologies resulting in **increased efficiencies and cost-savings**; technologies included fax services and colour scanning, which increased turnaround in ad presentation and makeup and **saved £125,000/year**.
- **Reduced annual operating costs by £500,000/year through offshore purchasing and vendor partnerships.**
- Successfully **sourced national and international vendors, negotiated and administered contracts** and executed **procurement strategies** on several large-scale capital projects: Development of a new £60 million facility; £97 million development project for implementation of new printing processes.
- **Directed international sourcing and managed logistics,** which included customs documentation and inspections.
- Served as **Project Manager in the design of a waste management system,** providing detailed specifications and managing project activities; **generated a significant increase in revenue.**
- **Overhauled the Security function** – outsourcing, modernizing equipment, establishing and training contract staff on new procedures and roles; significantly reduced costs, and nearly eliminated all incidences of theft.
- **Initiated and implemented the 'pay in advance' system** – now used internationally among all newspapers – which contributed to a significant increase in revenue.
- **Revamped First Aid and Safety programme,** and **implemented Staff Protection Programme.**
- Managed sale of assets from old facilities, building deconstruction, and **seamless relocation of 900 employees.**

Continued

Peter M Rabbit, page 3.

WORLD EXHIBITION, Manager, Site Operations Procurement   **1991 to 2005**

World Exhibition's six-month World Fair exhibition is orchestrated and attended by over 70 countries, each with its own on-site pavilion. Managed comprehensive procurement services for construction and start-up of operations. Held signatory responsibility for all purchases, and spearheaded profitable vendor partnerships.

- **Hired and established a procurement team and introduced new technology,** which facilitated shared communications and increased procurement and materials handling efficiencies; successfully managed procurement activities throughout liquidation and site deconstruction.

- **Orchestrated first-ever buyback contracts** for heavy equipment and machinery used by the Exhibition, regaining a full 50% of the initial purchase price; negotiated and received free maintenance, providing additional cost savings; **negotiated service contracts** for site equipment and operations.

- **Demonstrated creative problem-solving skills,** which enhanced operations ability to provide ongoing entertainment, while significantly reducing operating costs.

PAPER COMPANY, Project Budget Controller/Buyer   **1989 to 1991**

Provided project support for a £90 million operations implementation.

- **Led the development of an innovative financial tracking and control system.**

- **Controlled spending and ensured consistent use of the system, enabling a perfectly balanced budget.**

- Identified an opportunity to apply for a tax break, **saving an additional £600,000** at project's end.

Previous Experience

BIGWIG COMPANY, Project Expeditor, 1987–1989
CHEMICAL COMPANY A, Project Buyer, 1986–1987
CHEMICAL COMPANY B, Project Buyer/Expeditor, 1984–1986
BIG COMPANY, Materials Supervisor, 1983–1984

Technologies

Accpac, Crystal Report Builder, Dun & Bradstreet, EDI, Microsoft Office, Purchase Soft, RAL, Visio

Professional Development

Newspaper Purchasing Association
Society for Industrial Security
Business/Marketing Management Diploma

Management

Office assistant (initial CV)

After interviewing Barbara, it became clear that she did more than her CV reflected. Aside from her initial CV being poorly formatted, it lacked focus, an interesting summary, and a content-rich presentation of her experience.

BARBARA WINSTON
1 Any Avenue, Anytown AA1 1AA
• • • 55555 555555 • • •

OBJECTIVE TO OBTAIN AN OFFICE ASSISTANT POSITION, ENABLING ME TO USE MY SKILLS AND DEVELOP CAREER PROGRESSION.

SKILLS WORD PERFECT 5.0 AND 6.0
LOTUS 123
MICROSOFT WINDOWS 98
KEYBOARDING
DICTAPHONE, OFFICE PROCEDURES
KNOWLEDGE OF BUSINESS AND ORAL COMMUNICATIONS
MEDICAL FORMATS
WORK HISTORY

12/11 to Present CITY UNIVERSITY, BRENTWOOD
LIBRARY ASSISTANT

ORGANIZING CIRCULATION DESK. ATTENTION TO DETAIL, EDITING, DATA ENTRY, PHOTOCOPYING, FAXING, FILING, ASSISTING STUDENTS WITH RESEARCH, ADMINISTERING TESTS.

3/09 to 6/10 BRENTWOOD EDUCATION AUTHORITY, BRENTWOOD
TEACHING ASSISTANT

ASSISTED TEACHERS WITH SPECIAL EDUCATION STUDENTS, COMPUTER LAB, LUNCH ROOM MONITOR, PERFORMED DUTIES IN PUBLICATIONS DEPARTMENT, CLERICAL DUTIES SUCH AS COLLATING, HAND-INSERTING, AND PROOFREADING.

EDUCATION

10/07 *SECRETARIAL SCHOOL*
MORRISTOWN
Certificate In Information Processing

1/95 ABC TRAINING SCHOOL
BRENTWOOD
Certificate In Medical Information Handling

EXCELLENT REFERENCES AVAILABLE UPON REQUEST

Office assistant (revised CV)

The result of this before-and-after CV is dramatic in many ways. It has gone from a confusing document to a personal marketing tool that clearly expresses Barbara's skills. Most importantly, the experience section has become very detailed and interesting to read.

BARBARA WINSTON
1 Any Avenue, Anytown AA1 1AA ◆ 55555 555555 ◆ BWinston@anyserver.co.uk

◆ ◆ ◆

PERFORMANCE PROFILE
Extensive experience working in general public, educational and medical settings.
Interface well with others at all levels including clients, patients, professionals, children and students.
Caring and hardworking with excellent interpersonal communication, customer service and office support skills.

Core Skills
Windows 98/DOS, MS Word, Dictaphone, CRT data entry, basic Internet skills, and medical terminology.

Work Experience

Library Assistant, City University, Brentwood   **12/11–Present**
Provided information services and research assistance to the general public and students
- ◆ Assisted users in obtaining a broad selection of books, periodicals, audio-visuals and other materials.
- ◆ Catalogued library materials, prepared bibliographies, indexes, guides and search aids.
- ◆ Performed multifaceted general office support, and administered academic placement tests.

Teaching Assistant / Office Assistant, Brentwood Education Authority, Brentwood   **3/09–6/11**
Assigned to the Publications Department, Computer Laboratory and Special Education Resource Room
- ◆ Assisted teachers with clerical support in areas of document proofreading, duplication, collating and distribution, classroom management, student monitoring and miscellaneous assignments.
- ◆ Easily established rapport with students, and interfaced well with parents and staff.

Nursing Assistant, Our Lady of Consolation, West Islip   **6/00–1/06**
Physical Therapy Aide, Mother Cabrini Nursing Home, Dobbs Ferry   **3/95–6/00**

Held the following combined responsibilities at Our Lady of Consolation and Mother Cabrini Nursing Home:
- ◆ Obtained vital signs and followed up with timely and accurate medical records-keeping procedures.
- ◆ Interfaced extensively with patients, staff, orthopaedic surgeons and neurologists.
- ◆ Observed and reported changes in patients' conditions and other matters of concern.
- ◆ Performed ambulatory therapeutic treatments such as range of motion, gait training and whirlpool baths.
- ◆ Transported patients to and from the hospital for emergency care and scheduled tests.
- ◆ Ensured the proper use of equipment and medical devices such as wheelchairs, braces and splints.
- ◆ Assisted patients with personal hygiene, grooming, meals and other needs requiring immediate attention.
- ◆ Maintained sanitary, neatness and safety conditions of rooms in compliance with mandatory regulations.

Education

Certificate, Information Processing, 2007
SECRETARIAL SCHOOL, Morristown

Certificate, Medical Information Handling, 1995
ABC TRAINING SCHOOL, Brentwood

Office and administrative

Administrative assistant

Lillian V DiFrancesa
1 Any Street, Anytown AX0 0AA
020 8123 4567 • Lilli@mydomain.com
Administration Assistant

Performance Profile

Administrative assistant with strong organizational and interpersonal skills, able to multitask a variety of responsibilities and challenges.

Core Skills

- Types 65 wpm
- Transcription
- MS Excel
- Purchasing

- Planning and Scheduling
- MS Word
- Written Communication
- Customer Service

- Internet Research
- Filing
- Telephone Reception
- Interdepartmental Coordination

Professional Achievements

- Handled 30–50 daily incoming calls on a six-line telephone system, offered a customer-friendly greeting, and promptly routed calls to proper party among 65 employees.
- Scheduled weekly meetings for all employee levels and their clients, greeted and escorted visitors to staff members' offices, and provided hospitality service (food and beverage) as requested by staff.
- Composed and distributed interoffice memorandums via electronic, voice and traditional paper means, increasing delivery and receipt of important information, and preserving the confidentiality of sensitive data.
- Assembled media kits for marketing and public relations department, saving approximately £35,000 in additional labour costs.
- Scheduled 15–20 monthly client and internal meetings for both on-site and off-site locations, ensuring housing, catering and materials.
- Coordinated domestic and international travel arrangements for 10 senior-level executives on a weekly basis using internet travel sites that saved company an average of £100–£200 per round-trip airfare ticket.
- Established confidential electronic filing system for all correspondence and incoming faxes, creating a history for staff and eliminating excess paper and chance of exposing sensitive data to unauthorized personnel.
- Dispatched three messengers on bank runs and special assignments as requested by management, coordinating trips to ensure that multiple stops were made each time. This saved the company approximately £25.00 per messenger per day in excess travel expenses.
- Sorted and distributed mail for 65 employees.
- Ordered office supplies through the internet, taking advantage of online savings and using electronic means to ensure accuracy and distribution of supplies to employees. This logging process helped improve the accuracy of interdepartment charge backs.

Employment History

Administrative Assistant, ABC Associates, Easton	2007–Present
Secretary/Receptionist Logic Systems and Solutions, York	2002–2007

Education

City Community College, OND Business Administration

Receptionist

Office and administrative

Keisha A Jackson

1 Any Street ◆ Anytown AA1 1AA ◆ 55555 555555 ◆ kaj@anyserver.co.uk

RECEPTION/CUSTOMER INTERFACE

PERFORMANCE PROFILE

Responsible and dedicated office professional with 15 years' experience in high-volume, fast-paced environments. Cooperative team player who enjoys working with people and using direct telephone contact. Detail-orientated, thorough, and accurate in taking and relaying information. Well-organized and able to handle a variety of assignments and follow through from start to finish. Strong work ethic, with eagerness to learn and willingness to contribute towards meeting a company's goals.

CORE COMPETENCIES

- ◆ Visitor reception
- ◆ Multi-line phone system operations
- ◆ Data entry and retrieval (Word and Excel)
- ◆ Customer relations
- ◆ Sales department support

- ◆ Account maintenance/reconciliation
- ◆ Order processing and invoicing
- ◆ Research and resolution of problems
- ◆ Regular and express mail distribution
- ◆ Office supplies and forms inventory

WORK HISTORY

ABC GROUP, Chingford   2007–Present
Personal and commercial insurance company
Receptionist

- ◆ Represented the prestigious image of this company in a high-profile position requiring public contact with important clients in the sports and entertainment field as well as various other industries.
- ◆ Entrusted with opening the office daily and handling confidential material.
- ◆ Operated 24-line Premiere 6000 phone system, transferring calls/faxes appropriately, and relaying messages accurately. Saved managers' time by screening unwanted calls.
- ◆ Reorganized postroom to run more efficiently and operated automated labelling/tracking system (Powership), processing 5 to 50 outgoing packages daily.
- ◆ Ensured prompt delivery of express packages.
- ◆ Took initiative to update insurance certificates on computer.
- ◆ Participated in hiring a new assistant and trained her in company procedures.

XYZ LTD, Chingford   2004–2007
Nation's largest distributor of speciality paper
Telephone Account Coordinator (Customer Service Representative)

- ◆ As one of 80 employees in a busy call centre averaging 200 incoming calls per hour, handled the ordering process, invoicing, and issuing credits to ensure accurate account records.
- ◆ Consistently achieved excellent scores in the mid-90s on monitored activities.
- ◆ Provided support to sales representatives all over the country.
- ◆ For four months in 2005, assisted the product director, creative director and head of sales, providing them with daily sales activity reports and analyses, pricing updates, and sales strategy presentations for company's two divisions.
- ◆ Processed invoices and deliveries for international shipments.

ABC VENDING COMPANY, Chingford   2002–2004
Distributor of confectionery items sold in vending machines
Customer Service Representative

- ◆ Worked in a team of six, processing telephone orders from individuals and retailers, including four house accounts. Resolved invoice discrepancies.
- ◆ Offered information on promotions and discounts, which encouraged larger orders.

THE PLAYHOUSE, Kingston   1997–2007
Director of Nursery

- ◆ While raising a family, owned and operated a full-service day care centre for preschool children.
- ◆ Administered all aspects of the business (invoicing, accounts payable, accounts receivable, and maintaining client files).

Office support professional

JANET COOPER　　　　　　　　　　55555 555555 • jcooper@email.com
1 Any Street, Anytown AA1 1AA

OFFICE SUPPORT PROFESSIONAL
Receptionist ... Clerk ... Administrative Assistant

CORE SKILLS

Records Management

Customer Liaison

Front Office Operations

Workflow Planning / Scheduling

Troubleshooting / Problem Solving

Inventory Control

COMPUTER SKILLS

- Microsoft Word
- Cornerstone Proprietary Contact
  Management Software

TRAINING SKILLS

Annual training for receptionists and managers

Top-performing office assistant with a reputation for professionalism, integrity, creativity, resourcefulness and competence. Superior communication and listening skills. Strong client focus, with attention to detail and excellent follow-through.

PROFESSIONAL ACHIEVEMENTS

- Redesigned administrative processes to streamline functions, eliminate redundancy and expedite workflow. Initiated the conversion from manual processes to a fully computerized office. Implemented the automated HR Payroll Programme.
- Improved customer service by developing a new client survey, soliciting feedback to resolve client complaints quickly and ensure top-quality service and satisfaction.
- Launched an employee-of-the-month incentive programme to build unity and promote outstanding customer service.

PROFESSIONAL EXPERIENCE

Practice Manager – 2006–Present
Receptionist – 2005–2006
COMPLETE ANIMAL HOSPITAL, Torquay
(Veterinary clinic comprised of 6 vets, 10 technicians and 7 receptionists with annual revenues of £1.4 million)
Oversaw scheduling, managed inventory and trained receptionists. Accountable for financial reports including daily deposits, monthly invoicing and collections.

Receptionist – 2003–2005
WILLIAM SMITH, Torquay
(One-doctor veterinary clinic, 2 technicians, 2 receptionists)
Professional and cheerful first point of contact. Broad-based experience of answering multiple telephone lines, scheduling appointments and filling prescriptions.

RELATED EXPERIENCE

Administrative Assistant
ABC BUSINESS SYSTEMS, Torquay

Clerical Assistant
OSTEOPATHIC SCHOOL OF MEDICINE, Exeter

Customer service professional

Anne Granger

1 Any Street
Anytown, AX0 0AA

020 8123 4567
agranger@anyserver.com

CUSTOMER SERVICES

PERFORMANCE PROFILE

Customer service professional, skilled in problem solving and responsive to needs of clients, co-workers and management. Poised, resourceful and adaptable to any office environment. Organizational ability to handle multiple priorities and meet deadline schedules. Attentive to detail, with sharp awareness of omissions/inaccuracies, and prompt to take corrective action. A self-starter, eager to assume increasing levels of responsibility.

CORE SKILLS

Professional phone manner; data entry and word processing; updating/maintenance of files and records; composition of routine correspondence.

EMPLOYMENT HISTORY

CUSTOMER SERVICE ASSISTANT
ABC Insurance, Cheltenham *(2012–Present)*
Hired as a data entry operator and advanced to customer service position in less than a year. Took over problem desk, which had been inadequately handled by two previous employees. Worked closely with underwriters, answering client enquiries by phone or mail. Analysed complex situations affecting insurance coverage. Recognized opportunities to increase sales and advised clients when coverage was lacking in specific policy areas.

Key Accomplishments: During major restructuring of company resulting in 70% staff reduction, assumed more than triple the normal account responsibility, from 450 to over 1,500, while still in training. Simultaneously studied for insurance licensing course; passed exam on first try, with score of 95.

APPLICATIONS SCREENER
XYZ Insurance, Cheltenham *(2010–2012)*
(Applications processing centre for Mutual Surety Corporation)
Screened homeowners' new lines of business applications, verifying coverage. Filled in whenever needed for switchboard, typing and clerical assignments.

CHILD CARE RESPONSIBILITIES *(2003–2010)*

CENSUS TAKER
UK Census Bureau, Cheltenham *(2003)*
Visited individuals who had not filled out census forms properly. Worked in a multi-ethnic territory, overcoming language barriers and mistrust. Clarified discrepancies and ensured accuracy and completeness of reported information.

ADMINISTRATIVE CLERK
DEF Insurance Company, Middleton *(2001–2003)*
Started as receptionist and promoted shortly thereafter to handle various clerical assignments. Prepared paperwork for file with arbitration board. Kept ledgers up to date for auditors' review.

EDUCATION
City College – Diploma in Business Administration *(1999–2001)*
Completed 12-week basic course in Property and Casualty, Insurance Law, and Health Insurance (2013)

Customer service specialist

BRENDA FORMAN
1 Any Street
Anytown AA1 1AA   Phone: 55555 55555

CUSTOMER SERVICE PROFESSIONAL
SENIOR CUSTOMER SPECIALIST • INVOICING • CREDIT

Shipping and Dispatching • Inventory Control

PERFORMANCE SUMMARY

Top-performing customer service specialist with more than 20 years' experience in diverse environments. Outstanding reputation for maintaining excellent customer service standards. Experienced in working with high volume calls and answering detailed inquiries.

Train and observe other customer service staff. Take pride in order-processing accuracy and efficiency; receive excellent customer feedback. Punctual in meeting deadlines. Interact with the MD of my present company on a daily basis. Known to go the 'extra mile' for customers and colleagues. Dedicated, efficient, task-orientated employee.

Perform the functions of Order Processing Specialist, Diversified Account Specialist and Crediting/Invoice Specialist. Skilled planner with the ability to analyse client needs and achieve objectives.

CUSTOMER SERVICE SKILLS

- Customer Service
- Shipping Receiving
- Manufacturing Processes
- Troubleshooting Accounts
- Leadership/Supervision
- Sales Force Support
- Accounts Receivable
- Inventory Control Functions

- Pricing/Quoting Customers
- Processing Orders
- Expediting Deliveries
- Tracking
- Special Attention Order Entry
- Customer Service Observations
- Invoicing
- Written Reports

BUSINESS EXPERIENCE

ABC Ltd, Canterbury   **2005–Present**
Senior Customer Service Representative and Trainer
Team Leader
- Currently serve as a Team Leader for this fine art and supplies manufacturer. Responsible for training and observation of other customer service employees. Lead customer service meetings and prepare written reports of findings.
- Replace supervisor in her absence.
- Ensure that discounts are applied correctly, and credits are entered in a timely fashion.
- Work with orders from start to completion. Interact daily with Daler-Rowney sales force and district manager.

Continued

BRENDA FORMAN   **PAGE TWO**

- Handle customer requests. Take orders via fax, place on our system, send to purchasing; then send to warehouse, edit order, invoice, print, and send to customers.
- Process all orders from XYZ, our largest customer, through an EDI system.
- Work with internet order-processing systems including Microsoft Orbit program, Navision Financial Program, Trading Partners, Retail Link, Microsoft Word and Excel.
- Attend trade shows and handle special orders in the field. Work with export customers.
- Print back order reports on a weekly basis. Work with potential new clients and their sales representatives regarding administrative work.
- Process numerous order per day including 500–1,000 keyed lines. Write reports in Microsoft Excel and Word.
- Responsible for issuing all return authorization numbers. Research credits and input information into our system.

XYZ INDUSTRIES, Canterbury   **1996–2005**
Shipping/Receiving Coordinator
Customer Service Representative

- Responsible for a wide range of shipping/receiving and customer service functions for this carpet manufacturer. Handled an extremely high call volume. Processed orders, answered customer inquires, tracked inbound/outbound shipments, expedited deliveries and set up delivery schedules. Prepared shipments and participated in cycle counting and quarterly inventories.
- Attended trade shows and expedited special attention orders.
- Coordinated with and supported sales representatives in the field. Performed cash receipt reconciliations and resolved customer complaints, disputes or discrepancies.
- Received Employee of the Month Award out of 300 people.

ABC LIFE INSURANCE, Plymouth   **1994–1996**
Customer Service Representative

- Responsible for pricing/quoting customers, answering phone inquiries, processing orders and expediting deliveries along with troubleshooting accounts.

CHILDCRAFT, Plymouth   **1993–1994**
Customer Service Representative

- Duties similar to above. Position required ability to work in a high-pressure/fast-paced environment.

ACTION Ltd, Birmingham   **1990–1993**
Shipping/Receiving Coordinator/Accounts Receivable Clerk

~ LETTERS OF RECOMMENDATION AND REFERENCES UPON REQUEST ~

Customer service representative

JUANITA FLORES

1 Any Street • Anytown AA1 1AA

Home 55555 555555 • Mobile 5555555 5555 • jflores555@email.com

Customer Service Representative / Administrative Support Specialist

—Bilingual English / Spanish—

Highly reliable professional who consistently demonstrates integrity and sound judgement.

Verifiable record of low absenteeism and punctuality; performs tasks with enthusiasm and efficiency.

Well organized with good time-management habits; completes assignments in a timely and accurate manner.

Works well independently as well as collaboratively in a team environment.

Reputation for exceptional customer relations; easily establishes trust and rapport with public, demonstrating good listening skills.

Strong problem-solving abilities; can be counted on to follow through to resolution.

Computer Skills: Windows, Microsoft Office (Word, Excel, PowerPoint)

PROFESSIONAL EXPERIENCE

Administrative Assistant, Trust Division • 2010 to Present

ABC BANK, Leeds

Provide outstanding customer-service handling and directing incoming telephone calls, assisting clients with inquiries and requests, and processing account transactions.

Directly support two directors and team of trust specialists with administrative and clerical tasks.

Administrative Assistant • 2006 to 2010

XYZ NEWSPAPER, Tenerife

Provided sales and administrative support to advertising account executives. Assisted customers with inquiries and marketing information in Spanish and English.

Performed translation services.

Handled English and Spanish language correspondence.

Apartment Building Manager • 2006 to 2009 (*concurrent with above*)

DEF PARTNERS PROPERTIES, Tenerife

Collect rents, ensure grounds and units are well maintained, prepare vacancies for rental, screen applicants and write-up rental agreements.

EDUCATION

CITY COLLEGE

BA Business Administration

Retail manager

SCOTT KELLY

1 Any Street
Anytown AA1 1AA

55555 555555
ScottKelly@email.com

RETAIL ~ SALES & MANAGEMENT

Successful retail manager with over 14 years' experience in Sales, Purchasing/Buying, Customer Service, Inventory Management, Merchandising, Staff Recruitment and Supervision. Proven ability to increase sales revenue and improve profitability through effective sales consultation, merchandising, purchasing and inventory management. Demonstrate a high level of motivation and enthusiasm in all aspects of work.

- **Record of improving sales, successfully introducing new products and growing customer base.** Expanded business for large volume – wine speciality – off-licence.
- **Excellent leadership skills** – can communicate effectively with employees and motivate them to perform at their best. Can set direction for the team. Hands-on approach to training.
- **Established record of dependability and company loyalty.**
- **Experience in both general merchandising and speciality retail sales.** Extensive knowledge of the wine industry including suppliers, distributors and consumers; extensive product knowledge.

SALES MANAGEMENT CORE COMPETENCIES

- Sales
- Merchandising
- Purchasing
- Cash Management
- Budgets
- Promotional Events
- Security

- Purchasing
- Staff Recruitment
- Staff Supervision
- Product Introduction
- Sales Forecasting
- Competitive Pricing
- Training

- Customer Service
- Inventory Management
- Speciality Retail Sales
- Special-Order Purchasing
- Promotional Displays
- POS Technology

PROFESSIONAL EXPERIENCE

Manager (General Operations), *ABC Stores*, Woburn   **2006–present**

Direct the daily operation of a high-volume off-licence/wine speciality store, servicing over 1,000 customers per week. Manage staff of 15 in the areas of sales and customer service, cash management, budgeting, sales forecasting, employee relations, merchandising, promotions and security.

- Steadily increased revenues through strong focus on customer service, excellent merchandising and teamwork.
- Attracted new clientele to store through the development of a full-service wine department. Expanded product line, increased sales and special-order purchasing by implementing specialized sales methods, such as promotional wine-tasting events.
- Established strong reputation in the area as leader for extensive wine inventories at competitive pricing, including regularly stocked hard-to-find selections.
- Trained staff in selling through increased product knowledge and food and wine pairing.
- Participated regularly in trade tastings, shows and vintner dinners.

Manager (Stock and Display), *XYZ Department Store*, Oxford   **2004–2005**

Managed a staff of 12 in a large general merchandise store. Marketed and sold products; developed merchandise and promotional displays; maintained stock levels.

- Increased profits through effective displays and merchandising.
- Improved operations through effectively supervising daily staff assignments.

Stock/Inventory Manager, *DEF Gifts*, Oxford   **2002–2004**

Managed purchasing and supervised sales staff for a high-traffic speciality gifts store.

- Expanded customer base by offering a wide range of attractive product displays and creating a welcoming atmosphere that increased the comfort level of shoppers.
- Supervised staff of three, ensuring quality of store display and product inventory levels.

Additional experience includes entry-level inventory/shipping-receiving position at City University (2000–2002).

Merchandise buyer

Mary J Sanders

1 Any Street • Anytown AA1 1AA • 55555 555555 • mjsanders@anyserver.net

Assistant Buyer
Performance Profile

- Wholesale / Retail Buying
- Product Merchandising
- Inventory Replenishment
- Product Distribution and Tracking
- Sales Analysis & Reporting
- Regional Marketing Campaigns
- Information Systems
- Vendor Relations
- Order Management

Professional Experience

Assistant Buyer / Sales Analyst   7/10–Present
LONDON-AMERICAN COMMODITIES, LTD (LAC), London

Sales Tracking, Analysis & Reporting

- Perform LAC's weekly sales analysis on regional/local transactions, achieving a recovery of £1,800,000 from 2011 to 2014 from identification and resolution of accounting discrepancies.

- Develop sales books reflecting product lines, monthly promotions, discontinued items, order forms and transparencies used by sales teams and personnel throughout 26 store locations.

- Formulate price breakdowns and track sales levels to determine product volume adjustments, replenishments, and allocations with a demonstrated proficiency in internal networking systems.

- Researched, compiled and recorded LAC's historical data to develop innovative sales strategies through close examination of inventory and product availability, pricing and store promotions.

Assistant Buyer / Merchandise Coordinator   4/06–7/10
ABC BEDDING, York

Merchandise Buying / Coordination

- Report directly to ABC's Director of Sales, providing support in areas of commodities buying and merchandising activities that reach annual sales volumes of £3 million for the division.

- Collaborate with multiple buyers to facilitate the marketing of new products, and development of promotional calendars, product launches and employee incentive programmes.

- Maintain open lines of communication between manufacturers, sales teams, vendors and warehousing personnel to expedite product orders, distribution and problem resolutions.

- Reported directly to the Senior Buyer of ABC Bedding in charge of day-to-day retail merchandise buying and merchandising activities impacting bedding sales across 37 locations.

- Successfully trained 45+ employees on a complex LAN database management system.

Education

BA (Hons) Business Management, 2006
UNIVERSITY of YORK

Visual merchandising specialist

page 1 of 2

Jane Swift
123 Any Street, Anytown AT1 0BB
Tel: 020 8123 4567 jane@anyaddress.co.uk
VISUAL MERCHANDISER

PERFORMANCE PROFILE
Fifteen years' experience in Visual Merchandising Management.

- Coordinated all Visual Merchandising in Nairn's third-most-profitable store.
- Supervised visual aspects of a successful £1.5 million store renovation with responsibility for new fixtures and merchandising.
- Conducted seminar in Visual Merchandising for all new department managers in Nairn's Eastern region.
- Used innovative image control techniques that contributed to a new high-fashion store becoming the volume leader for its entire chain in one year.

PROFESSIONAL ACCOMPLISHMENTS
Visual Merchandising Manager of a Nairn's store with a £20 million sales volume, I coordinated fixtures, merchandising and seasonal changes for all 12 departments, along with responsibility for overall store image.

- Analysed stock levels to determine new fixture needs, prepared requirement reports and coordinated on-time deliveries of all fixtures.
- Reporting directly to the Director of Corporate Visual Merchandising, I supervised five Visual Merchandising Managers brought in from other stores to assist in the project.
- Interfaced with construction personnel while directing movement of departments under construction.
- Guiding all Department Managers through renovation and construction, I familiarized them with new fixtures and applicable merchandising techniques.

EARLIER ACCOMPLISHMENTS
As District Display Director for Daisy Chain, a 100-store speciality women's ready-to-wear chain, I developed fashion awareness, coordinated displays and trained staff, including new District Display Directors throughout the country. Reporting directly to the Corporate Display Director.

- Given responsibility for image control at the company's new flagship store in Oxford Street, where fashion image was crucial. My innovative merchandising and display techniques contributed to this store's becoming the number-one-volume store for the entire company by its first anniversary.

Continued

Retail and customer service

Retail and customer service

Jane Swift 020 8123 4567 page 2 of 2

- Recognized for my planning, organizing and coordinating abilities, I was involved in several new store openings throughout the UK and Europe.

As Display Coordinator/Visual Merchandising Manager with IMAGE Ltd, I progressed to having a five-store responsibility. Developing my functional skills, I was promoted to Visual Display troubleshooter for the region.

EMPLOYMENT
NAIRN LTD 2010–Present
DAISY CHAIN 2005–2010
IMAGE 2000–2005

EDUCATION
A graduate of Harpdale College, with a speciality in Fashion Design, I have also completed intensive course work in Architectural Technology, which has significantly contributed to my expertise in store renovation and floor plan know-how. Course work in photography has rounded out my background.

PERSONAL
Interests include fashion design and construction, sketching and free-hand drawing.

Restaurant waiter

Valerie W Butler
1 Any Street • Anytown AA1 1AA
222-222-2222 mobile • home 555-555-5555

⚘ Server ⚘

Professional Profile

Energetic and highly motivated **Food Server** with extensive experience in the food service industry. Expertise lies in working with the fine dining restaurant, providing top-quality service and maintaining a professional demeanour. Solid knowledge of the restaurant business with strengths in excellent customer service, food and wine recommendations.

Get along well with management, co-workers and customers. Well-developed communication skills, known as a caring and intuitive 'people person', with an upbeat and positive attitude. Highly flexible, honest and punctual, with the ability to stay calm and focused in stressful situations. Committed to a job well done and a long-term career.

Outstanding Achievements & Recommendations

- Served notable VIP clientele including clients associated with ABC Charitable Trust.
- History of repeat and new customers requesting my service as their waitress.
- Known for creating an atmosphere of enjoyment and pleasure for the customer.

'Valerie was warm, friendly, kind and very efficient.
We didn't feel rushed – she handled our requests and
we appreciated her genuine "Can I help you" attitude....'

Related Work History

Waitress • **Banquets** • Heath House • Maidenhead • *2010–present* • *Seasonal cuisine.*
Banquets • Dolce Vita • Stevenage • *2009–2010* • *Casual to fine dining restaurant.*
Waitress • Hidden House • Maidenhead • *2004–2009* • *Exclusive fine dining restaurant.*
Waitress • Falls Restaurant • Reading • *2003–2004*
Historic restaurant serving authentic French cuisine.
Waitress • The XYZ Restaurant • Oxford • *1 year*
World renowned award-winning fine dining restaurant.

Sommelier

Angelica's CV was arranged to look like a menu.

Restaurant and hospitality

Angelica Merceau
1 Any Street, Anytown AA1 1AA
Phone: 55555 555555 Email: wineangel@email.com

~~~~~~

Sommelier Extraordinaire

Piedmonts, Cheltenham
Master Sommelier, September 2006 – Present

➢ Expertise in all aspects of wine, including regions of the world and their products, grape varietals, fortified wines, methods of distillation, international wine law, cigar production, and proper storage and handling.
➢ Manage wine inventory averaging over 12,000 bottles, worth £2.5 million.
➢ Supervise and personally train staff of 25 sommeliers and wine stewards in pairing wines with cuisine, presentation of wine, brandies, liqueurs and cigars, and selection, preparation and placement of glassware.
➢ Coordinate all wine-tasting events, and varietal seminars.
➢ Handle all client inquiries and complaints.

Bordeaux Steak House, York
Sommelier, May 2004–January 2006
Lead Wine Steward, December 2002–May 2004

➢ Supervise and train staff of wine stewards in all aspects of wine presentation, pairing with cuisine, and glassware selection and placement.
➢ Choose appropriate cuisine and wine pairings, assist clients in selection of wines, brandies, liqueurs, cigars, properly present and decant wines, and select and place stemware.

Education, Certifications and Professional Development:

➢ City College
NVQ3 Food and Drink Service

➢ Institute of Master Sommeliers
Master Sommelier, 2006

➢ International Sommelier Guild
*Sommelier Diploma Programme, 2004
*Wine Fundamentals Certificate, Level II, 2004
*Wine Fundamentals Certificate, Level I, 2004

➢ Sommelier Society of Europe

Varietal Courses:
*Cabernet Sauvignon, 2004   *Sauvignon Blanc, 2004   *Chardonnay, 2004
*Merlot, 2004   *Sangiovese, 2004   *Syrah, 2003
*Pinot Noir, 2003   *Riesling, 2003

Professional Memberships
➢ *Association de la Sommellerie Internationale (ASI)*
Member, 2006 – Present

➢ *The Sommelier Society of Great Britain*
Member, 2004 – Present

Chef

JACKLYN LAFLAMME
Address   Postcode
Home Phone   Mobile Phone   Email Address

CHEF

*Fifteen Years' Management/Culinary Experience in Food Service Operations and Passion for
Food Preparation and Exemplary Guest Service in Executive Chef Position*

Quality-driven, guest-focused and award-winning chef with a track record of building and maintaining optimal guest satisfaction and excellent productivity/profit performance. Place uncompromising focus on guest needs fulfilment while striving to meet and surpass sales and production targets. Effective communicator, listener and troubleshooter. Able to manage multimillion-pound operations, prioritize multiple tasks in high-volume environments and relate to employees/guests with a wide range of backgrounds and personality types. Proficient in Execuchef, Cheftec and MS Office applications; thorough knowledge of kitchen equipment.

Core competencies and knowledge base include:

- Front-of-House Management
- Banquet Operations
- Team Building/Leadership
- New Operations Launch
- Guest Satisfaction/Retention
- Food Preparation & Preservation
- Staff Training & Evaluation
- Menu Planning & Pricing
- Service Improvements
- Purchasing & Receiving
- Quality Assurance Standards
- Time/Resource Management

Professional Experience

ABC HOTEL – London   2008–Present
Food operations included two restaurants, patio/café, 12,000 square foot banquet and catering space, in-room dining for 314 rooms, and 100-person employee cafeteria.

EXECUTIVE CHEF
Senior Food Service Executive with full accountability and decision-making authority for all food/kitchen operational functions, directing staff of three managers, three sous chefs and seven dish staff. Hold additional roles as Director of Purchasing/Receiving for all food and non-alcoholic beverages and Executive Steward. Established and implemented all systems guiding kitchen operations, instituted sanitation policies and HSE guidelines, and developed all menus for restaurants and banquet/catering functions.

- **New Systems Implementation** – Introduced software to manage inventory, labour/costing schedules, and recipe/plate costing, leading to 3.5% decrease in overall food cost, 4% reduction in kitchen labour cost, and overall increase in consistency.

Continued

Restaurant and hospitality

Jacklyn LaFlamme   Page 2

Professional Experience Continued

- **Food Cost & Labour Reduction** – Generated over £84,000 in food cost savings since restaurant's opening (01/09) through price modifications, improvements in portion control and negotiations with vendors to secure better purchasing deals, Reduced kitchen labour to annual rate of 9.84.

- **Operations Launch & Renovation** – Currently consulting with management on new hotel kitchen opening in 2015. Rewrote menus, designed recipes, trained cooking staff and set up other aspects of Courtyard by Marriott franchise. Directed two kitchen renovations to meet increased business.

- **Critic Reviews** – Led operations to receive outstanding reviews from leading local critics, including:
  - *ABC Journal*, rated 'Very Good'
  - *DEF Times*, rated 'Excellent'
  - *Cuisine*, featured 2010, 2011, 2012
  - *Food.Com*, rated 'Best Restaurant'
  - *City Paper*, rated 'Very Good to Excellent'
  - *AAA*, rated '3 Diamond Hotel'
  - *Mobil*, rated '3 Star Property'
  - *Where Magazine*, featured May, 2010

XYZ Restaurant: XYZ Hotel – Torquay   2008/2003–2004
Torquay's premier restaurant with food sales exceeding £3 million annually.

EXECUTIVE CHEF (2008) / **SOUS CHEF** (2003–2004)
Recruited for return after previously successful tenure as Sous Chef to lead all kitchen operations while assisting General Manager and Proprietor in developing strategies for profit and quality improvements. Supervised team of 170, created daily specials and standardized written recipes and operational procedures.

- **Menu Planning & Design** – Developed new bar, late night and café menus that provided additional revenue centres and led to £200,000 revenue increase; continued development on new menu of Creole and Acadian cuisine with modern influences.

- **Process Automation** – Introduced new inventory and recipe software that resulted in 3.2% decrease in overall food cost.

- **Formal Recognition** – Selected for Great Chef Culinary Series; chosen as one of five 'Great Chefs of Britain' for City Market dining promotion/festival.

- **Restaurant Reviews** – Achieved excellent reviews from local critics and publications:
  - *XYZ Journal*, '3 stars'
  - *MNO News*, '4 stars'
  - *PQR Times*, '4 stars' 'Best of Class 2008'
  - People Choice, 'Best in the West'
  - *DEF Magazine*, 'Best Bar/Restaurant'

Continued

Jacklyn LaFlamme   Page 3

Education & Credentials

Professional Development Courses:

- ServSafe Train the Trainer Sanitation Course – National Restaurant Association – 2012
- ServSafe Foodservice Sanitation Certification – National Restaurant Association – 2011
- Diversity Awareness Skills Training Seminar – MNO Hotel – 2010
- Big Tastes, Small Plates; Appetizers Class – The Culinary Institute – August, 2013

Affiliations:

- National Restaurant Association (NRA) – 2007 – Present
- Hotel Restaurant Association – Former member
- International Association of Culinary Professionals (IACP) – 2012 – Present
- Chef's Association – 2012 – Present

Recognitions:

- Selected as a Member of the Registry of Outstanding Professionals 2012, 2013, 2014
- Won 2nd Place – People's Choice Award 2014 – Sponsored by the Food and Drink Association – Sanctioned & certified by the Culinary Association
- Awarded 3rd Place Entrée Magazine's Dessert Contest – Sponsored by the Restaurant Association – Judged by the Culinary Institute, 2004
- Selected as a guest Chef for Culinary Great Chef Series, 2008

Presentations & Community Work:

- Hosting ABC Foundation Fundraiser Dinner, 2014 – 'Once In 100 Years' chef's dinner
- Featured on 'The Best Of' on the TV Food Network
- 'Great Chef of Ireland' – Dublin Food & Music Festival
- Best Chef Fundraiser
- Special Olympics Chef's Dinner
- Mentor for the ABC Charter Hospitality High School
- Volunteer cook for Salvation Army Christmas initiative

Hospitality management professional

Dianne Martino
1 Any Street • Anytown AA1 1AA
Home 55555 555555 • Mobile 5555555 5555 • DianneMartino@email.com

HOSPITALITY / HOTEL MANAGEMENT
Strengths in Operations / Sales / Marketing

Top-flight hospitality management professional with 10+ years' progressive experience and a track record of delivering measurable revenue and profit contributions. Team-building and leadership strengths with proven ability to hire, train and motivate top-performing teams. 'Big-picture' thinker, highly organized, with the ability to multitask in a fast-paced environment and respond quickly and effectively to problems. Learns quickly and thrives on challenges.

—Core Competencies—

Customer Service / Client Relations / Team Building / Hiring, Training & Motivating Operations Management / Marketing / Advertising / Time & Task Management / Policy & Procedures Revenue Optimization / Cost Containment / Productivity Enhancement / Problem Solving

PROFESSIONAL EXPERIENCE

CITY RESTAURANT, London
Achieved fast-track promotion to positions of increasing responsibility at world-renowned establishment.

Assistant General Manager (2009–Present)
Oversee day-to-day food and beverage operations of £5+ million fine-dining establishment that averages 250 covers daily. Train, manage and mentor cross-functional team of 60+, ensuring highest standard of customer service and brand integrity. Supervise food & beverage inventories, manage costs and maximize profitability, monitor safe handling best practices & procedures; prepare sales and labour forecasts. P&L accountability. Payroll responsibility. Accounting & POS support.

- Orchestrated scheduling initiative that minimized overtime, captured 10% increase in productivity and reduced payroll by over 10%.
- Hired, trained and supervised cross-functional front- and back-of-the-house staff of 60 with minimum turnover; achieved impact ratio over 100%.
- Generated mystery shopper score of 90+% annually.
- Slashed food cost by over £150,000 annually.
- Created marketing strategies that increased top-line sales.
- Consistently ensured excellent service within critical time frame for 300+ pre-theatre patrons as required.
- Organized alcohol perpetual inventory and streamlined daily procedures, capturing cost reduction of 2%.

Continued

DIANNE MARTINO
PAGE TWO • 55555 555555

Administrative Manager (2007–2009)
Promoted after nine months to initiate and manage administrative affairs for new location including daily cash and credit reconciliations, employee file maintenance, accounts payable, office administration, staff administration, recruitment processing, etc.
- Achieved 95% or better on all audits.
- Appointed as corporate administrative trainer; trained six managers during tenure.
- Authored Positouch Procedural Guide for use at all locations.
- Designed employee file initiative that was adopted for use company-wide.
- Implemented side work, floor plan and scheduling charts to organize restaurant opening.
- Assumed responsibility for health and safety initiatives that resulted in perfect scores on corporate audits.

Bartender (2005–2006)
Waitress (2005)

XYZ RESTAURANT, London • 2001–2005
Shift Supervisor / Bartender / Server
Advanced to shift supervisor with responsibility for opening/closing, scheduling staff, maintaining inventory, purchasing, reconciling cash drawer, etc, for busy city restaurant.
- Gained valuable experience in all aspects of restaurant operations.
- Developed 'spotter' system to eliminate theft that has been implemented by other establishments throughout the area.
- Increased sales through 'door to door' advertising programme.

Additional Experience – *Worked part-time as waitress at various establishments concurrent with university studies*

EDUCATION

UNIVERSITY OF LONDON
BA Humanities
Professional Development / Certifications
Stellar Service Training (2009)
Servsafe, FMP (Food Management Professionals) Certified Trainer

ADDITIONAL INFORMATION

Professional Affiliations – Member, NAWBO (National Association of Women's Business Owners)

Computer Skills – (PC and Macintosh), Word, Excel, Databases, POS Systems (Positouch, Squirrel, Micros), Restaurant Magic

Foreign Language Skills – Conversational Spanish in the workplace

Restaurant and hospitality

Communications

DEBRA JOY BISMARK

1 Any Street, Any Town AX0 0AA   020 8123 4567
E-MAIL: Bismark@email.com

Communications and writing professional

PERFORMANCE SUMMARY
- Research and Narrative Reports
- Academic Writing & Marketing
- Advertising & Promotional Writing
- Newsletters and Feature Stories
- Editorial Functions
- Community Relations
- Grant Writing
- Public Relations
- Proposals

CORE WRITING SKILLS
- Authored individualized newsletters for families of students with special needs
- Wrote detailed narrative reports citing student progress
- Wrote news stories, regular features for monthly newsletter with readership of 50,000 (Institute of Chemical Engineers, IChE)
- Wrote articles for student member magazine during six-year tenure as Communications Writer (IChE)
- Poetry published in *Without Halos*, *Worksheets*, *The Poet's Page*, and accepted into *Mediphors* and *Poet*
- Enjoy collaborating with colleagues to develop programmes and implement projects. Articulate ideas clearly and concisely

PROFESSIONAL ACHIEVEMENTS
- Turned technical papers into crisp copy – press releases received national recognition (IChE)
- Created and ran building code research business for York Architectural Support Services
- Designed brochure educating parents on early literacy
- Executive committee members wrote letters of appreciation for concept identifying a new engineering-in-schools campaign (Project VEGA, IChE)
- Won a company-wide logo competition (IChE)
- Created a proposal for a reading/writing clinic (South Somerset LEA)
- Trained and advised colleagues in strategies for supporting early reading and writing

CORE TECHNICAL SKILLS
- Proofread and edited technical articles for a scientific journal (IChE)
- Computer literate with working knowledge of Microsoft Word, Desktop Publishing (Ventura), Access database training
- Capable Internet researcher

PROFESSIONAL EXPERIENCE

2010–present	Programme Assistant (part-time)	THE INSTITUTE FOR ADVANCED STUDY, Somerset
2009–present	Reading Tutor	SELF-EMPLOYED
2008–2009	Teacher	FRIENDS SCHOOL, DOVER
2003–2008	Teacher	SOUTH SOMERSET LEA
1997–2003	Communications Writer	THE INSTITUTE OF CHEMICAL ENGINEERS
1996–1997	Editorial Assistant	THE INSTITUTE OF CHEMICAL ENGINEERS
1994–1996	Researcher	ARCHITECTURAL SUPPORT SERVICES

EDUCATION

MA, Social Work	City University
Teacher training	City College of Education
BSc Psychology	City University

Graphic designer/illustrator

Today every CV needs to be data-dense and appealing to the eye, and never more so than with a graphic designer; a beautiful example of form following function.

NORA PATTERSON

Address   Phone
Postcode   Email Address

ILLUSTRATOR   ✍   GRAPHIC DESIGNER   ✍   VISUAL ARTIST

CORE SKILLS

Textbook Illustration

❖ ❖ ❖

Scientific Drawings

❖ ❖ ❖

Museum Exhibits Illustration

❖ ❖ ❖

Book Illustration

❖ ❖ ❖

Cartoon Image Design

❖ ❖ ❖

Greeting Card Design/Illustration

❖ ❖ ❖

Artifact Replications

❖ ❖ ❖

Surface Colouration Restoration

❖ ❖ ❖

Original & Production Artwork

❖ ❖ ❖

Visual Aid Preparation

❖ ❖ ❖

Photo-Realistic Illustration

❖ ❖ ❖

Logo Design

❖ ❖ ❖

Full-Figure Drawing

❖ ❖ ❖

PERFORMANCE PROFILE

Creative, diverse illustrator and artist with extensive experience in designing and developing broad range of visual pieces to meet business and programme objectives of both employers and their clients. Particularly adept in creating original, vibrant artwork that captures attention from serious and casual viewers. Additional skills:

- **_Developing Products_** – Able to translate concepts into well-designed products by integrating various elements, including illustration, formatting, photography and typography. Combine innovative thinking with logical design elements.
- **_Conveying Messages_** – Create illustrations that articulate key ideas and earn recognition for aesthetic quality. Excel in reinforcing positive messages.
- **_Meeting Expectations_** – Maintain consistent track record of fulfilling organizational goals. Highly adaptable to changing needs and requirements.

SELECTED WORKS *(a full portfolio is available for immediate review)*

Marketing Material & Product Design

- International Colloquium for Biology of Soricidae – **Logo, image and product development** for line of merchandise used in international conference.
- Museum of Natural History – **Sweatshirt** *The Mastodon* for the museum's gift shop. Designed and produced original artwork for full line of products sold in association with the Ancient Egypt exhibition. Created full-sized, full-colour paintings for children's area the Discovery Room.
- Historical Centre – **Photo-mural retouching** activities to enhance key display areas.
- Children's Museum – Initial design and development of cartoon images for outside banner/T-shirt image and other museum merchandise.

Book & Magazine Illustrations

- *The ABC Magazine, XYZ Magazine* – Miscellaneous illustrations and graphics.
- *The DEF Times, Time, GHI Magazine, others* – Widely published illustrations through the United Press International.
- Dr LE McCullough – Instructional drawings for *The Making and Playing of Uilleann Pipes*, including musical notation.
- Dr Sandra Olson – Reconstruction illustration of Palaeolithic horse fetish for *Horses Through Time.*

Scientific Illustrations

- *National Geographic* – 11"x14" acrylic reconstruction of *Eosimias sinensis*.
- Cultural & Environmental Systems – Artifacts for Technical Series 56.
- Ancient Egypt exhibition – Scientifically accurate recreation of 18th dynasty tomb walls and entire hall as graphics artwork. Built complete scale models, coordinated all illustration production with various collaborators, and earned commendation from Egyptologists for accuracy of reconstruction.

Continued

Public relations and media

Nora Patterson   2

SELECTED PROFESSIONAL EXPERIENCE *(in order of professional importance)*

Illustrator/Exhibits Preparator, The Museum of Natural History
Built distinguished record of achievement and extensive portfolio of work. Employed with museum for 20+ years until 2012.
- *Work Summary* – Served as exhibits/scientific illustrator and designer for installation of travelling and temporary exhibits. Collected, researched and accurately reproduced artifacts (both for 3-dimensional and 2-dimensional venues) and vegetation for permanent installations.
- *National/Global Recognition* – Collaborated on production of life restoration for 40 million-year old fossil primate *Eosimias centennicus*, featured in *Science* magazine (2010) and receiving global coverage in the following:

National Geographic, Science et Vie (Paris), Earth, Today, Post-Gazette, Morning-News.
- Leadership Role – Supervised gallery technicians, staff and volunteers in general and specific activities, providing expertise and support to facilitate project completion.

Freelance Artist, Various Clients
Contracted to design and develop illustrations and artwork for broad range of companies, organizations and individual buyers. Period spanned from 2004 to 2014.
- Satisfying Requirements – Aligned client/employer needs with artwork to ensure satisfaction, leading to frequent repeat and referral business.
- Meeting Deadlines – Worked often under tight timelines; consistently exceeded expectations in delivering work on time with zero effect on quality.
- Earning National Recognition – Received placement in national, well-respected publications and garnered recognition for breadth/quality of creations.

Preparator, The JKL Museum
Oversee preparation and surface treatment of dinosaur cast exhibit specimens for university museum. Arrange artwork for display in large and small exhibits, prepare works on paper for exhibitions, and perform accurate replications of surface colouration for cast specimens. Work jointly with internal team members and external partners to ensure success of exhibitions. Hired in 2012; currently held position.

Held additional positions with ABC Ltd, XYZ Designs, Cultural & Environmental Systems, and DEF Gardens, among others. A full employment history will be provided on request.

EDUCATION & CREDENTIALS

Bachelor of Fine Arts
City School of Art

Former Affiliations
- Member, Guild of Natural Science Illustrators
- Member, Society for the Preservation of Natural History Collectors
- Member, National Association of Museum Exhibitors

Computer Summary
- Appleworks, Photoshop (rudimentary level), Internet research

Entry-level publishing/marketing

John Smith

1 Any Street, Anytown AX0 0AA 01234 567890 jsmith@email.com

Entry-Level in Publishing/Marketing
'Interned every summer; I'm energized, focused, hard-working and professional.'

Performance Profile/Performance Summary

➤ Professional work experience in Public Relations, Publishing, TV Production. Hard working and energetic, with a proven ability to produce results in a fast-paced environment with critical deadlines. Outgoing and articulate communicator who works well with public and co-workers at all levels. Equally effective collaborating in a team setting and working independently. Fluent *English, Spanish, French*.

Professional Skills

➤ Critical Deadlines	➤ Microsoft Office	➤ Bilingual English/Spanish
➤ Public Speaking	➤ Research & Analysis	➤ Press Kits
➤ Team Player	➤ Content Copy	➤ Merchandise Sourcing
➤ Enjoys Challenge	➤ Works Independently	➤ Client Hosting
➤ Writing	➤ Location Scout	➤ Styling Assistant
➤ Problem Solving	➤ Presentations	➤ Multitask
➤ Transcriptions	➤ Shoot Assistant	➤ Wardrobe
➤ Captions/Headlines	➤ Accommodation	➤ Word, Excel, PowerPoint

Education

BA Media Studies May 2012
University of the South of England

Professional Experience

Dynamic Publications/Sports Today Magazine, Surrey Summers 2013–2014

Assistant/Intern (for Editor-in-Chief)

Worked closely with Editor-in-Chief and Fashion Editor of teen magazine. Prioritized and coordinated multiple assignments including transcriptions, research and follow-up. Contributed story ideas that resulted in publication.

- Provided hands-on assistance to Fashion Editor at photo shoots. Contacted leading manufacturers to obtain sample merchandise; organized clothing for shoots; assisted with overall styling.
- Wrote articles for fashion feature of magazine. Arranged photo shoots for article including selecting locations and arranging staff housing. Attended editorial staff meetings, providing input on story.
- Contributed ideas for fitness feature. Wrote captions, explaining new trends in fitness training.

Continued

Public relations and media

John Smith   01234 567890   jsmith@email.com   Page 2

XYZ Marketing Associates, Maidehaid   Summers 2012–2013

Assistant to Managing Director

Assistant to MD of national marketing and public relations organization.

- Whatever the EVP needed, I made happen.
- Performed computer work, hosted clients, scheduled appointments, etc.
- Assembled press kits and EPKs.

Media Management Productions, Reading   Summers 2011–2012

Assistant to Director

Assisted in coordinating make-up and wardrobe for television commercial productions.

- Coordinated wardrobe selections with set decorators.
- Arranged specific selections and appropriate sizes for individual models.
- Assisted location scout with identifying locations and negotiating fees.

Additional Skills

Foreign Languages
Tri-lingual English, Spanish, French

Computer Skills
Microsoft Office: Word, Excel, PowerPoint
Social Networking

Event planner

George S Easton
1 Any Street, Anytown AA1 1AA
55555 555555

MEETING PLANNER

PERFORMANCE SUMMARY

Conferences ▪ *International Events* ▪ *Fundraising* ▪ *Golf Tournaments*

Fourteen years' experience in all aspects of successful event/programme planning, development and management. Excel in managing multiple projects with strong detail, problem-solving and follow-through capabilities. Demonstrated ability to manage, motivate and build cohesive teams that achieve results. Sourced vendors, negotiated contracts and managed budgets. Superb written communications, interpersonal and organizational skills. First-class client relation and teaming skills. Proficient in Access, Excel, PowerPoint, Outlook, MS Project, Publisher, MeetingTrak and Corel WordPerfect.

PERFORMANCE HIGHLIGHTS

Planned and coordinated local government, association and private conferences, meetings, events and fundraisers. Coordinated all conference activities, workshops, meetings, tours and special events. Trained, directed and supervised teams to accomplish goals. **Saved £72,000 on most recent meeting.**

Meeting Planning Management

Negotiated hotel and vendor contracts. Prepared and administered budgets. Arranged all on-site logistics, including transportation, accommodation, meals, guest speakers and audiovisual support.

- Coordinated 10 workshops for the Association for Disease Prevention.
- Coordinated 2014 National Conference on Smoking and Health. (2,000 participants)
- Organized 6,000-participant national annual conferences.
- Coordinated Youth Education Conference Training for 200 Third World participants.
- Developed and supervised education sessions at ABC's 2011 National Convention.
- Directed ABC's National Seminar Series.

Meeting Coordination

As Team Leader, coordinated production, distribution and grading of exam materials. Supervised registration and tracking of continuing education units. Negotiated hotel and vendor contracts. Prepared and administered budgets. Arranged all on-site logistics, including transportation, accommodation, meals, guest speakers and audiovisual support. Consistently came in under budget for each meeting planned.

- Developed and maintained 5,000 person database
- Developed, promoted and implemented ABC's National Certification programme
- Managed logistics for a Regional Training Company

Fundraising

Team player in the development, promotion and implementation of membership and retention programmes for XYZ. Coordinated fundraising events. Supervised high-donor club fulfilment benefits. Provided updated donor reports.

- Coordinated two fundraising golf tournaments.

Continued

Public relations and media

George S Easton   Page 2

EVENTS MANAGEMENT HIGHLIGHTS

2007–Present

- Association for Disease Prevention/Action on Smoking & Health
- XYZ Training & Technical Assistance Project
- Children, Youth and Families Centre for Development
- UK Centre for Health Education
- Association for Disease Prevention/National Centre for Health
- National Library of Medical and Health Information
- Urban Development Association
- ABC National Seminar Series
- ABC 2008 & 2009 National Conventions and Exhibitions

PROFESSIONAL EMPLOYMENT

XYZ SERVICES LTD ▪ London   2013–Present
Senior Conference Specialist

XYZ CONSULTING GROUP ▪ London   2010–2013
Logistics Manager
Senior Conference Coordinator

CONSTRUCTION SPECIALISTS LTD ▪ London   2007–2009
Assistant Coordinator of Education Programmes

NATIONAL ASSOCIATION FOR VOLUNTEERING ▪ Manchester   2007
Assistant Director, Fundraising

EDUCATION & CERTIFICATIONS

CITY UNIVERSITY ▪ Manchester
BSc (Hons) Psychology ▪ 2006

Programme Coordinator Certification ▪ 2014

Certified Group Facilitator – Pending Jan 2015

PROFESSIONAL AFFILIATIONS
- Meeting Professionals International
- Logistical Committee
- Educational Retreat Committee
- Member Services Committee
- Community Outreach Committee
- International Meeting Professionals Association (IMPA)
- Special Olympics – Volunteer
- Hands On – Volunteer
- Sport for All – Volunteer

Automotive service manager

TOM PARSONS

1 Any Street
Anytown AA1 1AA

AUTOMOTIVE SERVICE MANAGER

55555 555555
E-mail: dtjnpar@anyserver.co.uk

PERFORMANCE SUMMARY

Fifteen years' successful customer service management experience within the automotive industry; meeting challenges and creatively solving a variety of problems. Extensive knowledge of automotive warranty policies and procedures. Decisive hands-on manager with an interactive management style able to lead several service teams and administrative staff. Ability to motivate employees' performance levels and develop rapport with diverse audiences; excellent employee relations. Developed excellent product and service knowledge throughout career.

CORE COMPETENCIES

- Customer Service
- Problem Solving
- Leadership, Supervision & Training
- Service Repair Analysis
- Safety & Quality Control
- Warranty Expertise

- Product Knowledge
- Conflict Resolution
- Team Building
- Service Accounting (Expenses/Revenues)
- Technical Knowledge/Efficiency
- Operational Policies & Procedures

PROFESSIONAL EXPERIENCE

ABC & XYZ DEALERSHIPS, Keasby ~ 2012 to Present
Service Manager

- Manage 35 staff (Service Advisors, Service Teams, Cashiers, Receptionists & Detailers).
- Manage ABC and XYZ Service Departments while supervising service advisors and administrating client issues; ensure customer satisfaction.
- Solve product issues for both departments while working with company representatives and senior management.
- Improve department productivity and solve warranty issues when necessary.
- Monitor departmental budget, taking correct actions when required.
- Oversee the development and implementation of new XYZ franchise, and obtain required certification for service department.
- Achieve 2.2 hours' service time for each customer.
- Eliminate expense and waste while reducing employee time loss.
- Perform repair order analysis and monitor team efficiency, improving shop use and work in process times.
- Analyse monthly reports for ABC, and communicate findings with staff.

ESSEX COUNTY VANS, Stanhope ~ 2007 to 2012
Service Manager

- Responsible for 13 staff (Service Advisors, Service Teams, Cashiers & Detailers).
- Oversaw entire Service Department ensuring complete customer satisfaction.
- Communicated with ABC Service Representatives regarding product issues and warranty concerns.
- Improved departmental productivity, implementing several new programmes.
- Conducted repair order and service department analysis.
- Substantially increased service revenues and volume by 60% during first fiscal year.
- Maintained warranty expenses within manufacturers' guidelines.
- Transferred to another location to manage larger department.

HAYES XYZ DEALERSHIP, Heyes ~ 2002 to 2007
Service Consultant

- Handled and wrote over 20+ customer service orders per day.
- Sold service and maintenance plans to clients.
- Coordinated service orders with technical staff, ensuring quality control through entire service process.
- Prepared final accounting of orders.
- Implemented first nationwide service team model for dealerships.
- Transferred to new organization after company purchase.

Auto sales and service

JONATHAN THOMPSON

1 Any Street, Anytown AX0 0AA   020 8123 4567

SALES/SERVICE • CAR AND TRUCK PARTS

Professional Profile

Over 20 years' experience in the Car and Truck Parts industry specializing in locating the hard-to-find parts.

- Committed
- Dedicated
- Effective in fast-paced environment
- Efficient problem solver
- Even-tempered
- Excellent customer service
- Honest
- Learn and adapt quickly
- Persistent
- Personable

- Proficient under stress
- Reliable
- Resourceful
- Strong product knowledge
- Superb follow through
- TAMS Autolog and Triad Computer System
- Thorough
- Troubleshooter
- Trustworthy

Professional Experience

Sales Counter • GO Garage Parts, Ltd • Portbury • *2010–Present*
Answered phones, received parts orders. Researched parts and supplied recommendations. Worked with shop equipment sales. Supplied customer service support often recommending specific tools for certain jobs. Looked up service bulletins on All Data and assisted technicians. Specialized in obtaining hard-to-find parts.

Parts Controller • Clark's Discount Honda Repair • Portbury • *2006–2010*
Received orders and ordered parts. Maintained inventory control. Wrote service orders for customers. Test-drove vehicles. Company had six bays.

Sales Counter • Ed's Auto Parts • Greenway • *2001–2006*
Looked up parts for walk-in and telephone customers. Received and processed orders from dealers and other shops. Troubleshoot and provide solutions for customers. Deliveries and some machine-shop work.

Mechanic • Roy Farnam Supply • Greenway • *1995–2000*
Progressively promoted from initial position of **Stock Clerk/Delivery**
Mixed paint for custom colours. Worked extensively in machine shop. Operated overhead Broach cutter, performed valve jobs, installed valve guides and assembled two engines with excellent results.

Assistant Purchasing Clerk • Highways Department • Somerset • *1993–1995*
Purchased road repair supplies. Ordered parts for light to heavy trucks, Caterpillars, graders and rock crusher.

Personal driver

John Collins

1 Any Street, Anytown AX0 0AA • myemail@myemail.com • 020 8123 4567

PERSONAL DRIVER/CHAUFFEUR
TRANSPORTATION • DOT REGULATIONS • MAINTENANCE • CLIENT RELATIONS

Accomplished and dedicated Driver/Transportation Specialist with a proven track-record of increasing efficiency, quality and customer satisfaction. Skilled in all aspects of vehicle maintenance, Department of Transport regulatory compliance, driving operations, expense management, client relations and customer service within start-up and high-growth organizations. Results-orientated and driven professional with a solid work ethic and dedication to excellence. Professional communication, negotiation, conflict resolution, problem-solving and technical/ troubleshooting skills.

Core Competencies

- Professional Driver
- Expense Management
- Client Relations

- Chauffeur
- DOT Regulatory Compliance
- Customer Satisfaction

- Transportation Specialist
- Customer Service
- Vehicle Maintenance

Professional Experience

ABC – Farmington

2011 to Present

Full Service Driver
Manage a wide range of full-service transportation and customer service functions including collecting payments and delivering products.

Oversee routine vehicle maintenance and process all Department of Transport (DOT) regulations paperwork. Serve as an account manager with full responsibility for tracking and maintaining customer/order records and facilitating communications between owner/manager clients, sales and company management. Collaborate with technical and maintenance personnel to arrange machine repairs, replacements and new placements for services. Service machines and troubleshoot technical onboard computer problems. Operate forklifts to load and unload equipment. Train new employees in onboard computer operations and correct procedures/techniques.

Key Achievements:

- Recognized by the company for achieving a four-year safe driving record; received a letter of commendation.
- Played a key role in the suggestion and implementation of having off calls regulated instead of automated to significantly increase quality and customer satisfaction.
- Promoted to account management responsibilities due to dedication and professionalism.

Continued

Automotive and industrial

John Collins
page 2 of 2

XYZ – Missenden   2009 to 2011

Driver
Ensured correct products were delivered to the proper business locations and managed all aspects of vehicle safety and maintenance.

Recruited to manage daily transportation, warehousing, order-taking and customer service/client relations functions to ensure top-level service. Effectively learned warehouse layout to increase efficiency and operated forklifts to load and unload trucks. Assisted in unloading products at each stop and provided direct customer service to resolve issues at all levels. Managed petty cash receipts/reports and compiled/delivered all required paperwork.

Key Achievements:
- Recipient of a letter of commendation for 'Excellence in Customer Service'.

EDUCATION

Diploma: Business Studies • City College

Heavy equipment driver

TREAVOR BLACK
1 Any Street, Anytown AA1 1AA
55555 555555 + 5555555 5555 (M)

+ DRIVER / HEAVY EQUIPMENT +

PROFILE
- Skilled driver with Class A Commercial Driver's Licence (CDL).
- Over 2 million miles driving commercial vehicles loaded with general or refrigerated freight.
- Superior driving / safety / inspection record and on-time delivery.
- Excellent health and physical condition.
- Mechanically inclined and maintenance-minded.
- Customer-service orientated; personable with instructional communication skills.

VEHICLE EXPERTISE
• Several tractor / trailer rigs including refrigerated vans	32 years
• National 2003 Flatbed Trailer	3 years
• 2006 2T Ford F550 with Jerr-Dan Bed, Hydraulic Winch, Diesel	1 years
• 2004 35T Pete Wrecker with Nomar Bed, Hydraulic Winch, Diesel	3 years
• Racetrack road graders and water trucks	13 years

DRIVING EXPERIENCE

Driver, ABC RECOVERY, Birmingham   2008–present

Clean up heavy equipment accident sites and transport vehicle remains to ABC Recovery storage facility. In addition to using hydraulic winch, used refrigerated vans, trailers, flatbed trailers, and Jaws of Life as situation requires. Interface with customers and insurance providers. Maintain daily log and paperwork. Worked dispatch and accepted management responsibilities as needed.
- Receive consistent raises due to outstanding performance.
- Underwent police background check to secure driver's position.

Driver, DEF TRANSPORT, Birmingham   2005–2008

Leased refrigerated lorry to haul produce and meat products throughout UK and Europe. Maintained daily logs and trip sheets; and hired own loaders (lumpers) at docks.

Owner / Driver, XYZ HAULAGE, Birmingham   1998–2005

Leased out transport lorry during summers to clients that included ABC Transportation, WWW Haulage and DEF Transport. Drove during winters.

OTHER EMPLOYMENT
Promoter, CITY SPEEDWAY (summers)	2007–2008
Manager / Promoter, PLAINS SPEEDWAY (summers)	1995–2007
Auctioneer, Birmingham Area	2001–2007

EDUCATION
City College, NVQZ Transportation and Haulage	2003

Material handler

Glenda Pension

1 Any Street, Anytown AA1 1AA
Email: pen333333@email.com • 55555 555555

Material Handler

Professional Profile

Energetic, highly motivated and organized Material Handler with extensive experience in purchasing, inventory control and shipping / receiving. Strong liaison and negotiation skills for improving product delivery and lowering expenses. Well-developed tracking and research abilities. Outstanding communication skills. Personable, independent and committed to producing top-quality work. Positive and upbeat attitude; get along well with co-workers and management. Thoroughly enjoy a challenge and committed to a long-term career.

Core Competencies

- Accuracy
- Customer Service
- Dedication
- Export
- Import
- Inventory Control
- Liaison
- Negotiator
- Order Pulling
- Ordering
- Organization
- Purchasing
- Quality Assurance
- Receiving
- Shipping
- Tracking

Professional Accomplishments and Achievements

- Achieved IAA approval and Quality Control Certification on specific products.
- Secured credit, due to my personal reputation, for a company in receivership.
- Negotiated effective contracts to obtain product shipment with little or no shipping charges.
- Recaptured thousands of pounds in warranty monies for company.
- Developed and implemented inventory tracking system.
- Reorganized and set up efficient stock room.

Professional Experience

Enlargement Printer • ABC Ltd • Portsmouth • *2010–Present*
Temporary Associate • Manpower • Portsmouth • *2009–2010*
Inbound Auditor / Quality Control • DEF Sportswear • Portsmouth • *2008–2009*
Warehouse Supervisor / Quality Control • GHI Ltd • Portsmouth • *2006–2008*
Records Clerk • JKL Airlines • Slough • *2005*
Purchasing Agent • MNO Air Express Ltd • Gatwick • *2003–2005*
Japan Airlines Liaison for Inventory Management by PQR Airlines • PQR Airlines • Gatwick • *2001–2003*
Purchasing Manager / Warranty Administrator / Inventory Control • STU Airlines – VW-AIR Express • Heathrow • *1998–2001*

Education and Training

Warranty Training • City College • *2008*
Various classes offered by HSE and Japan Airlines
Hazardous Materials Training • City College • *2002*

Steamfitter

Fred G Jamisen
1 Any Street • Anytown AA1 1AA
55555 555555

Steamfitter

Professional Profile

Highly skilled, conscientious and precise **Steamfitter** with over six years' experience and 10,000 + hours of training in all aspects of Steamfitting. Familiar with all required codes, appropriate use of equipment, steamfitting techniques, safety standards and proper procedures to prevent injuries. Proficient in reviewing plans, blueprints and specifications for steamfitting projects with proven ability to provide expert recommendations. Well-developed troubleshooting skills with accurate and precise repairs. Experienced EMT willing to volunteer EMT services on the job. Excellent communication skills, personable, trustworthy, adaptable and committed to a long-term career.

Core Competencies
- Air Conditioning and Refrigeration Systems and Equipment
- Boilers
- Commercial and Industrial
- Conduit Flex, Duct and Controls
- Electrical and Electronic Contracting
- HVAC, Air Conditioning and Refrigeration
- Instrumentation
- Outdoor Installations
- Overhead and Underground
- Process Systems and Equipment
- Steam and Heating Systems and Equipment
- Troubleshooting and Maintenance
- Welding Processes including Orbital Welder Arc 207
- Wire Pulling, Wiring Devices, Removal and Finish

Licences

Pressure Vessel and Boiler Licence Class V
United Association of Steamfitters

Employment History

2009–Present   **Steamfitter** • United Association of Steamfitters • Portsmouth • *Six years* assignment to various companies and projects as needed.

2004–2009   **Paper Machine Operator** • ABC Ltd • Weston • *Six years previously owned by XYZ Paper Company*
EMT *(Emergency Medical Technician)* • Served as volunteer EMT for the paper mill.

2000–2004   **Sales Representative** • DEF Bottling Company • Portsmouth • *Five years* beverage sales.

Military

Specialist E-4 – Nuclear Missile Technician • *Honourable Discharge* • *2000*

Education

BA (Hons) • Humanities
City College and Weston Community College

Property management

Jane Swift
127 Any Street, Anytown AT1 0BB
Tel: 020 8123 4567   jane@anyaddress.co.uk

PROPERTY MANAGEMENT

PERFORMANCE SUMMARY

- More than six years' experience assisting in the management of multiple rental properties.
- Thoroughly familiar with both tenant and landlord laws and guidelines; experienced in collections and county court procedures.
- Extensive business background in general management, customer service and support, and subcontractor supervision.
- Advanced computer skills and demonstrated proficiency in streamlining administrative tasks through the application of technology.
- Resourceful and innovative in problem solving; adapt quickly to a challenge. Strong prioritization, delegation and planning skills.
- Relate warmly to diverse individuals at all levels; respectful yet assertive communication style.

CORE COMPETENCIES

- Perform background, reference and credit checks; select quality tenants and maintain high occupancy rates.
- Show available properties to prospective tenants; negotiate lease and rental agreements.
- Handle tenant communications; respond to requests for maintenance and answer questions.
- Troubleshoot and resolve disputes, including evictions and cleaning/demand deposits.
- Research legal issues using Infolaw, file court documents and represent property owner in court.
- Schedule and supervise subcontractors; oversee upgrades, maintenance and renovations.
- Plan and manage budgets; execute general accounting functions.
- Set up and maintain computerized property management systems.
- Coordinate and track rent collection, maintenance and repairs. Proactively address security issues.

PROFESSIONAL EXPERIENCE

Assistant Property Manager (2011–Present)
Owen & Gains, Portmere
Assist in the management and oversight of multiple residential rental properties. Set up efficient administrative systems, coordinate rent collection, handle tenant disputes and resolve legal issues.

Owner-Manager (2003–2011)
Computer Works, Danesford
Founded and managed this micro/mini-computer sales and systems integration company. Achieved status as a South East Bell Master Vendor.

EDUCATION

City Technical Community College (2001–2002)
OND in Business Administration

Property management (joint CV)

Pamela and Katherine needed a combined CV for their Team Managers application. This format was highly effective.

Pamela Heshe & Katherine Heshe

| 1 Any Street | Anytown AA1 1AA | 55555 555555 |

Property Managers

PROFESSIONAL PROFILE

- Highly motivated, dynamic and energetic with over 30 years' combined experience successfully working with diverse personalities.
- Experienced management and maintenance of various houses and flats.
- Possess strong organizational skills and effective record-keeping techniques.
- Expert bookkeeping abilities.
- Skills include: minor repairs, simple plumbing, light electrical, painting and decorating, landscaping, strong maintenance and clean-up experience.
- Effective in checking new lease applicants and collecting rents in a timely fashion.
- Personable, loyal, honest, committed, creative, able to maintain property impeccably, and get along well with tenants and management.
- Computer literate.

Pamela Heshe	*Katherine Heshe*
EMPLOYMENT HISTORY	**EMPLOYMENT HISTORY**
Sales Consultant • Plymouth • *1993–2007*	**Accounting Manager / Administrative Assistant**
• ABC & Co • Plymouth • *2002–2007*	• National ABC Ltd • *2003–2004*
• XYZ Ltd • Plymouth • *1993, 1994, 1998, 2000, 2002*	Willington
• PQR Stores Group • Dartmouth • *1999–2000*	**Bookkeeper** • *2001–2003*
• NOP • Dartmouth • *1994–1998*	• DEF International
	Willington
EDUCATION	**Bookkeeper** • *1979–2000*
South West Community College • *1988*	• GHI Ltd
• A levels: English and History	Dalloway
	Clerical Assistant • *1974–1978*
Graduate	• JKL Ltd
• BA(Hons) History South West University	Plymouth
	EDUCATION
	Bookkeeping and Accounting • *1979*
	• South West Community College

Property development

MICHAEL WILSON

1 Any Street, Anytown, AX0 0AA
Home: 020 8123 4567 Mobile: 55555 555555 E-mail: mwilson@anyserver.com

PROPERTY DEVELOPMENT

PERFORMANCE PROFILE

- Organized, take-charge professional with exceptional follow-through abilities and detail orientation; able to plan and oversee a full range of events from concept to successful conclusion.
- Demonstrated ability to efficiently prioritize a broad range of responsibilities in order to consistently meet deadlines.
- Dynamic negotiator; effective in achieving positive results.
- Demonstrated capability to anticipate and resolve problems swiftly and independently.
- Possess strong interpersonal skills; proven ability to develop and maintain sound business relationships with clients, anticipating their needs.
- Highly articulate, effective communicator, experienced presenter; possess excellent platform skills.
- Highly adept in using state-of-the-art software packages for industry-related functions, from data and finance management to CADD. Hands-on-experience with Argus and Project.

CORE COMPETENCIES

- Research
- Urban Development
- Accounting
- Bankruptcy
- Tax Issues

- Mediation
- Legal Writing
- Analytical Writing
- Financial Analysis
- Small Business Development

- Mergers and Acquisitions
- Small Business Planning
- Corporate Finance
- Administrative System Design
- Foreclosure

PROFESSIONAL EXPERIENCE

May 2012–Present
SMITH & ASSOCIATES, Overland Park
Special Projects Consultant for well-respected communications consulting firm. Firm authored two critically acclaimed standards in the marketing/business field: *The New Positioning* and *The Power of Simplicity*.

- Perform directed internet and other research in preparation for an upcoming book.
- Analyse research and draft description for inclusion in articles and future book.
- Specifically recruited for special projects on basis of past performance.

Continued

Michael Wilson 020 8123 4567
Page 2 of 2

PROFESSIONAL EXPERIENCE (continued)

September 2011–Present
RIVERVIEW LTD, Overland Park
Assistant Manager for firm affiliated with the ABC Design Centre.

- Collaborate with decorative artist on projects in the £75K range, custom-building business furniture, conference rooms, mahogany libraries, etc.
- Perform multitude of skilled operations from rough milling to fine-detail finishing and veneer application.
- Assist in project estimates and sales proposals.

June 2010–December 2010
MATHEWS, WATERS & MILLS, Kirby
Paralegal

- Gained valuable experience in bankruptcy proceedings.

January 2010–May 2010
HENRY, MARGOLIS & WHITE, Lincoln
Paralegal

- Legal research and writing on legalities relating to general equity matters.

September 2009–December 2009
GIARDELA & ROSE, Lincoln
Paralegal

Summer 2009
SETTON, BIGGS & RUTTER, Overland Park
Clerk

EDUCATION

UNIVERSITY OF THE SOUTH
Higher Certificate in Paralegal Studies   2011

METROPOLITAN UNIVERSITY
BA, Political Science   2008

REFERENCES

Excellent references will be furnished on request.

Fitness trainer

Anna Mead   1 Any Street, Anytown AA1 1AA • 55555 555555 • fitness77@anyserver.net

FITNESS SPECIALIST

Eighteen months of ENERGETIC professional experience delivering health and wellness programmes yielding enthusiasm, commitment and results. Proficient in the use of PC and Macintosh computers.

PROFESSIONAL CERTIFICATION
BSc kinesiology
December 2009, *City College*
IDEA Personal Trainer
Yoga Fit Certified Instructor
Advanced Personal Trainer Diploma
CPR and First Aid

PROGRAMMES DEVELOPED
• **Volleyball League** for health club members
• **Women's Self Defence**
• '**Silver Hearts**' group exercise class for mature members over 60 years of age
• **'HealthPlex Holiday Challenge'**
• **'Suit Up for Summer'**
• **Personalized exercise programmes for clients**
• **'Tiny Mites' gymnastics for preschool**
• **'Gymnastic All-Stars Cheerleading Programme'**

GROUP EXERCISE CLASSES

• Yoga for Fitness	• Rock Bottoms
• Muscle Pump	• Aquafit

PROFESSIONAL ACHIEVEMENTS
• Develop strategic weightlifting programme for male clients.
• Implement customized fitness programmes for group and individual clients.
• Manage personal training programmes, results and profiles for 13 clients.

Continued

Anna Mead Page 2 of 2

PROFESSIONAL PHYSICAL FITNESS EXPERIENCE

EXERCISE PHYSIOLOGIST
- **Develop, produce and implement** internal and external marketing plans.
- **Instruct and create** programmes for Cardiac Rehabilitation Phase III members.
- **Organize** Fitness Team and Health Assessment Testing schedules
- **Exceed expectations** and **deliver excellent customer service**.

PERSONAL TRAINER
- **Develop** personalized exercise programmes for each client.
- **Monitor** the progressions of each client into new, more effective exercises.
- **Prepare** exercise prescriptions.

FITNESS INSTRUCTOR
- **Instruct** various Group Fitness and Yoga classes.
- **Conduct research** on the latest trends and newest exercises.

GYMNASTICS COACH
Advanced Personal Trainer Diploma

CLIENT PROFILES
Profile: Female, age 33 – Stay-at-home mother
Goal: Lose weight and get in shape after birth of baby.
Results: Within 4 months, weight: 147 to 128 lbs; body fat: 30.8% to 18.9%.

Profile: Senior male, age 57 – Retired
Goal: Exercise to maintain and get the benefits for his heart.
Results: Developed regulated fitness programme to reach target heart rate.

Profile: Female, age 40 – Professional
Goal: Lose weight (100 lbs) and get in shape.
Results: Lost 12 lbs and 14 inches in a six-week period.

PROFESSIONAL EXPERIENCE
ABC HEALTHPLEX – Richmond   **January 2010–Present**
DEF GYMNASTICS – Richmond   **2006–2009**
GHI GYMNASTICS – Richmond   **2004–2006**

Fitness and beauty

Beauty therapist

ANITA KELLER

1 Any Street, Anytown AA1 1AA
55555 555555 • akeller@123.net

BEAUTY THERAPIST

PERFORMANCE PROFILE

Beauty therapist experienced in service-driven, team-centred spa / resort settings. Consistently exceeds client expectations; recognized for a gentle, soothing touch and pleasant attitude.

CORE SKILLS

• skin care / facials • body treatments / wraps • waxing • lymphatic drainage • chemical peels • masks • aromatherapy • multivitamin treatments • make-up • acupressure and oriental massage treatments

PRODUCTS

• Dermalogica • Murad • Obagi • Trucco • Jan Marini • Epicuren • Bio Elements • Biomedics • Skinceuticals • MD Forte • Neo Clean • Magica

MEMBERSHIP

- Beauty Therapists Association
- Complementary Therapists Association

EXPERIENCE

ABC DAY SPA, 3/08–Present   Richmond
XYZ, 4/08–7/11   Putney
Beauty Therapist
Working by appointment, provided comprehensive aesthetology services, from oxygen facials and anti-aging skin treatments, to waxing, body wraps, and aromatherapy for these luxury spas.

- Noted for customer service excellence to build a loyal customer base.

OTHER

DEF AGENCY, 7/11–Present   Richmond
Personal Assistant
Provide production support for advertising agency, monitoring media placement, preparing and analysing invoices and coordinating/scheduling talent for ads.

- Additionally serve as **make-up artist / stylist** on location/photo shoots to maximize visual impact.

Continued

ANITA KELLER Page 2 of 2

EDUCATION
ITEC Diploma for beauty specialists, 2010
Classroom and hands-on training in:

• European Skin Care Techniques • Vitamin Therapy for Skin Health • Aromatherapy
• Body Therapy • Wellness Therapies for Body, Mind, and Spirit • Results-orientated Tips for
Maximum Prescriptive Retailing

ITEC Diploma in Body Treatments, 2008
Course work encompassed:

• Microdermabrasion • Salt Glow Body Scrub
• Advanced Skin Care • Make-up Techniques
• Colour Theory • Contouring and Corrections
• European Skin Care Techniques • Vitamin Therapy for Skin Health
• Aromatherapy • Body Therapy
• Wellness Therapies for Body, Mind and Spirit
• Results-orientated Tips for Maximum Prescriptive Retailing

Senior-level company executive

DONALD T THOMAS
1 Any Street
Anytown AA1 1AA

Home: 55555 555555   *donaldthomas@gmail.com*   Mobile: 5555555 5555

SENIOR-LEVEL EXECUTIVE
FINANCE, CORPORATE STRATEGY & DEVELOPMENT
Expert in Leading & Partnering Corporate Finance with Enterprise Strategies, Initiatives, Transactions & Goals

PERFORMANCE PROFILE	CORE COMPETENCIES
Strategic Finance Expert – Dynamic CFO with extensive experience and exceptional success in conceiving, planning, developing and executing strategic and tactical finance initiatives that drive top-line performance and bottom-line results. Technically proficient in all aspects of the finance and accounting functions, and expert in partnering corporate finance with enterprise strategies, initiatives and objectives.	Vision, Strategy, Execution & Leadership
	Strategic Corporate Finance
	P/L & Performance Improvement
	Financial Forecasting, Analysis & Reporting
Corporate Strategy & Development Specialist – Characterized as a rare visionary, strategist and tactician. Consistent originator of bold, innovative business strategies that have extraordinary results on growth, revenue, operational performance, profitability and shareholder value. Heavy transactions background including start-up financing, industry rollup, merger of equals, acquisition and sale.	Cost Analysis, Reduction & Control
	Treasury, Tax, Internal Audit
	Corporate Development & Strategic Alternatives
	Due Diligence, Deal Structuring & Negotiation
Consummate Management Executive – Top-performer and valuable contributor to corporate executive teams. Extremely versatile with high-calibre cross-functional management qualifications, experience-backed judgement and excellent timing. Outstanding role model. Talented team builder, mentor and leader.	Financial & Legal Transactions
	Growth Management & Business Development
	Organizational Design & Transformation
Diverse Industry & Situational Experience – Public and private; small and FTSE 100; start-up, rapid growth, turnaround, post-IPO, post-acquisition integration, bankruptcy – consulting services, property, hospitality, resort/vacation property, travel companies doing business in highly regulated industries in UK, European and global arenas.	Turnaround & Restructure
	Crisis & Change Management
	Internet Strategies & IT Projects
Extraordinary Personal Characteristics – Articulate, intelligent, ambitious, self-driven and creative. Outstanding corporate ambassador to customers, industry groups, regulatory bodies, private investors, analysts, board members and other internal and external stakeholders. Speak conversational French and German.	Team Building & Leadership
	Investor, Analyst & Board Relations
	Executive Advisory & Decision Support

PROFESSIONAL EXPERIENCE

ABC Management Consulting, London   2005 to Present
Successful Management Consulting Firm – Significant Repeat Business and Value-Added Partner to Leading Consulting Firms (eg, XYZ Partners, PQR Consulting) – Retained by Start-up, Small-Cap, and FTSE 100 in United States, UK and Asia

MANAGING DIRECTOR

Operate an independent firm specializing in the delivery of a full range of consulting services – strategic business planning; strategic finance; corporate strategy, development and financing; organizational design; operational and financial turnaround; marketing; and market research and strategy. Identify and acquire new business, and manage all aspects of the project lifecycle – from scope of work through provision of deliverables, follow-up, and relationship management – for large-scale, long-term projects. Engaged by corporate clients representing a broad-range of industry sectors – travel and tourism; hospitality; property development; marketing services; and technology and internet.

Management Successes

- Developed professional reputation contacts worldwide to build and grow a successful management consulting firm.
- Acquired significant repeat business and positioned the firm as a value-added partner to high-profile management consulting firms in the United States and UK (eg, ABC Partners, DEF Consulting).

Continued

Key Engagements

- **Turnaround & Change Management** – Retained (by principal consultancy group) to evaluate a key strategic business unit of a £500 million resort/vacation sales company in receivership. Performed in-depth analyses of operations, identified deficiencies and risks, and presented recommendations for restructure and turnaround of call centre operations, programme management, inventory control and member services functions. Engagement contract was extended to serve as Chief Business Architect during execution and recovery phases.
- **Operational Start-up & Financing** – Retained by UK-based client of a £10 million marketing services business to advise and participate in creating a business plan, raising capital, and executing a start-up in the global event management and incentives sector.
- **Corporate Strategy & Finance** – Retained by independent US resort developer to determine the viability and ROI of expanding into international markets. Analysed business, financial, marketing, competitive intelligence and geopolitical issues impacting the world tourism and hospitality sectors. Pinpointed key target markets, and authored business strategy and financial plan for launch of a luxury boutique hospitality brand.
- **Corporate Strategy** – Engaged in joint consultancy project with ABC Consulting in developing a full-scale corporate strategy plan for £500 million public hospitality company. Researched and analysed internal and external organizations, market opportunities, competitive differentiators, business models and challenges.

CDE Group, Ltd, London   2004 to 2005
Venture Capital–Backed Dot-Com Start-up Operating in a Niche Sector – Fine Arts and Antiques Online Sales/ Auction

MANAGING DIRECTOR

Held full P&L accountability – recruited by and reported to the investor group and Chairman of the Board – for an early-stage internet company. Developed and executed strategy, managed finance and operations, directed sales and marketing, steered technology development, and managed relationships with internal and external stakeholders. Led a core team of three executives – Director of Sales, Director of Operations, Manager of Finance & Administration – and provided indirect oversight to team of 18 in sales, operations, IT, finance and administrative roles.

Strategy & Leadership Successes

- Revised corporate strategy to develop core competencies – a well-established network of dealerships and virtually unlimited source of product – and position the firm as inventory and distribution solution to another company.
- Conceived and executed viable exit strategy – vs minimum requirement of additional 2+ years' investment to achieve breakeven – by identifying a buyer and negotiating sale of the company to a US-based business. Provided investors with ROI on their original investment/commitment of 660%+.

STUV Ltd, London   2002 to 2004
£500 Million Company – One of Largest Resort Development/Sales Companies in Europe – in Rapid Growth Through International Expansion

DIRECTOR – BUSINESS DEVELOPMENT

Key member of the executive committee – retained in company's buyout of UK-based LSI Group – in charge of the strategic and tactical business development activities during period of dynamic growth and change. Crossed-over functional lines to address product development, marketing, branding, sales, corporate communications, legal and regulatory matters. Administered £10 million business development budget. Reported directly to the CEO, led a team of five Director-level executives, and interfaced with Board of Directors, analysts and strategic alliance partners.

Strategy & Leadership Successes

- Led the company's single most significant post-IPO strategic initiative – conceptualization, development and execution of transformation of the company's infrastructure, business model, product offering and marketing strategy – without negative impact on sales, operational performance or customer service during execution.
- Shifted the business model and organizational structure – from a disconnected collection of resort properties – to a membership-based holiday sales company with an exclusive, points-based product, and strong value proposition with single marketing message.

Business Development Results

- Credited with personal contributions to explosive growth – from £330 million in 2002 to £500 million in 2004 – by spearheading the development and rollout of an innovative holiday ownership product and complementary offerings.
- Expanded market reach and brand recognition by initiating and developing relationships with high-profile strategic business partners – ABC Airlines, DEF Travel, GHI Communications and others in the travel, hospitality and marketing services industries.

Continued

Executive

Executive

DONALD T THOMAS	Page 3 of 3

XYZ, Ltd, Lancaster   1999 to 2002

£65 Million, Privately Held Enterprise – One of Largest Vertically Integrated Holiday Ownership Companies in Europe – Specializing in Development and Management of Resorts, and Marketing and Sales of Timeshares and Travel Services

DIRECTOR – BUSINESS DEVELOPMENT (2000 to 2002) CHIEF FINANCIAL OFFICER (1999 to 2000)

Held two key executive positions on the management team – both reporting to CEO (one of two principal shareholders) – following a major debt restructure, physical relocation and preparation for sale. As CFO, managed all aspects of the corporate finance and administration functions (including treasury, tax, statutory reporting and internal audit) for headquarters and 10+ overseas branches. Directed the preparation and analysis of financial statements, budgets, forecasts, desktop 'dashboards' and other essential management reports. Hired, trained, mentored and managed a team of 28 including three senior financial and accounting professionals.

As Director of Business Development, identified, created and capitalized upon both innovative and traditional business opportunities. Conceived, developed and managed strategic and tactical messaging, branding, marketing, sales and relationship-building initiatives. Directed product development, positioning and go-to-market strategies, and launched a series of breakthrough concepts and techniques – trial membership, incentive-driven referral programme, customer/prospect profiling, direct-to-consumer sales, interactive multimedia presentations.

Strategy & Business Development Successes
- Key contributor to providing deep due diligence to ABC in its purchase of LMN Group – activities and relationships that led to recruitment to executive position with the acquiring company.
- Credited with personal contributions (strategy, finance, operations, business development) – to growth – from £40 million to £65 million – profitability – from 5% pre-tax margin in 1994 to 11% in 1997 – and shareholder value – from £15 million to £55 million at sale of the company in mid-2002.

Finance & Operations Results
- Built and managed a best-in-class finance and accounting function. Managed the complete turnaround of the corporate finance organization to include new systems, technologies, processes and personnel.
- Provided the executive team and stakeholders with comprehensive, meaningful decision support by restructuring virtually all financial reporting systems.

WXY Group, London   1992 to 1999

One of London's Largest Public Accounting and Business Consulting Practices – Professional Services for Entrepreneurial Public and Private Companies in Property, VC Funding, Hospitality, and Leisure Travel Sectors

Rapidly Advancing Levels of Seniority to:
MANAGER – CORPORATE FINANCE & INVESTIGATIONS DEPARTMENT (1997 to 1999)

Managed client engagements involving deep due diligence for numerous acquisition and funding transactions. Provided a full range of advisory services and functions including creating/opining on corporate development strategies, authoring business plans, preparing projection models, and performing operational and financial assessments. Developed expertise in fraud and litigation support, debt workout and internal audit. Interfaced with firm's partners, investment bankers, private investors, senior-level corporate executives, board members, industry specialists and regulatory officials.

Key Engagements
- **Debt Restructure** – Contributed to restructure of £100+ million debt with complex asset security position.
- **Fraud Investigation & Litigation** – Provided support on several high-profile engagements including collapse of a private financial services firm (represented WXY as the client) and a Formula One motor-racing team.
- **Corporate Recovery** – Contributed to financial and operational turnaround of several hospitality and leisure firms.

EDUCATION & CREDENTIALS

British Chartered Accountant – ACA – (CPA equivalent), Institute of Chartered Accountants in England and Wales
G Mus (Hons) – Four-year degree in Music (with honours), Royal Northern College of Music, Manchester, England
Training in Corporate Finance and Treasury, Association of Corporate Treasurers

PROFESSIONAL AFFILIATIONS

Institute of Chartered Accountants in England and Wales (ICAEW); Resort Development Association (regular speaker and panelist at conventions); Marketing Association; Chamber of Commerce; Association of Chartered Accountants; and Financial Management Association (FMA)

Senior executive–scientist

SAMUEL HARRINGTON, PhD

Office Address
XYZ Laboratories
Any Street, Anytown AA1 1AA
Office: 55555 555555
harringtons@universityserver.co.net

1 Any Street
Anytown AA1 1AA
Home: 55555 555555
Mobile: 5555555 5555
harringtonsam@anyserver.co.uk

SENIOR EXECUTIVE – SCIENTIST
Chief Science Officer – Executive Director – Programme Manager – Senior Scientist/Researcher
Biotechnology Enterprises – Molecular Research & Diagnostics Organizations

---

PERFORMANCE PROFILE & DISTINCTIONS

- Dynamic, entrepreneurial business professional with high-calibre general management qualifications ... strong orientations in finance and technology ... proven leadership talents. Led the start-up of three biotechnology R&D organizations and turned around an existing test/surveillance laboratory.
- Accomplished senior-level scientist and recognized innovator in modern technical and managerial strategies, principles, methodologies and processes for the biotech industry. Designed and developed numerous scientifically/commercially significant diagnostic reagents and assays.
- Professional experience spanning diverse clinical and technical settings; private biotech firms ... large R&D operations ... public health organizations ... hospitals ... academic facilities ... National Security projects.
- Accustomed to, and effective in high-profile scientist executive roles ... managing large organizations ... overcoming complex business/technical challenges ... gaining respect from competitors and peers ... communicating complex concepts to technical and non-technical audiences ... maintaining impartiality in politically charged environments ... fostering consensus and generating cooperation from multicultural, multidisciplinary teams.
- Confident, assertive, diplomatic and outgoing with exceptional communication, public speaking and interpersonal relations skills. Multicultural, bilingual professional – speak fluent Arabic and English.

MANAGEMENT COMPETENCIES

Entrepreneurial Vision, Strategy & Leadership	P&L and Operations Management
Financial Planning & Management	Budget Planning, Analysis & Control
Programme & Project Management	Process Design / Improvement – Business & Technical
Staff Training, Development & Supervision	Technology Investments & Solutions
Team Building, Mentoring & Leadership	Marketing, Communications & Public Relations

SCIENCE COMPETENCIES

Molecular Diagnostics R&D	Molecular-Based Surveillance
Disease Investigation & Management – Infectious & Genetic	DNA Fingerprinting & Gene Banking
Laboratory Management Quality Improvement & Assurance	Regulatory Affairs & Compliance
Advanced Laboratory Procedures & Technologies	Crisis / Emergency Preparedness & Response
Security Strategies, Policies & Programmes	

PROFESSIONAL EXPERIENCE

2004 to Present

DIRECTOR OF MOLECULAR DIAGNOSTICS
Department of Health

Hold full P&L accountability for public health reference laboratory – infectious disease testing and surveillance services, bioterrorism detection, prevention and response. Manage all aspects of business operations (eg, strategic planning, budgeting, financial reporting, staffing, workflow, administrative affairs, internal/external customer service, quality, regulatory reporting/affairs). Provide technical and managerial oversight to six primary areas of laboratory operations: test development, disease surveillance, disease outbreak investigations (including emerging infections, air-water-food-borne infections), and testing for biothreat organisms/bioterrorism. Manage £600K capital budget and £250K annual budget for operations. Lead a three-person management team and provide indirect supervision to seven technical and non-technical support employees.

Continued

Executive

SAMUEL HARRINGTON, PhD   Page Two

DIRECTOR OF MOLECULAR DIAGNOSTICS – *Continued:*

Management & Leadership Successes:
- Distinguished the facility as one of the best labs in the nation, and one of the first public health organizations to receive government funding for bioterrorism testing and preparedness.
- Evolved a very basic laboratory operation into a dynamic scientific organization staffed with talented, highly trained professionals using state-of-the-art technologies and contemporary methodologies to perform sophisticated testing and surveillance of emerging infections.
- Led an ambitious campaign to secure £600K+ investment in technology. Achieved financial accountability and discipline throughout the organization in order to maximize ROI.
- Equipped the organization and prepared the staff to handle both routine and emerging infections (including potential bioterrorism organisms) despite the challenges of operating under serious financial and staff constraints.
- Converted the test development strategy from a successive to concurrent approach. Re-engineered laboratory processes and workflows enabling completion of 80,000+ tests in 2006/2007.
- Designed and led intensive training and career development programmes – trained/qualified four professionals in advanced molecular testing – and provided team coaching and one-on-one mentoring.
- Served as an effective representative/spokesperson for the organization to internal and external parties – scientific community, government agencies, other public health laboratories, regulatory officials, media and the public – and continue to advocate on behalf of the laboratory and its activities, budgets, personnel and projects.

Clinical Projects & Achievements:
- Distinguished, top-ranking science officer providing consulting, advisory and leadership services on matters related to molecular diagnostics.
- Led the entire development cycle – design, validation, application, training, troubleshooting – of molecular diagnostics-based assays for rapid investigation, diagnosis and surveillance of emerging/re-emerging infectious diseases including E. coli, salmonella, West Nile virus and Noro virus.
- Participated in validation of new rapid tests developed by CDC for BT organisms including anthrax, smallpox and the emerging virus responsible for SARS.

City University Medical Centre (CUMC)   1997 to 2003
PROGRAMME COORDINATOR – DEVELOPMENT
Division of Molecular Diagnostics
Key member of a seven-person management team for a key division within this large, diverse healthcare organization comprised of several regional hospitals and specialist institutions (including the Cancer Institute and the Transplant Institute). Managed the business, clinical and technology aspects of test development. Led a team of 13 full-time technologists.

Management Achievements:
- Established the developmental laboratories from the ground up – lab was a model followed by other laboratories throughout the UK – and provided the vision and operational framework for accommodating emerging technologies and future expansion.
- Contributed to planning, development and control of annual budgets of nearly £1 million for operations – including £200K for capital equipment.
- Developed/presented formal training programmes – one-month courses in lecture and wet lab formats – to physicians on topics related to emerging/advanced molecular diagnostics methodologies, technologies and applications.

Clinical Projects & Achievements:
- Developed DNA fingerprinting method to distinguish between closely related isolates of *Legionella pneumophila* – causative pathogen for Legionnaire's Disease.
- Developed test for identifying four most common gene mutations of Gaucher Disease among Ashkenazi Jewish populations. Delivered £110K+ per year in revenue from laboratory test fees.

Continued

Executive

SAMUEL HARRINGTON, PhD | **Page Three**

The City Transplant Institute | 2000 to 2003
SCIENTIST/CONSULTANT

Contributed expertise in molecular diagnostics to a multidisciplinary team of professionals – immunology, molecular biology, genetics, cell biology, other disciplines – working clinical R&D activities for the oldest/largest comprehensive international organ transplant programmes in the world. Developed customized specialty reagents used in research at the Institute.

Clinical Projects & Key Accomplishments:

- Developed two-hour assay – vs existing test requiring 24+ hours – for detecting presence of low-level HCV in donated livers to be used in transplantation.
- Established custom oligonucleotide design and synthesis service. Generated £150K+ in annual revenue (commercial value exceeded £300K).

Applied Genetics Laboratories, Inc (AGL), Melbourne | 1996 to 1997
PROJECT LEAD/STAFF SCIENTIST

Managed a five-year, £2.5 million project funded by the National Institute of Environmental Health Sciences (NIEHS) for R&D of early cancer detection/treatment methods. Provided technical and managerial oversight to all aspects of the project lifecycle. Tracked and controlled project budgets. Supervised four laboratory technologists.

Clinical Projects & Key Accomplishments:

- Designed and executed protocols for searching for TSGs in mice genome and detecting mutations enabling early diagnosis of cancer in humans.
- Participated in presenting annual project report to National Institute of Environmental Health Sciences in North Carolina.

Kuwait Institute for Scientific Research, Shwaikh, Kuwait | 1990 to 1992
RESEARCH SPECIALIST
Department of Biotechnology

Established and managed Kuwait's first molecular genetics laboratory. Developed research strategies and managed projects. Provided consulting/advisory services on business and scientific issues. Built and led a team of 10 scientists, and hired/managed administrative support staff.

Research Projects & Key Accomplishments:

- Distinguished as the only molecular biologist in Kuwait, and independently started and managed mission statement, business/clinical strategy, business/laboratory operations, policy/procedure formation, budget, staff, equipment for this, the first molecular genetics laboratory in the country.
- Co-Principal Investigator on three-year, £480K+ project involving establishment of basic tools and methodologies for subsequent production of high-value compounds – single cell proteins – for use as animal feed supplements.

TEACHING EXPERIENCE

University of London | 2005 to Present
ASSOCIATE PROFESSOR
Department of Microbiology

Served in a consulting role as a biotechnology subject-matter expert. Led presentations to faculty and graduate students on topics related to molecular diagnostics, public health and bioterrorism. Provided advice on technical issues and made recommendations for academic/scientific programming.

City University | 1992 to 1996
RESEARCH ASSOCIATE

Supervised graduate students and taught undergraduate coursework in chemistry. Worked with senior scientists on projects.

Kuwait University Faculty of Medicine, Jabriya, Kuwait | 1990 to 1992
LECTURER

Provided classroom and laboratory instruction in biochemistry and molecular biology to undergraduate students. Led/participated in scientific research with focus on rheumatic fever.

Continued

Executive

SAMUEL HARRINGTON, PhD   **Page Four**

EDUCATION
PhD – Medical Biochemistry, City University, 1988
MSc – Biochemistry, London University, 1984
BSc – Biochemistry, Kuwait University, Khaldiya, Kuwait, 1982

PUBLICATIONS – *a partial list*
Samuel Harrington. Molecular Diagnostics of Infectious Diseases: State of the Technology. *Biotechnology Annual Review*, Elsevier Publishing Company (2005).

Samuel Harrington, Robert Lanning, David Cooper. Rapid detection of hepatitis C virus in plasma & liver biopsies by capillary electrophoresis. *Nucleic Acid Electrophoresis Springer Lab Manual*, Dietmar Tietz (ed), Springer-Verlag, Heidelberg (2003).

Samuel Harrington, William Pasculle, Robert Lanning, David McDevitt, David Cooper. Typing of *Legionella pneumophila* isolates by degenerate (D-RAPD) fingerprinting. *Molecular and Cellular Probes*, 9 405–414 (2000).

John A. Barranger, Erin Rice, **Samuel Harrington,** Carol Sansieri, Theodore Mifflin, and David Cooper. Enzymatic and Molecular Diagnosis of Gaucher Disease. *Clinics in Laboratory Medicine*, 15 (4) 899–913 (2000).

Samuel Harrington, Robert W. Lanning and David L. Cooper. DNA Fingerprinting of Crude Bacterial Lysates using Degenerate RAPD Primers (D-RAPD). *PCR Methods and Applications*, 4 265–268 (2000).

Samuel Harrington, Carol A. Sansieri, David W. Kopp, David L. Cooper and John A. Barranger. A new diagnostic test for Gaucher Disease suitable for mass screening. *PCR Methods and Applications*, 4 (1) 1–5 (1999).

David L. Cooper, **Samuel Harrington.** Molecular Diagnosis: a primer and specific application to Gaucher disease. *Gaucher Clinical Perspectives*, 1 (3) 1–6 (1998).

PRESENTATIONS – *a partial list*
Samuel Harrington and Krista Marschner. 'A new, two-hour test for *Bordetella pertussis* using the SmartCycler', 103rd General Meeting of the Society for Microbiology (SM), London, May 2008.

Samuel Harrington. 'Methods & Applications of DNA Fingerprinting Techniques', Five 1- and/or 2-week-long workshops presented at the University of Puerto Rico, 2002 to 2008.

Samuel Harrington and Denise Bolton. 'Development of a duplex real time RT-PCR test for surveillance of West Nile and Eastern Equine Encephalitis viruses using the SmartCycler', 102nd General Meeting of the Society for Microbiology (SM), London, May 2007.

D.K. Voloshin, A.W. Pasculle, S.P. Krystofiak, **S. Harrington** and E.J. Wing. 'Nosocomial Legionnaire's disease: an explosive outbreak following interruption of hyperchlorination', Interscience Conference on Antimicrobial Agents and Chemotherapy, San Francisco, CA, October 2000.

S. Harrington. 'Genetic identification technologies: PCR and DNA fingerprinting', Second UN-sponsored Conference on the Perspectives of Biotechnology in Arab Countries, Amman, Jordan, March 1998.

S. Harrington, G. L. Rosner, D. L. Cooper and J. A. Barranger. 'A new PCR-based diagnostic test for Gaucher Disease (GD)', Amer. J. Hum. Genet. 53 (supplement) 1755, 1998.

G. Bahr, **S. Harrington**, A. Yousof, I. Jarrar, J. Rotta, H. Majeed and K. Behbehani, 'Depressed lymphoprolypherative responses in vitro to different streptococcal epitopes in patients with chronic rheumatoid heart disease', Conference on Infectious Diseases in Developing Countries, Kuwait City, Kuwait, March 1992.

PROFESSIONAL AFFILIATIONS
Member, Society for Microbiology – SM   Member, Association for Molecular Pathology – AMP

Consultant, INTOTA Corporation Group   Member, Council of Healthcare Advisors

INDEX